# The Great War
# and the Search
# for a Modern Order

# The Great War and the Search for a Modern Order

## A History of the American People and Their Institutions 1917–1933

### SECOND EDITION

## Ellis W. Hawley
University of Iowa

WAVELAND

PRESS, INC.

Prospect Heights, Illinois

For information about this book, write or call:
Waveland Press, Inc.
P.O. Box 400
Prospect Heights, Illinois  60070
847/634-0081

*To my wife, Sofia*

ISBN 0-88133-973-3

Printed in the United States of America

7  6  5  4  3  2

# Preface

America at the beginning of 1917 was a nation mobilizing for war. It was also a nation potentially capable of developing the world's first mass consumption economy. Institutionally and ideologically it was a nation facing one of the central problems of industrial societies with liberal-democratic commitments. For a quarter of a century it had been shifting power to a new set of organizational and technical elites, thus undermining traditional forces of discipline and social integration. But it had yet to develop new institutions capable of ensuring that the new sources of authority would be used to further the ends of liberal democracy and national progress. For these institutions the quest was continuing, though punctuated by dire warnings about the evils of statist intervention, bureaucratic centralism, and market subversion.

My purpose in the following pages is to reexamine America's historical development during the years from 1917 to 1933, focusing in particular on wartime mobilization and action, the rise and collapse of the world's first mass consumption economy, and the continued search for a modern managerial order geared to the realization of liberal ideals. This search moved away from the paths projected by the New Nationalists and New Freedomites of the prewar period. But from the wartime experience came an enhanced vision of enlightened private orders enlisted in the national service and working with public agencies to advance the common good, and the economic expansion of the postwar period seemed to support this vision. Not until the subsequent economic contraction had unmasked the weaknesses in New Era ideology and practice did the search move onto other paths. Even then it could not ignore the legacy left by New Era organizers and policymakers. Much of what followed would consist of increased support for those still seeking to realize the New Era vision, and much that did break from this pattern would be limited and shaped by the organizational framework erected between 1917 and 1933.

v

This is not to say that I propose to ignore the reaction, alienation, and moral blight commonly emphasized in histories of the 1920s. Behind the popular mythology that surrounds these are substantial realities, which I hope to convey. But the focus in this book is not on bohemians, Babbitts, and bootleggers; nor is it on alienated cultural critics, incipient New Dealers, or intolerant nativists and fundamentalists. It centers instead on the development of managerial institutions and values, drawing particularly from the work of historians who have come to regard that development as constituting the core of modern American history. Underlying such treatment is the view that the 1920s are best understood not as the Indian summer of an outmoded order or even as the seedtime of the reforms of the New Deal but rather as the premature spring of the kind of modern capitalism that would take shape in America in the 1940s and 1950s. The importance of the 1920s, I have come to believe, lies in the ideological and institutional foundations then laid for post-1940 developments, and in this sense they may well constitute the more innovative and significant of the two interwar decades.

Recent work in social, cultural, and policy history, however, has altered somewhat the interpretive view that I had when writing the first edition. More, I believe, should have been made of the facts that managerialism advanced over "contested terrain" could never subdue the "unruly pluralism" that was also a part of American organizational development, and often accommodated itself to persisting elements of the nineteenth-century political and social order. More, I also believe, should have been said about the experiences of women, minorities, and the working class — particularly about the gap between New-Era rhetoric and reality and about the struggles for greater equality that were of significance for the future. My efforts to deal with these matters appear in a number of revisions and additions and particularly in a new chapter (Chapter 9) on the persistence of unequal states.

The underlying ideas and judgments expressed in this book have taken shape through years of study, research, and teaching. In ways too numerous to detail, I am indebted to students, colleagues, and archivists, in the latter category especially to those who have made available the rich resources on this period housed at the Herbert Hoover Presidential Library. In addition, I am indebted to a number of trailblazing scholars who have helped me to see the period in new ways and from new perspectives. In particular, I have been influenced by the work of Robert H. Wiebe, Samuel P. Hays, Louis Galambos, Alfred D. Chandler, William Appleman Williams, Joan Hoff Wilson, Robert F. Himmelberg, Barry D. Karl, Robert H. Zieger, Robert D. Cuff, Carl P. Parrini, Edwin T. Layton, Grant McConnell, Philippe Schmitter,

Charles S. Maier, Morton Keller, Alan Dawley, and David Montgomery. I have also learned much from other scholars, among them Michael J. Hogan, Melvyn P. Leffler, Bruce A. Lohoff, David Burner, Craig Lloyd, Burton Kaufman, Robert H. Van Meter, Martin L. Fausold, Murray Rothbard, Gerald D. Nash, Peri Arnold, Haggai Hurvitz, Guy Alchon, and David Hamilton.

Finally, I want to express my gratitude to the reviewers of this edition: Guy Alchon, University of Delaware; JoAnne Brown, Johns Hopkins University; David Lundberg, Massachusetts Institute of Technology; David Reimers, New York University; Herbert J. Rissler, Indiana State University; and David Zonderman, University of Wisconsin, Madison, and to Vincent P. Carosso for his editorship of the first edition. My thanks are extended to the editors at St. Martin's Press for their assistance and their patience with my failures to meet deadlines, and to my wife, Sofia, for her tolerance and good temper while the book was being written.

Ellis W. Hawley
*University of Iowa*

# Contents

# The Great War
# and the Search
# for a Modern Order

# CHAPTER 1

# The Heritage of
# the Progressive Era

At 8:35 P.M. on April 2, 1917, President Woodrow Wilson ascended the Speaker's platform to address a joint session of the U.S. Congress. He began by reading from a manuscript held firmly in both hands, peeling off each page as he finished. First came an indictment of the new German policy under which "vessels of every kind" were to be "sent to the bottom without warning and without thought of help or mercy for those on board." This, he declared, was a "war against all nations" and a "challenge to all mankind." Next came a linking of these wrongs to a larger and irrepressible conflict between autocracy and democracy. Finally came a call to action. It was necessary not only to right wrongs but to "make the world safe for democracy," and America, as a great democratic nation, must necessarily fight for the principles that gave her birth and happiness. "God helping her," she could "do no other."

In Congress a few members still argued for peace. But four days later, at 1:18 P.M. on April 6, the president signed a war resolution that had passed the Senate by a vote of 82 to 6 and the House of Representatives by 373 to 50. Some thirty-two months after the onset of the Great War in Europe, a conflict that Wilson had labeled "the most terrible and disastrous of all wars," the United States had become a full-fledged belligerent. Looking back from later vantage points, a good many historians and participants would come to feel that the war period constituted a great watershed in both American and world history. For some it was the dividing line between an era of reform and one of reaction, for others the threshold of a new urban and managerial order, and for still others the end of a promising epoch of human progress and the beginning of an era in which the forces of progress were nearly submerged by irrational destruction and social malignancies.

It is not easy to quarrel with such perceptions. In many ways the world of 1919 was a different world from that of 1914, and clearly the

1

America of Warren Harding and Calvin Coolidge was not the America that had elected Theodore Roosevelt and Woodrow Wilson. Yet if the nation was entering on a new stage of its history, it was also bringing with it a heritage that would continue to shape and limit the unfolding of that history. The major concerns of the prewar years had revolved around the challenges posed by industrialization, urbanization, immigration, and pluralistic diversity. It was the search for new institutions to cope with these challenges that had produced much of what was called "progressive reform." And while the paths along which this search moved were altered by the war experience, the quest itself persisted and continued to shape both the institutions and the political behavior of the 1920s. Nor did the other developments of the postwar years constitute anything approaching complete breaks with the past. Such phenomena as the technological and moral revolutions, the advent of a mass consumption economy, and the revolts staged by urban minorities and cultural rebels all had their roots in the prewar era.

A history of post-1917 America, then, must begin with an examination of the era that preceded it and the heritage that this era transmit-

President Woodrow Wilson reads his war message to Congress, April 2, 1917.
*(Brown Brothers)*

ted to its successor. In particular, it is necessary to look at the economic transformation that had taken place by 1917, at the institutional and ideological responses to this change, at the social and cultural tensions seeking resolution, and at America's new concerns about international order.

## The Economic Heritage

By 1917 the American nation had already passed through a remarkable period of economic change, an era that had witnessed the rapid transformation of a land of farmers, villages, and small entrepreneurs into one of factory production, burgeoning cities, and new and powerful masters of industry and finance. In 1870 some 72 percent of America's 40 million people lived on the land or in rural villages, some 53 percent of its work force consisted either of farmers or farm laborers, and only its railroad companies had approached the status of big business. By 1917 the rural population had grown, but that of the nation as a whole had expanded much more rapidly. Swollen both by natural increases and by a massive influx of immigrants, it had reached a total of 103 million, approximately half of whom were now living in urban places. And of the work force in 1917, a force that had come to consist increasingly of employees rather than the self-employed, only 27 percent remained engaged in agricultural pursuits. On the eve of their participation in the Great War, Americans had become a predominantly industrial and urban people, and with the acquisition of new tools and new forms of economic organization their output and productivity had undergone remarkable growth. The national product in 1917 was nearly eight times as large as it had been in 1870, and output per person was nearly three times as great.

Contrary to some expectations, moreover, this growth had continued even after the frontier was closed and the railroads were built. In the two decades prior to the war, American had taken the lead in developing new industries committed to the mass production and consumption of consumer durables and middle-class services. These had become the "new frontier," and while a part of their growth could be attributed to the size of the American market and the American middle class, some of it was undoubtedly due to the activities and policies of key industrialists. In the American context they had been able to escape the restraining hand of business restrictionists and exploit the potential for growth.

One side of their activities was the installation of revolutionary production techniques. By 1910 improvements in machine tools and

new techniques of "scientific management," developed and popularized by such management engineers as Frederick W. Taylor, had laid
the groundwork for striking advances in productivity. And beginning in
1913, something approaching a new system of production had taken
shape at the Ford Motor Company. Concentrating on a standardized
product, the company had implemented continuous assembly, a tech-
nique that involved ever-moving conveyors, minute specialization of
labor, and rigorous coordination. In Henry Ford's own words, it focused "the principles of power, accuracy, economy, system, continuity
and speed" on a manufacturing project, and one result was a Model T
that eventually sold for less than one-third its previous price.

The other side of the new frontier was the introduction of marketing techniques aimed at producing consumers willing and able to buy
large quantities of goods once regarded as luxuries. One strategy was to
cut distribution costs, primarily through large-scale operations and the
elimination of intermediaries. A second was mass advertising designed
to create new wants and overcome ingrained spending habits. A third
was new forms of consumer credit. Finally there was the disposition of
a new set of managers to raise the wage level and hence the purchasing
power of worker-consumers. Again Henry Ford was a pioneer. In a
much-heralded move in 1914, he had raised the pay of his workers to a
minimum daily rate of $5 while reducing their workday from nine to
eight hours.

Also growing by 1917 was another sector of the economy that
would become increasingly prominent in the postwar years, a sector
devoted to the provision of mass services and mass cultural and recreational activities. Taking shape between the older high and folk cultures was a new mass or middle culture, and catering to its wants and
needs was an expanding array of commercial enterprises and social
agencies. Already, for example, motion pictures were emerging as a
huge industry based on entertainment. Already professional sports,
with baseball leading the way, were becoming large business enterprises. And already in the process of rapid expansion were such fields as
health care, secondary and higher education, a press tailored to mass
tastes, and the service trades catering to tourists and travelers.

Growth, then, was still under way. Americans in 1917 had inherited an economy that was entering a new stage of expansion, becoming
more productive, and providing an increasingly rich material life. Yet
economic performance in the two decades prior to the war had not
been especially impressive. Growth had also led to weakening of older
social relationships and older justifications for social hierarchy, and
with it had come new problems of squalor and misery, corruption and
exploitation, monopolistic combinations and destructive economic

warfare. These aspects of the process had generated waves of protest and discontent, and from the 1890s on, as dissatisfaction was crystallized first by an economic crisis and then by a wave of muckraking, there had been a running attack on the adequacy of the existing polity and society to deal with the problems engendered by economic change.

A key part of this attack had challenged the notion that resources and product shares were being efficiently and equitably allocated through an autonomous and apolitical market system. Some groups, it was believed, had acquired substantial power over the process and were using this in antisocial and unproductive ways. The result had been both efforts at market restoration and efforts to find and install a better substitute for market allocation. The years from 1890 to 1917 had brought not only a new antitrust bureaucracy but also an array of regulatory commissions, public enterprises, and special benefits, and of greater importance for the war and postwar years, they had witnessed the emergence of private organizational elites claiming that they could serve as the builders of a new and better social order. What some historians have called the "organizational revolution" was well under way by 1917, a "revolution" that was shifting power and status from old-style entrepreneurs and community leaders to the leaders of financial institutions, corporate bureaucracies, and functional or occupational organizations, while at the same time containing "revolutions" envisioning new class, gender, and racial relationships. Thus to understand post-1917 developments, it is necessary to understand the major features of this organizational heritage.

## The Organizational Heritage

In the business sphere, the prewar search for greater order had brought forth three new elites, each aspiring to the role once filled by master entrepreneurs and leaders of local communities. For many businessmen and for business-supported social science, the great enemies had become "social chaos," "destructive competition," and "defective coordination." It was these disorders that were threatening both liberty and progress, and in different ways the developments that brought forth master financiers, systematic managers, and associational bureaucracies were all responses to these perceptions of social need and group interest.

In the background of the first development lay the wreckage engendered by the financial panic of 1893 and the concurrent rise of powerful investment banks, especially such organizations as the House of Morgan and Kuhn, Loeb and Company. Understandable desires to mitigate "destructive competition" developed simultaneously with institutions capable of controlling a large share of the savings stream; the result, as these institutions were used to mobilize the capital needed for mergers and reorganization, was a consolidation movement going far beyond that of the 1880s. Out of it had come a regrouping of the railroads, a set of supercorporations dominating their respective industries, and a system of interlocking investments and directorates that allowed financial leaders to exert considerable control over managerial decisions. Agitation against this "money power," moreover, had not brought its dissolution. On the contrary, the new financial elite had won substantial acceptance as part of a new and more socially conscious national leadership. During the panic of 1907 it had been called on to check economic demoralization. Subsequently it had become a partner of the State Department in efforts to stabilize troublesome areas abroad, and under the new Federal Reserve Act of 1913 it was to work with public representatives in exercising expert and apolitical controls over the money supply and credit availability.

Meanwhile, a second and at times competing elite was also emerging, primarily in the large corporate organizations with their expanding array of technical specialists coordinated and directed by professional administrators. Here a new "managerial elite" was taking shape; addressing both the desire for continued economic development and concern with its social impact, the elite's leaders were offering themselves as instruments through which an orderly and healthy growth could be organized and directed. Given positions of greater influence, it was argued, they could transform an exploitive and wasteful system into one of humane and uplifting efficiency.

The third development in the business sphere was an immense growth of business associations. Businessmen organized partly for defensive reasons, especially for protection against labor unionizers, political reformers, and rival business organizations. But they also hoped to achieve greater mastery over their environment and to enhance their ability to predict, plan, and control economic behavior. By 1917 these impulses toward organized cooperation had produced hundreds of industrial and trade associations, many with continuing programs, professional staffs, and bureaucratic outlooks. Emerging from this structure, moreover, was a further array of cooperative business councils and national coordinators. Of particular importance was the formation in 1912 of the United States Chamber of Commerce, designed as an association of associations through which organized business could serve the cause of national progress.

In the meantime, as businessmen organized, other groups also tried to develop similar structures. In agriculture the collapse of populism had been followed by a wave of association building, organizing the more businesslike farmers into commodity associations and farm bureaus. In the labor field an elite of skilled workers had turned to "business unionism," developing in spite of employer resistance a network of business-oriented craft unions joined together in the American Federation of Labor. Among the new managers and technicians a variety of professional and technical societies took shape, and in the field of social work a new array of professionally directed organizations were replacing or absorbing the older philanthropic and charitable agencies. The watchwords of the progressive era were *organization* and *professionalism,* and by many Americans the period's business-oriented "organizers" and "professionalizers" were perceived as the new agents of social progress.

The emergence of an organizational society had also had its effects on political institutions. Moving beyond demands for honest and economical government, the new organizational elites had sought managerial aids and allies in the public sector, thus helping to bring into being a variety of technical, fact-finding, and promotional agencies. Seeking a government more responsive to their interests and needs, the elites had also supported reforms designed to break up the older partisan organizations and city machines, shift policymaking to administrators and technical experts, and provide themselves with regularized access to the arenas of decision making. American government at the end of the Progressive Era had not yet been completely "rescued" from the practitioners of mass and party politics; nor had the "new state" escaped from the constraints of judicial power, local autonomy, and fragmented authority. But in important respects the nation's meaningful political units were becoming those generated by the "organizational revolution" rather than those described in the civics books.

Institutionally, then, the America of the prewar period was a society reorganizing around functional identities, shifting power to new organizational elites, and forging rationalizations to justify these changes. For better or worse, the land that had idealized yeomen farmers and rugged individualists was becoming a land of "organization men." And though some people believed that this must necessarily lead either to a new tyranny or to a socialist commonwealth, the more general assumption was that it could be kept within the framework of a liberal democracy. The benefits of the organizational revolution, progressive theorists were insisting, could be obtained without sacrificing the essentials of America's liberal heritage. There could be a middle way between the prescriptions of classical liberalism and those of its socialist critics, and by 1917 several forms of this "new liberalism" had taken shape and were being offered as the road to future progress.

## Visions of a New Liberalism

In one such prescription a marketplace that was succumbing to restrictive organization was to be revitalized through governmental action. The "nightwatchman state" of classical liberalism would give way to active and continuous governmental intervention, primarily to thwart would-be monopolists and keep the marketplace expanding. In this way, it was argued, the discipline and safeguards of an "unseen hand" could be reestablished and sustained. There could be, in the words of Woodrow Wilson, a "new freedom" under which society would again reward "brains and efficiency" rather than "water-logged giants." After Wilson articulated this view in the presidential campaign of 1912, he had sought to provide the needed governmental tools. Such was the aim of the Clayton and the Federal Trade Commission acts in 1914 and of other legislation that dealt with trade barriers and unfair competitive advantage.

For some progressives, however, such a prescription was more suited to the nineteenth than the twentieth century. It amounted, according to Theodore Roosevelt, to "a kind of rural toryism," incapable of realizing the uplifting and liberating abundance made possible by modern technology. And from 1905 on, as the workings of the antitrust laws became a major political issue, a second and competing prescription took shape. Designated as a "new nationalism," it called for the creation of a national regulatory and welfare apparatus that might achieve the liberal ends no longer attainable through nineteenth-century institutions. Underlying it was the assumption that a new kind of governmental bureaucracy, staffed with professional experts and responsive to a properly enlightened people, could become the instrument not only of greater efficiency and productivity but also of better social adaptation to economic change. This had been the approach advocated by the Progressive party in 1912; and though it had initially lost out to the "new freedom," its advocates were heartened by Wilson's subsequent support of special farm aids, protective labor laws, and an expert tariff commission.

Also discussed during the period was a third prescription, one that rejected the statism of the other approaches yet agreed that the attainment of liberal ends now required a regulatory and welfare apparatus. The answer, according to this third theory, lay in cooperative institutions that would allow each functional bloc in society to see its proper role and work with other blocs to realize a new abundance and an ordered freedom. As its proponents put it, a "new individualism," developed and disciplined in private associations and guided through scientific inquiries and coordinating councils, would provide the tools for continued progress.

In the immediate prewar period, moreover, economic difficulties combined with concerns about radicalism, statism, and European developments to propel this form of a new liberalism to the fore. Convinced that social action was needed yet fearful of where government intervention could lead, a variety of organizational leaders had begun articulating a nonstatist and nonradical alternative to classical liberalism. The period had brought forth "solutions" of this sort for the problems of unemployment, industrial waste, and "destructive competition," for those posed by labor-capital conflict and industrial violence, and for those stemming from new developments abroad. The answer to all of these, it was being argued, was not in strong government but rather in the consignment of social duties to properly enlightened private orders. The role of the truly progressive state was to serve as the agent or "midwife" for bringing such arrangements into being. Public policy, moreover, did seem to be moving in this direction. Through such bodies as the Commission on Industrial Relations, the National Foreign Trade Council, and the Council of National Defense, the state was being linked to the new organizational blocs in society and used to legitimize a quasi-public role for private "partners" and "copartnerships."

Ideologically, then, the heritage of the Progressive Era consisted of continuing commitments to a liberal order coupled with growing doubts that it could be realized through the classical prescriptions and with competing efforts to design mechanisms of greater effectiveness. Although America was not without its radicals and reactionaries, liberal values had remained dominant. And though the old liberalism continued to have its adherents, the central debate had become that between advocates of a new freedom, a new nationalism, and a new individualism. It remained to be seen which of these or what combination of them could reconcile the new economy and the organizational revolution with the nation's liberal heritage.

## The Heritage of Ethnocultural Tensions

Also inherited from the Progressive Era was a set of ethnocultural tensions that would become central features of the postwar period. In the years from 1886 to 1916 nearly 19 million immigrants had entered the United States, mostly from eastern and southern Europe and mostly with religions, cultural traditions, and ways of life that diverged markedly from those of northern Europe and Anglo-America. Overwhelmingly they were Roman Catholic or Jewish and hence suspect in a society that had developed an informal Protestant establishment. Overwhelmingly, too, they were uprooted peasants or agricultural laborers whose heritages hampered their functioning in urban settings. Yet what opportunities they could find had been in the great industrial metropolises of the Northeast, where much of the industrial working class had come to consist of recent immigrants. This transformation not only heightened class and ethnocultural divisions within the cities but also strengthened the antiurban attitudes of the hinterland.

Added to the disintegrating effects of rapid industrialization and urbanization, then, were the tensions and anxieties generated by a largely immigrant labor force whose traditions, values, and ideals clashed with those of the host society. To natives with roots in an older America, order seemed to be dissolving into chaos. Collapsing, so it seemed, were not only the traditional structures for ordering economic and social life but also the religious and cultural traditions on which national well-being allegedly rested. Alarmed by what they felt to be the corrupting and disorganizing effects of the cultures that were being imported, many Americans were inclined to listen to demagogues preaching bigotry, intolerance, and discrimination. In the name of progress, patriotism, or pseudoscientific racism, they lent their support to measures that would either "Americanize" the new ethnic minorities or bar them from positions reserved for "real Americans."

In its harsher forms this anti-immigrant sentiment found expression in such organizations as the American Protective Association. But it also had a softer side, seeking through education and reform to rescue worthy immigrants from their benighted conditions. This softer side permeated much of prewar progressivism. It helped to spark the attacks on urban political machines, big city vices, and working-class saloons. It fostered new kinds of vocational education, social work, and citizenship training; rejecting the notion that all should be welcome in the "land of opportunity," its adherents lent their support to measures that would not only reduce the number of incoming immigrants but also select those most amenable to Americanization.

At best, however, such actions had produced a tenuous and uneasy compromise between majority demands and minority aspirations. They had not brought the kind of "melting" that dissolved ethnic loyalties or the kind required to make nativists feel secure and unthreatened. In the political arena the continued tensions were reflected in bitter contests over such issues as prohibition, immigration restriction, and parochial schools. By 1917 all indications were that the tensions were mounting rather than receding. Although the war and postwar experiences would add to them, one could already discern a loss of support for the softer solutions, increased resistance and activism by urban ethnic groups, and the beginnings of the nativist crusade that would become so prominent in the political life of the 1920s.

Also mounting at the time were the tensions inherent in a system that professed liberal democracy yet still denied it to most of the 10 million Americans who were black. Along this fault line, efforts to achieve social peace had been built around the so-called Tuskegeeism of black educator and spokesperson Booker T. Washington, a formula that relegated blacks to the status of an "emerging race" and stressed advancement through vocational training. Yet in practice the formula had brought neither peace nor much improvement in black living standards. In the South political disfranchisement and formalized seg-regation were accompanied by a growing use of lynching and violence as methods of race control. And among blacks the decade preceding the war witnessed both growing criticism of Tuskegeeism and increasing migration from the rural South to the urban North. In these develop-ments lay the bases for new forms of black protest and activism. But at the same time they would also spark new efforts to keep blacks "in their place," new defenses of discrimination and white supremacy, and a general spread of racial violence to the North.

At issue as well in 1917 were the arrangements governing the status of women and their role in a changing society. From 1912 on, a wide variety of women's groups had coalesced behind the movement for equal suffrage; while some saw this primarily as an aid to attaining political and moral reforms, others viewed it as one step toward ending all forms of sexual discrimination and discrediting the social myths that narrowly circumscribed women's opportunities and behavior. Accom-panying the political militance were movements to reform women's dress, family relationships, housework, and the double standard for sexual and social behavior. Emerging in response to such movements, however, was opposition on both the preservationist and the modern-izing sides, the latter seeking especially to develop new forms of "women's work" appropriate to a society of "organization men." Dur-ing and after the war, women's issues would continue to be a major source of cultural conflict.

Freedom for women had also become tied to larger protest against Victorian ideals and the cultural establishment that had helped to sus-tain them. By 1917 the city had become not only the home of discor-dant ethnic minorities and women's liberationists but also the spawning ground of a new cultural modernism that attacked the very notion that art should promote established moral principles. In New York City's Greenwich Village the vanguard of the cultural rebellion had proclaimed a "New Renaissance," one that would allegedly free creative individuals from restrictive traditions and usher in a "new freedom," a "new art," a "new morality." Indeed almost anything new was to be celebrated, especially if it embodied the virtues of spontaneity, intuition, and sensuality; artistic endeavor was now to be either its own reason for being or an instrument for changing national sensibilities. Much that would flourish in the 1920s had its roots in this prewar assault on "genteel" traditions and standards, and much of the cultural fragmentation that would characterize modern America was already becoming discernible. As modernists and traditionalists fought over the custody of high culture, both were losing contact with the emerging popular culture to which large numbers of middle-class America is were turning.

Culturally, then, the heritage of the Progressive Era consisted of mounting tensions between the established order of the Victorian age and the challenges posed by immigration, the activism of submerged minorities and women's groups, and the attitudes emanating from cultural modernists and promoters of a pleasure ethic. These were tensions that many Americans still hoped to resolve, especially through organization and education for a coming age of harmonious abundance. But for the most part the prewar formulas for doing this had brought only uneasy and tenuous compromises. The America that entered the Great War was a potential candidate for bitter and divisive ethnocultural conflict, and the developments that followed would result in much of this potential being realized.

## The Heritage of Progressive Diplomacy

As America entered the war, it was also a country that had gone through what one historian has called its "first great revolution in foreign policy." In the 1890s a policy of continental isolationism had given way to a new imperialism; although the impulse toward acquiring and managing colonies had quickly faded, the progressive presidents had continued to be active interventionists in the international arena. Under Theodore Roosevelt the Caribbean had been turned into an "American lake," the navy had continued to grow, and the United States had become an active participant in big power politics. Under William Howard Taft the diplomatic establishment had been used to push American capital into new areas, ostensibly for the purposes of uplifting and stabilizing them. And under Woodrow Wilson a renunciation of this "dollar diplomacy" had been accompanied by new forms of trade promotion, a policy of withholding recognition from morally reprehensible regimes, and military intervention in Santo Domingo, Haiti, and Mexico. For much of America the isolationist creed retained great appeal. But gradually the nation had also acquired a set of policy-makers who were no longer inclined to uplift by example or merely to react to developments abroad. America's power, they insisted, must be used to shape its international environment and promote international progress, and with the support of a variety of interested groups they were attempting to translate these ideas into practice.

Running through much of this outlook was a vision of America taking its place among the great powers and joining with them to bring civilization and progress to the backward areas of the world. America, in essence, was to become part of the competitive process through which the world's rulers and regulators were selected, demonstrating its fitness for the role and taking up the duties and responsibilities that went with it. Yet it was also assumed that this competitive process would not lead to a major world conflagration, that it could be contained and ordered within a framework of rational negotiations, international rules, and peacekeeping mechanisms. Those who emerged from the process and took up their international duties would be equipped to build these barriers against irrational and destructive behavior. And America, it was thought, could bring a special competence to the task. Its previous isolation from Europe, its achievements in domestic governance, and its freedom from irrational hatreds and "entangling alliances" had all made it a nation to which the European powers might look for moral leadership and disinterested guidance. Such were the arguments often made by the American peace movements, and one side of progressive diplomacy had concentrated on the production of arbitration agreements, cooling-off treaties, and other peacekeeping mechanisms.

Despite such claims, however, the United States had not remained entirely aloof from the alliance systems that had divided Europe into two armed camps. Between 1900 and 1913 American relations with Britain had steadily improved, while those with Germany had rapidly deteriorated. America's interests, so its diplomats had come to believe, were generally compatible with a British-dominated Atlantic and with British trade and balance-of-power politics; they were not compatible with the German bid for imperial glory. And even though most Americans did not believe that the Anglo-German rivalry would end in a resort to arms, it was already clear that if such a war did come, the United States was likely to be tied to the British system rather than to its German rival.

In 1914, then, as an obscure assassination in the Balkans activated Europe's competing alliances and brought the unexpected war, the sympathies of most Americans and especially of those in charge of foreign policy were with Britain and France. And in the months that followed, as British propaganda played on American emotions and British sea power ensured that American merchants could trade only with one side, these sympathies became stronger and more intense. Growing numbers of Americans came to see the Central Powers— Germany, Austria-Hungary, Turkey, and Bulgaria—as aggressor nations seeking to conquer and enslave democratic peoples; and though the other major Allies—Russia, Italy, and Japan—were difficult to perceive as champions of democracy, their imperialistic ambitions aroused far less concern. Although British violations of neutral rights brought protests from the United States, the notes were usually couched in friendly language without threats of reprisal, and such friction as they did engender failed to curb a growing conviction that America could not permit a German victory. Such administration leaders as State Department counsellor Robert Lansing, U.S. ambassador to England Walter Hines Page, and chief presidential adviser Edward House became early advocates of intervention on the British side, and while Wilson vacillated between commitments to the Allied cause and the idea of a "peace without victory," he was clearly opposed to actions that might contribute to the defeat of Britain and France. The chief spokesman for noninvolvement was Secretary of State William Jennings Bryan; when he was replaced by Lansing in 1915—his resignation coming as a protest against Wilson's position on maritime rights —the nation moved closer to intervention.

By 1916 American nonbelligerence had come to hinge on Germany's willingness to withhold its submarines from effective use and allow the United States to function as an Allied arsenal and granary. From early 1915 on, the United States had insisted that naval warfare be conducted in accordance with rules of visit and search that submarines could not meet, and in the face of American protests, the Germans had given the *Arabic* and *Sussex* pledges (the former in September 1915 and the latter in May the following year) committing themselves not to sink unresisting passenger or merchant vessels without warning and rescue operations. This arrangement, however, was not destined to endure. It rested on the German hope that a favorable peace might be negotiated, perhaps in a conference called by President Wilson. When this hope faded, German policymakers decided on an effort to starve the British into submission even if this meant full-scale American belligerence. On January 31, 1917, the German government informed the United States of its intention to resume unrestricted submarine warfare, and from this decision war quickly followed. On February 3, Wilson announced the severance of diplomatic relations; on March 1, the State Department released proof of German intrigues for an alliance with Mexico; on March 18, German submarines sank three American merchant vessels with heavy loss of life; and on March 20, the president's cabinet was unanimous in urging a declaration of war. On March 21, the president issued a call for a special session of Congress, and on April 2, the day the session convened, he delivered his war message.

Viewed from almost any angle, the movement into war represented a failure of progressive diplomacy. The events of 1914 had given the lie to assumptions about great power behavior, and those of early 1917 had demonstrated America's inability either to correct the unexpected misbehavior or to escape its consequences. Yet the custodians of the new diplomacy now proposed to turn one of history's darkest hours into a new beginning. As early as September 1914, Walter Hines Page had come to regard the war as a blessing, an opportunity to strangle "the Hohenzollern idea" and destroy the German militarism that had become the chief obstacle in the path of human progress. It was this view of the matter that Wilson now used to sanctify and ennoble the resort to arms. In essence, the war that progressive diplomacy had failed to prevent was now perceived as a "progressive war," a struggle through which the forces of light and progress would destroy the great obstacle in their path, redeem past errors and failures, and build institutions capable of realizing the progressive dream. In Wilson's most famous words, it would not only make the world "safe for democracy" but also "end all wars" and bring "peace and safety to all nations."

In other areas, too, the effort to turn seeming regression into a new beginning quickly became evident. While some Americans deplored and resisted the militarization of American society, others viewed it not only as a requirement for survival but as a steppingstone to the social order that the Progressive Era had envisioned but failed to achieve. A system of war management, they came to believe, could be adapted to the peacetime management of social progress, and the story of this attempted adaptation would form one of the central themes of the postwar era.

CHAPTER 2

# "A Progressive War"
## 1917–1918

If the Progressive Era laid the basis for modern America, the war experience of 1917 and 1918 catalyzed the process of organizational change and set the pattern for future economic and social management. It brought, above all, a new reliance on the private organizational elites that had emerged in the prewar years. For as old institutions failed the test of military exigency, it was these elites who built a system capable of breaking the deadlock in Europe and forcing Germany to sue for peace. The story of America at war was a story of courage and misery in the trenches of northern France, of heightened xenophobia and intolerance at home, and of diplomacy that aroused expectations it could not fulfill. But it was also the story of a people organizing in ways that would shape its destiny.

### Early Decisions

In large measure the wartime pressure for organizational change stemmed from two decisions about the type of war that the nation would attempt to fight. In the first place, it was decided, the stream of war matériel moving across the Atlantic must be substantially expanded. America must seek, in particular, to meet the urgent requests of the Allies for new credits, more ships, and a larger flow of foodstuffs. Second, it was decided shortly thereafter, the United States must raise a large expeditionary force and deploy it in France. Without such actions, so the reasoning ran, the war could not be brought to a successful conclusion, nor could America expect to play a major role in shaping the peace. The consequences, however, were to subject the economy to massive demands for a new type of consumption, and from the outset

16

it was widely conceded that trying to meet these demands through existing economic and political institutions was likely to bring economic chaos and social breakdown. Temporarily, at least, America would have to construct its own version of the war collectivism to which Europeans had turned.

For the raising of military manpower, this meant conscription, and despite protests of "Prussianization," Congress proceeded to follow the president's recommendations, defeating efforts to force reliance on volunteer units and enacting a selective service law for the first time since the Civil War. This, it was said, constituted "modern democracy" in action, and in practice implementation of the law proved easier than expected. When June 5 was proclaimed Registration Day, Senator James Reed of Missouri predicted that the nation's cities would be "running red with blood." But nothing of the sort happened. On the appointed day, some 9,660,000 American males between the ages of 21 and 31 went to their polling places. As one commentator put it, there they were "exhorted by their mayors, prayed for by their clergymen, and wept over by sundry females," after which they filled out the

A Brooklyn, New York recruiting station in March of 1917. Miss Viola McGuckin in charge. *(UPI/Bettmann)*

proper forms and awaited the decisions of local draft boards. Eventually the draft boards would register over 24 million men between the ages of 18 and 45, and of these about 2.8 million would be inducted. Approximately 2 million more volunteered, thus bringing the total who saw service to about 4.8 million.

The government also moved quickly to establish special agencies of information management. On April 13 the veteran journalist George Creel took charge of the newly established Committee on Public Information, whose primary tasks were to manage war information, mobilize public opinion behind war measures, and "sell the war" to those not yet convinced of its justice and necessity. It quickly organized a system of "self-censorship" for the newspapers and began turning out a steady stream of releases, posters, films, speeches, pamphlets, and other materials. As Creel saw it, he was running "the world's greatest adventure in advertising." But for those who refused to buy the product or tried to offer competing images, there was little toleration. With official encouragement, a number of "loyalty" organizations sprang up to catch domestic traitors, expose "slackers" and "shirkers," and force would-be dissenters into line. And with presidential support, Congress moved promptly to make legal sanctions available. In June 1917 it passed the Espionage Act, providing heavy penalties for "false statements with intent to interfere with the operation or success of the military or naval forces" and empowering the postmaster general to withhold mail privileges from any materials "advocating or urging treason, insurrection, or forcible resistance to any law of the United States."

To the conscription of money there was more resistance. But after heated debates over how the burden should be distributed, Congress produced a war revenue act that raised both income and excise taxes and allowed approximately 31 percent of the war's cost to be met from current revenue. The remainder, a sum that would eventually total about $23 billion, was borrowed, partly through the sale of war bonds to the public and partly through the exchange of such bonds for newly created bank credit. To curb private demands for capital, the Federal Reserve Board also created the Capital Issues Committee, eventually empowered to block the employment of capital in nonessential enterprises.

Meanwhile, the country was also groping toward new mechanisms that could reduce the competition for scarce materials and bring production into line with the new demands. The mere placing of orders through competitive bidding, so most leaders had concluded, could not bring this about. Yet it would be difficult and dangerous, if not impossible, to build a state bureaucracy equal to the task. The "American way," so Wilson was being told, was through voluntary cooperation between public agencies and enlightened private organizations, building in particular on the ties of the prewar Council of National Defense to the leadership of functional blocs and private institutions.

By early fall, administrative and legislative action had brought several of these exercises in public-private cooperation into being. In May the President had entrusted the organization of a food program to Herbert Hoover, recently director of the Commission for Relief in Belgium. In July the Council of National Defense created the War Industries Board, responsible for the functioning of key raw material and manufacturing industries. In August the Lever Act not only gave a statutory basis and new powers to the Food Administration but also authorized the creation of a separate program for fuels. And in early October the president established the War Trade Board to control exports and imports and wage economic warfare against the enemy. In addition, the reorganized Shipping Board was entrusted to Edward Hurley, one of the prewar period's most articulate spokesmen for business-government cooperation; and the Railroads War Board assumed the task of reordering rail traffic. Although production bottlenecks and bureaucratic disorders were still much in evidence, the nation was being organized along lines that would eventually be hailed as eminently workable. And though much was made of the expanding public sector, the heart of the new order was a network of cooperating industrial committees that linked the war agencies to private organizations and drew on both public and private power to enforce agreements reached by consultation and bargaining. Official encouragement and support was now given to the association building that antitrusters had previously regarded as unhealthy, and antitrust immunity was granted to combinations certified to be in the public interest.

While moving toward administered markets, the emerging war system was also engaged in creating new mechanisms of social management. The kind of national efficiency being sought, it was decided, required not only a managed economy but also the management for war purposes of the home, the workplace, the playground, the school, the church, the community, and the social service agency. For each of these a new managerial apparatus appeared, typically consisting of the management-minded professionals in the field linked to business and civic organizations and to the social mobilization arms of the major war agencies. For home economists, employment and recreation managers, school, church, and health administrators, and much of the social worker community, the system created new openings both for professional advancement and for pushing an "American brand" of social engineering.

Where labor associations fit into this picture was more controversial. But by late 1917 a series of decisions had directed government policy toward working with and through "enlightened" unions rather than trying to suppress unionization or to extend military conscription to the industrial sphere. The goal, so it was early declared, was to achieve full utilization of manpower without depriving workers of rights and living standards already won. To achieve this goal the war agencies proceeded to recognize the leaders and unions of the American Federation of Labor as legitimate partners worthy of joining with business and public representatives to implement war programs. Radical and obstructionist unions, by contrast, were to have their organizations destroyed. In September 1917, after a series of bitter conflicts in the copper industry, federal authorities conducted a mass raid on the offices of the Industrial Workers of the World (known as the "Wobblies"), arrested the union's leaders, and used the wartime statutes to convict and imprison some ninety-five of them. Subsequently, mob attacks on what remained of the IWW and like-minded groups became common.

## The War Economy in Action

When Congress reconvened in early December, it could take note of several layers of organizational growth. Yet performance was clearly below expectations, and during the ensuing winter, as one crisis followed another, the organizational machinery came under severe criticism from the public and from congressional investigators. On December 26 a monstrous transportation snarl brought federal seizure and operation of the railroads. Two days later the worst blizzard in forty-one years aggravated both the transportation and fuel crises. In mid-January the Fuel Administration was forced to close eastern business plants for a five-day period and for nine subsequent Mondays. Through it all, bitter quarrels developed on the labor front and over the issues of priorities, pricing, and purchasing. It seemed "such a hopeless tangle," wrote Bernard Baruch, then a Wall Street broker who was in charge of developing raw materials controls, that men who were offered war positions refused to take them and those in charge of the war agencies were eager to leave.

Gradually, however, federal orders did untangle the transportation difficulties, and between February and July 1918 a series of actions brought greater effectiveness while retaining much of the reliance on private organizational resources. On March 4, Baruch became head of the strengthened and more effective War Industries Board. Shortly thereafter, the heads of the principal war agencies began meeting with the president as a war cabinet, thus providing a higher degree of coordination and integration. In addition, Congress established the War Finance Corporation to mobilize and allocate needed capital, the Shipping Board's controls and programs began operating more smoothly, the postmaster general was put in charge of the telegraph and telephone industries, and to handle the problems that had developed in the labor field, the president established two new bodies that were to become models for future federal action. One was the National War Labor Board, made up of labor, management, and public representatives and charged with fostering collective bargaining and resolving labor disputes. The other was the War Labor Policies Board, established to serve as a coordinator and harmonizer for the labor and welfare programs that had been undertaken in particular industrial sectors. During the winter crisis there had been much support for taking the direction of the war effort out of the president's hands and lodging it in an independent body. But by April such proposals were fading, and in May the administration succeeded in getting through the Overman Act, a measure giving the president almost unlimited power to organize the nation's resources.

While these actions were being taken, the Food Administration was also engaged in dramatic operations that were making Herbert Hoover the best known of the nation's war managers. Operating under the Lever Act, the Food Administration had organized the food industries for collective action, forcing dissenters into line through its licensing powers and using governmental marketing agencies to hold prices at specified levels and enforce industrial agreements. But of greater concern to the general populace, the Food Administration was also attempting to organize farmers for greater productivity, consumers for greater conservation, and communities for action against profiteers. Working with the Department of Agriculture, it had drawn farm groups into the machinery through which incentive prices and production goals were set and had subjected them to infinite variations on the theme "Food Will Win the War." It had conducted massive pledge campaigns, enlisting the support of individual households for Wheatless Mondays, Meatless Tuesdays, and Porkless Thursdays and Saturdays. It had urged and helped communities to form "price interpretation boards" that compiled and published lists of firms engaged in unfair pricing. In addition, agricultural war work brought a rapid expansion of the farm bureaus served by county extension agents and thereby laid the basis for the American Farm Bureau Federation.

The system that had emerged by the summer of 1918 was far from fully satisfactory. Shippers were still dissatisfied with the Railroad Administration. Consumers complained about profiteering and the rising cost of living. Antitrusters worried about a government-fostered system of "trusts." Northern and western interests disliked Wilson's concessions to powerful southern congressmen and their regional constituencies. And disgruntled business, labor, and farm groups saw themselves as not being adequately rewarded. Yet production and delivery graphs were moving upward now, lending credibility to the claim that America was meeting war needs through a system that still left much decision making in private hands. The food program, after all, was able to triple the export of foodstuffs. The coal shortage yielded to price pegging and other ministrations of the Fuel Administration. And although the projected flow of new ships and aircraft was just getting under way as the war ended in November 1918, the overall output of war goods, measured in constant 1914 dollars, rose from $4.1 billion in 1917 to $9.7 billion in 1918.

As finally organized, the war machinery also provided a workable system of industrial relations — partly, to be sure, through suppression of dissenting labor groups and threats that workers would be drafted, but also through better working conditions, collective bargaining agreements, and wage and profit policies that by raising prices, shifted much of the war's burden to civilians living on savings or relatively fixed incomes. Government support for a basic eight-hour day with time and a half for overtime made this the established practice in most industries. Similar support for reducing worker discontent brought improved factory conditions, expanded programs for employee welfare, and new systems of personnel management. And out of the wage-setting apparatus came increases that allowed the average industrial worker's income to rise a bit more rapidly than the 40 percent jump in the cost of living. Very little of this improvement, however, came at the expense of business profits. Although income, inheritance, and excess profits taxes were substantially increased, the most important "tax" was inflation. Profits were protected from this through cost-plus contracts and similar guarantees.

In addition, the war's "organization men" found much to admire in the new arrangements. Union officials congratulated themselves on their quasi-governmental positions and on an AFL membership that had grown from around 2 million in 1916 to over 2.7 million by the end of the war. Trade association executives saw the roles being played by their organizations as indicative of a new spirit of cooperation that could yield great social benefits. Engineers, economists, scientific managers, and other technocratic professionals welcomed the system's use of their expertise. And at the center of the system, said its admirers and defenders, stood a service-minded managerial elite working to integrate the products of the organizational revolution into a harmonious and productive whole. In these respects the system appeared to be a realization of prewar prescriptions for progress rather than a repudiation of them.

## The War and Ethnocultural Conflict

While seeking to integrate organizational blocs, the war managers also urged harmony and cooperation among ethnic and racial groups. Pageants and parades featured "nationalities" sections symbolizing the unity desired, official propaganda stressed how America had emerged from the amalgamation of many nationalities, and the Division of Work with the Foreign-born set out to organize "loyalty leagues" in America's many ethnic communities. In three ways, however, the war had the effect of enhancing ethnocultural conflict rather than reducing it. In the first place, its ideals and demands further weakened the older arrangements for keeping subordinate groups in their place. Second, it aroused suspicion and distrust of ethnic groups that could be identified with foreign enemies or were in conflict with foreign friends. Third, it spawned a repressive loyalty apparatus that tended to fall into the hands of nativist groups or social traditionalists and be used in their actions against what they regarded as "un-American elements."

As the war proceeded, the arrangements governing relations between whites and blacks came under particular stress. On one side, the need for black manpower, the ideal of a war for democracy, and the intensified migration of blacks to northern cities provided new weapons to support demands for racial justice. Despite strong southern resistance, the lure of war jobs and greater freedom had set in motion a black northward exodus involving a third of a million people and much optimism about a better future. Yet as black expectations rose, the defenders of existing arrangements took alarm and reacted with new outpourings of racial abuse and new efforts at race control. Although blacks were drafted and black officers were trained, the armed forces remained segregated institutions in which black units served chiefly as labor battalions. And though blacks benefited financially from war employment, their arrival in northern cities frequently aroused hostilities that exploded into rioting and violence. At East Saint Louis in 1917, nine whites and more than forty blacks lost their lives in a riot over employment in a defense plant. By the end of the war there was increased militance on each side, setting the stage for an eruption of racial violence in 1919.

Arrangements defining the status of women and upholding established moral and cultural standards also came under increased stress.

Again, the war system tried to make a place for women, especially through its enlistment of women professionals, its establishment of the Women in Industry Service, and its use of a Council of National Defense Woman's Committee to organize women's "volunteer" activities. Approximately 1.4 million women became involved in war work and military-related activities. But to a women's movement that also drew new strength from the war's ideals and demands, such action did little to alter gender roles or power relationships. Demands for greater equality intensified, and on the suffrage issue women were able to win presidential support and set the stage for passage of the Nineteenth Amendment in 1920 granting women the right to vote.

In addition, the war experience made life vastly more difficult for the defenders of Victorian morality and ideals. Although they could seek to shield training camps from prostitution and other vices, a job undertaken particularly by the Commission on Training Camp Activities, the traditionalists found it increasingly difficult to hold the line against urban sophistication, the new morality, and cultural deviance. To these the war gave an added impetus, and among the defenders of an older America there was mounting alarm.

Meanwhile, the outpouring of anti-German propaganda was having pronounced effects on Americans of German ancestry and admirers of German culture. In the eyes of Theodore Roosevelt, men who tried to be "both German and American" were "not Americans at all, but traitors to America and tools and servants of Germany against America." Superpatriots attacked German families and organizations, producing a series of infamous cases of vigilantism. Near Saint Louis, for example, a mob seized and stripped a man named Robert Prager, bound him with an American flag, dragged him stumbling through the streets, and eventually lynched him. In addition, many states prohibited church services in German and the teaching of German in the public schools. For the duration sauerkraut became "liberty cabbage" and the hamburger a "liberty sandwich," German measles became "liberty measles," and hundreds of individuals and firms hastily anglicized their German-sounding names. In the words of the historian Arthur Link, the majority of Americans seemed to lose "not only their tolerance but their sense of humor as well."

Along with the propaganda, moreover, the government continued to develop an elaborate loyalty apparatus directed not only against suspected German-Americans but also against antiwar radicals, dissident Irish-Americans, conscientious objectors, black protestors, and others charged with obstructing the war effort. In the spring of 1918, Congress passed both a sabotage and a sedition act, the former aimed at the remnants of the IWW and the latter forbidding any disloyal or abusive remarks about the United States and its system of government. Under such statutes the Justice and Post Office departments carried on extensive security operations, eventually prosecuting over 2,000 persons. And linked to these operations was an extensive network of state loyalty agencies, local defense councils, and such cooperating private orders as the National Security League. As in other areas of war administration, the machinery that evolved tended to collapse distinctions between the public and private sectors, which meant in practice that "disloyalty" was defined and punished not only by legally constituted bodies but also by what amounted to vigilante groups. Supplementing the prosecutions were organized lynchings, floggings, tarrings, and other extralegal acts of vengeance, all part of a behavior pattern that would reappear in the postwar Ku Klux Klan.

It was perhaps inevitable, too, that such actions against disloyalty should become confused and intermixed with nativist efforts to restore and maintain "national purity." In any event, nativist leaders frequently appeared as leaders of the loyalty organizations, and in the name of patriotism the country adopted a number of the measures long urged by nativist groups. In early 1917 a measure establishing literacy requirements for incoming immigrants was passed over President Wilson's veto. In mobilizing the schools, much emphasis was put on Americanization programs. And advanced now as an anti-German measure (taking advantage of the fact that many breweries had German names) as well as an efficiency enhancer and social purifier, prohibition finally became a part of national law: In the summer of 1917 the prohibitionists successfully amended the Lever bill to forbid the use of foodstuffs in the manufacture of distilled liquors, and in December of that year Congress adopted and submitted to the states a constitutional amendment prohibiting the manufacture, sale, or transportation of all alcoholic beverages. The loyalty apparatus was already becoming part of a new nativist crusade, one that would purportedly make America safe for "100 percent Americans."

## War Aims and Coalition Diplomacy

While they attempted to enforce domestic harmony, America's wartime leaders were also much concerned with inter-Allied harmony and, beyond that, the international harmony that could bring lasting peace. One goal of wartime diplomacy was a coordinated and effective military effort. The other was the translation of military success into a progressive and stable world order, which meant, above all, finding ways to protect liberal and peace-loving peoples from the twin scourges of German-style imperialism and antiliberal radicalism. Most Americans agreed on these ends, but about the means for attaining them there was much less consensus.

At the core of Woodrow Wilson's solution was the vision of a democratized enemy, freed of its militaristic and authoritarian proclivities and brought into a new concert of democratic power capable of providing collective security and administering peaceful progress. This was the vision implicit in Wilson's prewar pronouncements on international organization and "peace without victory," and it continued to inform his thought concerning the kind of peace that the United States should seek and help to enforce. It was a vision, however, that clashed with Allied plans for territorial and economic gains and for crushing and limiting German power rather than democratizing it. It also clashed with the propaganda image of a brutal and depraved enemy utterly incapable of participating in democratic processes. And during the war, Wilson was loath to point up these incongruities or insist on resolving them.

This did not, however, reduce the president to silence, especially in the face of the moral and emotional crisis engendered by the Allied military reverses of late 1917, the revolution of the Bolsheviks in Russia that November, and the subsequent publication of secret Allied treaties by the new Russian rulers. The Allies, it was revealed, had agreed among themselves to partition Turkey, divide up Germany's colonies, and pay for Italian, Japanese, and Romanian belligerence with territories taken from the Central Powers. The allies seemed to be only another set of greedy imperialists. Having failed to persuade the Interallied Conference in Paris to formulate a reply, Wilson decided to do so independently. On January 8, 1918, he went before a joint session of Congress to enumerate and explain his famous Fourteen Points.

In this document Wilson specified not only the general principles of a liberal world order but also the changes necessary to free subject peoples from foreign domination. In points 1 through 5 he called, respectively, for open diplomacy, freedom of the seas, equality of economic opportunity, reduction of armaments, and the impartial adjustment of colonial claims. Point 6 demanded German evacuation of Russia and self-determination for the Russian people. Under points 7 and 8 the Germans were to evacuate Belgium and France and restore Alsace-Lorraine to France. Points 9 through 13 called for adjusting Italy's boundaries, granting autonomy to the subject nationalities of Austria-Hungary, restoring the Balkan nations that had fought on the Allied side, liberating the subject peoples of the Turkish Empire, and creating a free and independent Poland. Finally, as a capstone to the edifice, Wilson added and stressed a fourteenth point. It called for a general association of nations that would afford "mutual guarantees of political independence and territorial integrity to great and small states alike."

In the months that followed, the Fourteen Points became the great manifesto of the war, extensively used as a weapon of propaganda. Yet the European Allies gave no indication that they were willing to use them as a basis for peace. And American behavior, especially the mistrust that American authorities had of interallied bodies and their continued insistence on remaining an "associate" rather than an "ally," raised strong doubts about the readiness of the United States to participate in a collective security system. Nor was harmony easily achieved on other matters. American insistence on fielding an independent army in France caused much friction with the British and the French. Interallied coordinating bodies were slow to be established and were frequently torn by bitter dissension over shipping and supplies. And there were mutual suspicions that much of the idealistic rhetoric, whether American or European, amounted to a smokescreen for imperial and commercial ambitions.

In addition, differences developed over appropriate responses to Russia's withdrawal from the war and to the internal struggles there. American military leaders strongly opposed any diversion of Allied troops to Russia. But under pressure from the British and French, Wilson finally agreed to limited military operations designed to keep supplies out of German hands, assist friendly forces, and rescue a Czech legion seeking to extricate itself from Russia via the Trans-Siberian Railroad. By September 1918, American contingents had joined Allied expeditionary forces both in the Russian north, at Murmansk and Archangel, and in Siberia. In the latter expedition Japanese forces were prominent, and the American decision to participate was in part motivated by a desire to curb Japanese ambitions. Although Japan and the United States were now associates in the war against Germany, American diplomacy continued to oppose Japanese expansion in the Far East, and the Americans were soon having second thoughts about an agreement of November 1917 (the Lansing-Ishii Agreement) under which Japan was recognized to have "special interests" in China.

## The Fighting Fronts

Meanwhile, despite continuing problems on the diplomatic and home fronts, American troops were being transported to France and brought into military action. In May 1917, General John J. Pershing was chosen to head the American Expeditionary Force, and in June he arrived in

France with some 15,000 American troops. By October the number had grown to 87,000. But action was still confined to defense of a quiet sector of the front east of Verdun. There Pershing had established an American command, and throughout 1917 he successfully resisted efforts to have American soldiers fed into the other Allied armies in small groups.

During 1917 the major contribution of Americans to actual fighting was on the seas. There the German submarine campaign had initially seemed to be paying off. It was sinking ships at a rate of nearly 900,000 tons a month, a rate that could mean the destruction of the British merchant marine and hence of British fighting power. But gradually, through a combination of patrolling, convoying, and mine laying, Allied shipping losses were reduced to tolerable levels: 400,000 tons in December 1917 and less than 200,000 tons by April 1918. The flow of foodstuffs and materials was sustained, and eventually about 2 million American troops crossed the Atlantic and were deployed in France.

In the spring of 1918, however, the American forces numbered only about 300,000, and at this stage it seemed that the Germans might still win the war. The withdrawal of Russia allowed the transfer of large German armies from the east to the western front. Beginning on March 21, 1918, the Germans used them to launch a series of major offensives designed to break through the Allied trench systems and end the long defensive stalemate. In the face of these German drives, the Allies established a unified command under General Ferdinand Foch, and with some reluctance Pershing now agreed to the detachment and use of American units wherever they were most needed. Beginning on May 31, the American Second Division and several marine units helped the French turn back the Germans at Château-Thierry and Belleau Wood, and between July 15 and August 6 some eight American divisions participated in battles that contained the last of the German offensives and forced a German retreat from the Marne River to the Vesle. By early August the German offensive power had been broken, and with American reinforcements now arriving in large numbers, the Allies were rapidly achieving the superiority necessary to take the initiative.

The result was a series of Allied offensives, forcing German retreats along the Somme River, from the area between the Oise and the Aisne, and from western Belgium. Reinforced by new American divisions, the British and French were now sweeping forward. Farther east, the newly constituted American First Army was at last involved in operations of its own. In mid-September it attacked and wiped out the German salient at Saint Mihiel. Later in the month it undertook the massive Meuse-Argonne offensive, driving north along the Meuse River and through the Argonne Forest toward Sedan. By early November it had destroyed a major portion of the German defense system and contributed substantially to the German decisions that led to the armistice.

In its military operations the United States suffered far fewer casualties than the other major belligerents. A total of 112,432 Americans died while in service, nearly a third of them in training camps and many as a consequence of the influenza epidemic that began in September 1918. The other belligerents bore the major losses associated with the war's trench-line slaughterhouses and the breaking of German military might. Yet the American contribution indisputably provided the margin of Allied victory. It was a major factor in foiling the German gamble on submarine warfare, it provided the reinforcements needed to contain the last German offensives, and it provided the margin of military superiority that finally broke the stalemate on the western front.

## Peace and Beyond

Even before the October reversals, the German military command had concluded that only an armistice could keep the Allied armies out of Germany itself. This had been demanded by General Erich Ludendorff as early as September 29; five days later, following the formation of a new government under Prince Max of Baden, the Germans indicated their willingness to restore peace on the basis of President Wilson's Fourteen Points. An exchange of notes followed, with Wilson insisting on German evacuation of occupied territory, an immediate end to submarine attacks, and proof that the government requesting terms really represented the German people rather than their "military masters and monarchical autocrats." To these conditions a reorganized German government agreed, and on October 23, Wilson turned to the task of obtaining their acceptance by the other belligerents.

This proved difficult. In the American camp General Pershing was now calling for unconditional surrender, and during deliberations in Paris the British, French, and Italians all voiced strong objections to Wilson's peace proposals. Finally, however, threats that the United States would make a separate peace, coupled perhaps with fears about where a potential revolution in Germany could lead, produced a conditional acceptance. On November 4 the Allies agreed to a peace based on the Fourteen Points with two reservations, the first being an exclusion of point 2, in regard to freedom of the seas, and the second stipulating that Germany must pay for all civilian damages caused by its aggression. In addition, it was agreed, the armistice terms must prevent the Germans from resuming hostilities.

Such terms were not what the Germans had hoped for. But by the time they were offered, the German condition had become desperate. By November 7 the other Central Powers had already surrendered, mutiny was sweeping the German navy, and revolution had broken out in Munich. On November 8 a German armistice commission was received by Marshal Foch in his railway coach in the Compiègne Forest, and the following day, while the commission considered Allied terms, Germany became a republic. Under pressure the Kaiser abdicated and subsequently fled to the Netherlands. At 5:15 A.M. on November 11 the German delegates signed the armistice offered them, and less than six hours later, at 11:00 A.M. on November 11, 1918, the Great War came to an end.

As the guns fell silent, jubilant throngs celebrated the coming of peace. Liberal democracy, so it was stated and restated, had triumphed over the forces bent on its destruction. Among those who had helped to organize and administer the instruments of victory, there were many who believed that their handiwork could be adapted to the problems of postwar reconstruction and used to organize and administer peaceful progress. Diplomats and foreign policy experts seemed confident that an association of victors could serve as the instrument for realizing Wilson's international goals, and in the government-encouraged labor unions, welfare organizations, associational bureaucracies, and professional societies hopes for a "new liberalism" in which their particular orders would play key roles ran high.

If the new forms of association raised hopes, however, they also produced fear, resentment, and disillusionment. Substantial minorities had come to see them not as building blocks of a progressive order but as instruments of monopoly, tyranny, terrorism, injustice, profiteering, or sectional advantage. In the Midwest, in particular, a heritage of isolationism had combined with anger over the wheat program and the loyalty measures to produce a marked revulsion against Wilson and his war managers. Elsewhere, both at home and abroad, the drift of politics in late 1918 did not bode well for the hopeful visions emanating from Wilsonian reconstructionists. Despite Wilson's plea for a Democratic Congress, it was the Republicans who won the congressional elections that fall; and despite Wilson's faith that the world's peoples were with him, power in Europe was gravitating toward extremists who preached either nationalistic revenge or international social revolution.

The war to end wars was over. But it remained to be seen whether it would achieve its goal or whether the forces it had unleashed would bring greater disorders.

# CHAPTER 3

# Conflict and Frustration

## 1918–1920

Although the armistice of November 1918 ended the war with Germany, it did not usher in a period of tranquillity. The world inherited by the peacemakers was one in which questions of economic and social reconstruction were generating intense political heat and civil strife. And the American nation inherited by the demobilizers was ready to erupt into industrial, social, and political conflict. Both abroad and at home the architects of the war machinery tried to build comparable tools for resolving peacetime conflicts and administering national and international progress. But for the most part, their handiwork either collapsed or was repudiated, and by 1920 they were giving way to social designers who were more attuned to the postwar resurgence of individualistic, antistatist, and isolationist values.

## Peacemaking

On December 4, 1918, President Wilson, the American Peace Commission, and a large body of technical experts sailed for Europe hoping that the peace envisioned in the Fourteen Points could be translated into reality. Upon arriving at Brest, Wilson made triumphal tours of the European capitals, and in January 1919, as the peace conference assembled in Paris, his hope of integrating a democratized enemy into a new community of power or league of nations remained high. At home, however, Republican partisans had won control of Congress and were bitter over Wilson's exclusion of their leaders from the peace commission, a situation unlikely to strengthen his position at the peace table.

And in the other victorious nations, supporters of the Wilsonian design were now losing ground to those who called for revenge, heavy reparations from Germany, and a permanent reduction of German power. In Britain the elections of December 1918 demonstrated the political potency of such slogans as "Hang the Kaiser" and "Make Germany Pay." In France, Premier Georges Clemenceau headed a government bent on retribution and ironclad guarantees of future French security, and in both Italy and Japan emphasis was being put on obtaining the territories and other concessions that had lured them into the war.

As the conference met, moreover, the fate of Russia and the impact that bolshevism might have on the rest of Europe remained huge question marks. German instability, Russian calls for world revolution, and short-lived communist takeovers in Hungary and Bavaria were all aspects of a larger threat that worried the peacemakers. Even as they quarreled over how to rid the world of kaiserism, they became involved in running disputes over how best to contain and put an end to the communist menace. For Wilson and his supporters the answer was to liquidate the Allied military intervention in Russia, relieve the human misery on which bolshevism fed, and build a strong democratic Germany that could act as a stabilizing force. But for other Allied leaders, especially the French, it was military measures to contain and then overthrow Russia's communist regime. While the United States proceeded to extract its troops from northern Russia and seek stability through large-scale food relief programs, Clemenceau and his supporters urged increased Allied military and economic aid for the Russians and other eastern Europeans who were fighting the Bolsheviks.

As negotiations proceeded, Wilson's opposition limited what the French could do in eastern Europe. The Allied military interventions did come to an end, and while a chain of anticommunist states emerged along Russia's western border, the new Poland was shaped more by Wilson's designs that by those of the French. In regard to Germany, Wilson yielded much to French demands. Although American and British opposition killed Clemenceau's plan for buffer states in the German Rhineland, the final settlement called for a fifteen-year occupation and permanent demilitarization of the region, return of Alsace-Lorraine to France and French acquisition of the coal mines in the German Saarland, and strict limitations on the future size of Germany's army and navy. In addition, Germany was to lose territory to Belgium, Denmark, and Poland and was not to unite with the remnants of Austria. It was to be stripped of its overseas colonies and forced to pay for its past aggression. To guard against any future German revival, Britain and the United States were to give guarantees of the security of France.

Wilson's presence undoubtedly prevented an even harsher treaty. But clearly more reliance was being put on keeping Germany weak than on integrating a democratic Germany into a new community of democratic power.

On two other key issues — colonial areas and reparations payments — Wilson also yielded much ground. He agreed, in effect, that Germany's colonial empire and much of the Turkish Empire should be divided up among the Allied nations, whose only concession was that the areas should be held as mandates from the League of Nations rather than as outright possessions. Wilson also conceded that the Japanese might take title to German economic concessions in the Shantung area of China, provided that they promised to return political control to the Chinese. And in assessing reparations Wilson gradually gave way to the extreme Allied demands. He acquiesced in a "war guilt" clause under which Germany was forced to acknowledge that it alone had caused the war. He agreed to large exactions of reparations in kind, and he did not insist that the reparations be set at a fixed sum payable in a specified time. Eventually a reparations commission would fix Germany's obligations at the astronomical figure of 136 billion gold marks, approximately $33 billion.

Another major issue at the conference concerned the territories formerly held by the Austro-Hungarian Empire. Boundaries had to be set for the successor nations of Austria, Hungary, Czechoslovakia, and Yugoslavia, a process that was difficult in view of the diverse ethnic groups involved. And particularly burdensome for the peacemakers was the clash between Yugoslavia and Italy over the city of Fiume at the head of the Adriatic Sea. Wilson resisted the Italian demands, even going so far as to make a direct appeal to the Italian people. Despite a protest walkout from the conference by Premier Vittorio Orlando, Wilson remained unwilling to compromise. The issue was finally left for direct negotiations between the Italians and Yugoslavs.

As the peace settlement took shape, Wilson recognized that it contained inequities and defects. Yet these, he believed, were correctable if the right kind of international organization could be established. For him the covenant of the League of Nations had become the central and redeeming feature of the conference's handiwork, and this he had been able to shape in accordance with his own prescriptions. In early confrontations he had insisted on an organization open to all nations, not just a league of victors. He had also insisted that the league be an integral part of the peace treaty and the agency for its implementation and, subsequently, following a brief return visit to the United States, he had obtained provisions designed to accommodate America's Monroe

Doctrine and to exempt domestic issues, allow U.S. withdrawal from the League, and permit rejection by the United States of any League mandate.

As finally written, the League covenant called for an organization that would function through two major organs, an Assembly made up of all members and a Council consisting of the major powers as permanent members and four smaller nations chosen on a rotating basis by the Assembly. There would also be an administrative secretariat, an international court, and a variety of technical agencies. And at the heart of the organization, providing the foundation on which cooperative structures were to be erected, would be a mutual guarantee by all members of each other's independence and territorial integrity. The League would not have its own army or police force. But its decisions would have behind them the force of international law, moral right, and world public opinion, and in cases of aggression it might call on its members to take appropriate action against the aggressor.

By the end of April 1919, the peacemakers had written a treaty for Germany, and on May 7 it was formally presented to delegates from the new German Republic, who protested strongly, arguing that it was a dictated and punitive peace wholly out of keeping with the one promised in prearmistice negotiations. But there was no alternative to acceptance, and on June 28, in the Hall of Mirrors in Versailles Palace, the formal signing took place. Wilson believed that he had helped to forge a lasting peace structure, but it was certainly not the one envisioned in his Fourteen Points. Critics, then and since, have insisted that for all the difficulties involved, more of the original design could have been realized. Wilson, they have charged, traded much of it away for the pipe dream of a League of Nations, and as a bargainer he failed to mobilize and use what might have been his most effective weapon. At a time when the Allies were financially dependent on the United States, he made no serious effort to apply the economic pressure that could have brought political concessions.

Whatever the merits of such charges, the big question now was whether the treaty could win approval in the U.S. Senate. At home Wilson faced a Congress controlled by an opposition party eager to discredit him. He also faced growing sentiment for withdrawing from abroad and isolating America from Europe's "social diseases." As written, the treaty was satisfactory neither to the advocates of a harsh peace serving narrow national interests nor to those who had shared Wilson's hopes for a new international order. From one side he was accused of serving the interests of the Germans and the Bolsheviks; from the other, of helping greedy Allied imperialists to hatch an "inhuman monster."

## The Peace Treaty in the Senate

On July 10, 1919, Wilson formally presented the Treaty of Versailles to the United States Senate. To reject it, he said, would "break the heart of the world," and he left little doubt about his opposition to any amendments or reservations. Equally clear, however, was his opponents' determination not to accept the treaty as written. Their first resort was to lengthy proceedings before the Senate Foreign Relations Committee, a body chaired by Senate Majority Leader Henry Cabot Lodge. When it became clear that a large majority of the Republican senators favored reservations of varying strength, Senator Lodge placed himself at the head of the "strong reservationists." The treaty, so his group insisted, must explicitly recognize congressional prerogatives and the nation's autonomy in immigration and tariff matters. It must not commit the United States to preserving the British Empire or Japan's hold on Shantung, for example. And above all, Congress must have the right to evaluate each situation that might possibly require the use of American forces. The League guarantees must not become blank checks for future American participation in collective security measures.

By making a few mild concessions, Wilson might have enlisted the support of a number of the reservationists. His decision instead was to take his case to the people; for three weeks in September 1919, as his new speaking tour moved across the country, it seemed that he might indeed check the rising cynicism and force favorable action in the Senate. His health, however, was fragile. He had a long history of cerebral vascular disease, including several earlier episodes that some historians have seen as being partly responsible for his growing intellectual rigidity, and attacks of illness now brought his tour to an end. On September 25, after making an address in Pueblo, Colorado, he became too ill to continue, and on October 2, shortly after his return to Washington, he suffered a severe stroke that paralyzed the left side of his face and body. For two weeks he was close to death, and for six weeks more he remained seriously ill, with his wife and physician shielding him from most of the business of government.

With Wilson sidelined, the outcome in the Senate was probably a foregone conclusion. The "irreconcilables," who opposed the treaty under any circumstances, now joined with the reservationists to add fourteen reservations, twelve of them proposed by Senator Lodge. The choice, it seemed, had become a treaty with the Lodge reservations or no treaty at all. Yet Wilson still refused to accept the former or to allow his supporters to do so. On November 19 his followers joined with the irreconcilables to defeat the treaty with the reservations included, and immediately thereafter a Democratic resolution to ratify without reservations also failed. As matters stood, neither Wilson nor Lodge could muster the necessary two-thirds majority.

During the next four months a number of individuals and groups tried to arrange a compromise. Others pleaded with Wilson to give in, and from the Allied nations came indications that they would welcome ratification on Lodge's terms. But to Wilson this still amounted to nullification, and when a new vote was taken on March 19, 1920, the results were basically similar to the vote in 1919. Although twenty-one Democrats broke ranks and voted for the treaty with Lodge's reservations, the number sticking with Wilson was sufficient to prevent ratification. To end the state of hostilities, Congress then adopted a resolution repealing the declarations of war against Germany and Austria-Hungary. But this the president vetoed, thus leaving the nation in a technical state of war. The coming elections, he had declared, would be a "great and solemn referendum" on the League issue, but he was unable to make them so. The United States would not ratify the Treaty of Versailles and would never join the League of Nations.

Whether or not Wilson himself was responsible, his vision of a new international order would remain unrealized. Taking shape instead would be two weaker and more national-oriented systems, one built around the Anglo-French alliances and their extension in the League apparatus, the other around a new set of American-sponsored treaties, expert commissions, and cooperative arrangements. The building of a progressive world order, so the policymakers of the 1920s would insist, was taking place without sacrificing the benefits and safeguards of national autonomy. But the structures erected were to prove incapable of preventing a world depression and a second and greater world war.

## Reconstruction at Home

At the same time that the peacemakers were laboring to create international order, a number of America's war managers had been trying to adapt wartime structures to the tasks of postwar reconstruction and peacetime management. From mid-1918 on, they had been discussing which features of war collectivism should be retained as instruments for implementing a "new liberalism." By the end of the war they had produced a variety of blueprints. Being planned or discussed were such agencies as a "reconstruction council," a "peace industries board," a "labor relations tribunal," a "peace policies inquiry," and a "living conditions commission."

Even as these designs were being elaborated, however, the obstacles to their realization were becoming insurmountable. Groups that had been critical of the war administration were in no mood to tolerate a peacetime counterpart. Congress was unsympathetic and eager to regain its prewar role in policymaking. Private organizational leaders were under increasing pressure to abandon collaboration with class enemies or rival interests. And disintegrating now, as the business volunteers who had served for a dollar a year ended their service, was the administrative elite that had facilitated public-private cooperation and dampened traditional fears of statism and collective action. Indeed, within the Wilson administration itself there were strong doubts that such agencies were needed or desirable or even politically attainable. Bernard Baruch, who had been looked to for leadership, was unwilling to urge extension of wartime industrial arrangements. Nor had the president been persuaded. On December 2, partly perhaps to placate conservative opposition to his foreign policy, Wilson dissociated himself from reconstruction planning and proposed to leave readjustment problems to the individual efforts of "spirited businessmen and self-reliant laborers."

Not surprisingly, then, early efforts to install postwar substitutes for the war organizations were unsuccessful. These efforts could neither halt liquidation of key war boards nor establish new agencies of reconstruction. Yet this initial failure did not end the search for domestic managerial tools. As it turned out, reconversion left to businessmen and laborers became punctuated by bitter industrial conflicts and massive fluctuations in employment, demand, and prices. In response, a number of the former war managers kept trying to resurrect modified segments of the war machinery.

In early 1919 the three most urgent problems were those posed by unemployed veterans and war workers, canceled Allied orders for American foodstuffs, and business fears of impending deflation. That something had to be done was widely conceded, and the actions ultimately taken did involve limited extension or resurrection of the war apparatus. What remained of the War Labor Administration joined with private and local partners in campaigns to step up expenditures on public works. What remained of the food and war credit machinery became closely linked to relief and rehabilitation activities in Europe, continuing through them to support agricultural and export markets. In the Commerce Department a group of former dollar-a-year men succeeded in creating an industrial board designed to change business psychology through negotiation and support of "fair prices." From its labors came a steel price schedule, defended by board chairman

George Peek as being scientifically determined. But when the Railroad Administration disagreed and the attorney general threatened antitrust action, the board's operations came to an end.

Efforts to convert these forms of collective action into ongoing stabilizers received little help in Congress. There the emphasis was on economy and tax relief, not managerial tools. Yet economic difficulties persisted. By late spring, concern with finding replacements for military demand was giving way to overoptimism and a speculative boom with rapidly rising living costs. By fall the nation was suffering through one of the worst bouts of price inflation and labor turmoil in its history. And while one response was to look for "subversives," another was new attempts to install managerial tools modeled after those of the war period. One new creation was the High Cost of Living Division through which the Justice Department tried to resurrect the wartime network of profit restraints, conservation activities, and price interpretation boards. The Fuel Administration was also revived temporarily. And through two industrial conferences, one meeting in October 1919 and the second studying the situation from December 1919 to March 1920, efforts were made to resurrect the wartime system of labor tribunals and labor-management cooperation.

Again, though, managers were unable to surmount the obstacles that blocked implementation of their designs. The industrial conferences did not bring forth the contemplated machinery, and the problems of the revived Fuel Administration, the High Cost of Living Division, and what remained of the wartime food organizations were such as to make these agencies more enemies than friends. In 1920 they all expired, their demise signaling another major defeat for reconstruction management. When Congress adjourned, the War Finance Corporation was still functioning, but the hope was that new investment cooperatives, to be formed under the Edge Act of December 1919, would soon take its place. The only other major survivals of the war state were agencies and arrangements authorized to continue under the Transportation and Merchant Marine Acts of 1920. For railroads and shipping, Congress had rejected nationalization schemes and proposals for national transportation planning, but it had authorized a continuing mix of public aid, regulatory restraint, and government-fostered cartels and cooperation.

With the war over, traditional fears of big government had reasserted themselves and been spurred along by taxpayers and regulated interests who believed that they stood to gain from shrinking the public sector. Many had come to believe that economic dysfunctions were best corrected by shrinking government rather than by expanding it. And for the time being, this antistatism had blocked not only the advocates of new social programs but also those who would use the state to coordinate and support private organizational elites. Antistatism, however, did not necessarily mean a scrapping of the private side of war organization. Over whether to do this, in whole or in part, other battles were being waged.

## Antiunionism and National Purification

One such battle involved the fate of war-fostered unionization, specifically whether it should become part of a new organizational order or should be scrapped as something appropriate only for a national emergency. Workers were seeking to make their wartime gains permanent, and through strikes and strike threats they were initially able to expand the area of collective bargaining. For much of the public, however, unions had no rightful place in a peacetime system. Drawing on this sentiment was a growing antiunion movement, operating both through business associations committed to the nonunionized "open shop" and through groups urging company unions, corporate welfare programs, and new approaches to personnel management. By mid-1919 labor's position was rapidly weakening. Unions no longer had government support; they were being blamed for the rising cost of living and lagging productivity, and to a public inflamed with anti-Bolshevik hysteria the distinction between good American unions and those bent on social revolution had become increasingly blurred.

The stage was set for major labor defeats. In late 1919, as the issue of communism diverted even more attention from legitimate grievances, unionism suffered one setback after another. The great steel strike, which began on September 22, was soon crumbling under the weight of massive public disapproval, stern repression of union activities, and armed protection for strikebreakers. In Boston a strike of the police force brought intervention and union busting by Governor Calvin Coolidge. There was, he said, "no right to strike against the public safety by anybody, anywhere, anytime." And in November, when the coal miners struck for higher pay, Attorney General A. Mitchell Palmer used the Lever Act to obtain court injunctions ordering them to cease all strike activity.

In the wake of such defeats unionism did not disappear. In 1920 the American Federation of Labor had 3,260,000 members (over 500,000 more than at war's end), and some unions retained enough power to create major crises. Yet efforts to organize the basic and mass production industries had clearly been thwarted. The dream of converting the war-fostered unions into components of a new organizational system was not to be realized. As antiunionism gained new impetus during the post-1920 recession, labor organization would soon recede to roughly the same position it had occupied before the war. What the New Era would take from wartime labor developments was not independent unions; it was rather management-organized employee associations, vertical committees in which management exercised leadership, and new personnel work with its vision of creating a labor force for which unions would have no appeal.

Meanwhile, even as the fate of the wartime labor system was being decided, American society was being rent by conflict of other sorts. Ethnic divisions were being acerbated by ethnic-related quarrels over the peace settlement, new demands for immigration restriction, and new efforts to convert "hyphenated Americans" into "real Americans." Cultural divisions were taking on a new intensity, especially over the war-fostered victories of the prohibitionists and feminists and the war-promoted assaults on Victorian morality and rural provincialism. Religious conflict was mounting, sparked particularly by a new fundamentalist militancy against modernist error and creeping secularism. Racial tensions now, built up during the war period and exacerbated by clashing postwar expectations, were producing not only racist rhetoric and agitation but violent and destructive race riots as well. In Chicago rioting that began on a Lake Michigan beach on July 27 led to a thirteen-day reign of terror, and between July and December 1919 some twenty cities exploded into orgies of burning, looting, and killing, leaving 120 dead and thousands homeless. Many feared that America was coming apart, the prey of those who hoped to benefit from chaos and anarchy. In the context of such fears, the champions of order were busily engaged in finding new uses for the wartime loyalty apparatus.

In particular, it was said, America needed purgatives and antidotes to deal with the social and political poisons now undermining its national life. In the spreaders of such poisons, especially in the newly formed Communist parties and other radical groups, America faced a national enemy too insidious to be tolerated or absorbed into the body politic. It was an enemy that would have to be fought through special agencies similar to those established during the war. By late 1919 a new network of such agencies was in operation. In the Justice Department, Attorney General Palmer had put J. Edgar Hoover in charge of a new antiradical division. Arrayed around it were cooperating federal bureaus and state agencies, and attached as quasi-official extensions were the wartime loyalty organizations plus such newly formed groups as the Allied Loyalty League and the American Legion.

For a time the network's operations enjoyed strong support. In the spring of 1919 a series of terrorist acts, including the mailing of bombs to prominent officials and the bombing of Palmer's Washington residence, had generated widespread public alarm. When General Leonard Wood called for a policy of "S.O.S. — ship or shoot" — deport or kill the foreign radicals supposedly at the root of political unrest — many Americans seemed to agree. Protest remained minimal as vigilante groups moved into action, state and local officials conducted antiradical raids, and federal officials invoked wartime statutes and began dragnet arrests and summary deportations. Nor were the courts inclined to see such actions as violations of constitutional liberties. In the Schenck and Abrams cases of 1919, the Supreme Court held that any action constituting a "clear and present danger" to the social order did not enjoy the protection of the First Amendment; by applying this doctrine, it upheld convictions under the wartime Espionage and Sedition acts.

As hysteria mounted, then, "red scare" justice frequently replaced that grounded in the traditions of Anglo-Saxon jurisprudence. In Centralia, Washington, IWW agitator Wesley Everest was dragged from the town jail, castrated, and hanged from the girders of a railroad bridge. In the coroner's report he was alleged to have "jumped off with a rope around his neck and then shot himself full of holes." In New York thousands cheered as the U.S.S. *Buford*, the so-called Soviet Ark, departed for Hangö, Finland, with a cargo of 249 deportees. Included were not only such notorious "propagandists by deed" as Emma Goldman and Alexander Berkman but also more than 200 people whose only offense was espousal of radical ideas. In Detroit the great majority of some 800 people seized and held amid wretched conditions in city buildings turned out to be what a citizens' committee called "plain, ignorant foreigners" rather than "dangerous radicals." And in South Braintree, Massachusetts, police searching for the murderers of a shoe company paymaster arrested Nicola Sacco and Bartolomeo Vanzetti, both Italian aliens and both avowed anarchists. Later the prosecuting attorney would make the defendants' radicalism the cornerstone of his case, and they would be convicted and sentenced to death.

Amid tragedy and moral outrage there was also some comic relief. In Chicago "patriotic" prisoners rioted, taking violent exception to having "reds" put in the same cells with them. "There are some things," one newspaper remarked, "at which even a Chicago crook draws the line." In New Brunswick, New Jersey, the scene of raids on a socialist club, seized papers that were thought to be plans for "various types of bombs" were finally identified as drawings for an improved phonograph. But such ridiculousness was lost on the great majority of Americans now caught up in fear, hysteria, and zealotry. It was not until January 1920, when the Labor Department refused to cooperate in holding and deporting the 6,000 victims of the largest raids, that such antiradical measures provoked much concern about civil liberties, and it was several months more before the perceptions used to justify the antiradical operations began to change.

Antiradicalism also became a weapon in the hands of antifeminists, used particularly by such ultraconservative groups as the Women Patriots. Though it could not prevent ratification, achieved on August 26, 1920, of the Nineteenth Amendment granting women the vote, it did lead moderate feminists to distance themselves from former allies and contributed to the breakup of the coalition that had won suffrage for women. The National Woman's Party under Alice Paul would continue to work for full equality to be guaranteed by an equal rights amendment to the Constitution. But other women's groups saw this as a threat to hard-won protective legislation, and still others turned their energies away from politics to concerns of taking advantage of cultural and economic change. Gains for women in the 1920s would come primarily by adapting to the "modern" roles created by corporate bureaucratic needs, new cultural ideals, renewed economic growth, and persisting managerial impulses, not by exerting unified political pressure in pursuit of a common female mission or by breaking down the barriers between men's work and women's work.

As the "red scare" began to recede, loyalty groups had greater difficulty in obtaining governmental support and keeping their quasi-official status. Yet "un-Americanism," as some groups were now defining it, had come, once again, to include more than espousals of radical doctrine. It had become partly a matter of ethnicity, race, religion, and social values, all areas where the "100 percent American" must be separated and saved from impure and contaminating elements. It was as safeguards against and controllers of this "un-Americanism" that the organizations born of the war and strengthened during the intimidation of 1919 — groups such as the National Security League, the American Protective League, the Allied Loyalty League, and the American Legion — would remain active in the 1920s. Unlike the federal war agencies and the war-fostered labor unions, they would not only survive but would also remain a major political force.

## Visions of a New Individualism

Running through much of the postwar assault on government, unionization, and "un-Americanism" was a recurring appeal to America's tradition of economic individualism. It was an appeal that could also be used to attack business organization, and for a time, in 1919 and 1920, such attacks did bring a revival of antitrust activities and attitudes. Schemes for permanent relaxation of the antitrust laws met with strong opposition. And responding to allegations that business combines were responsible for the economic troubles of the reconversion period, the nation's antitrust agencies stirred from their wartime sleep and began attacking collusion and conspiracy in sales of foodstuffs, fuels, textiles, and building materials. By early 1920 some federal and state investigators were hunting "monopolists" almost as zealously as others were hunting "reds."

Unlike labor organizers, however, business organizers were able to erect shields against their antagonists and preserve much of what the war had brought about. Legally they won an expanded "rule of reason," enunciated especially in the U.S. Steel Corporation case of March 1920. Under this rule no merger seemed too large to be legal, provided that it did not unduly restrain competition. And ideologically such corporations managed to cultivate images that distinguished their bureaucracies from other kinds and depicted them as sustainers and improvers of individualism rather than underminers or destroyers of it. Unlike the old "trusts" and "rings," so the argument ran, the new business organizations were service-minded, public-spirited, growth-oriented, technically progressive, and scientifically managed. Their emphasis was on improving the informational and moral base of economic individualism, not supplanting it. And through them the American people might meet modern social and national needs while retaining business independence and the traditional curbs on big government and monopolistic conspiracies.

In business, then, association building did continue, and by 1920 was producing a wide variety of cooperative informational exchanges, waste elimination programs, and better business rules, all justified as in the public interest and as encouraging healthy competition. In agriculture too, where cooperationists had tough going despite antitrust exemptions, the immediate postwar period brought both a federation of the farm bureaus and continued growth of commodity groups and marketing associations. In these areas the war-fostered associational development was sustaining itself, and it was being argued that this could bring about the "new individualism" envisioned by some prewar progressives. It could, in the words of the publicist and educator Glenn Frank, bring needed ordering mechanisms and community action while restraining "political government" and could thus save America from "a rampant unsocial individualism on the one hand and an inefficient bureaucracy on the other."

Often joined with such arguments, moreover, were calls for national coordinating bodies, envisioned now as taking the place of the war state yet remaining nonstatist in character. In one set of proposals, coordination would be achieved through collaborative councils, special tribunals, and advisory planning boards. In another, much of the coordinating role would be assigned to apolitical research institutes such as the newly established Brookings Institution, Twentieth Century Fund, and the National Bureau of Economic Research. In yet another such professional groups as the American Economic Association, the Taylor Society, and the engineering associations would serve as coordinators. The engineers in particular were eager to play a part. In 1920 they brought their societies together in a national federation, elected Herbert Hoover its first president, and began a waste survey designed to stimulate and guide associational activities. Out of it and similar surveys, Hoover argued, could come "a plan of individualism and associational activities" that would preserve "the initiative, the inventiveness, the individuality, the character of man" yet would also "enable us to synchronize socially and economically this gigantic machine that we have built out of applied science."

Also surfacing was the notion that if government lacked managerial competence, it could play a constructive role in promoting and servicing the organizational developments needed in the private sector. Indeed, it was argued, doing so was the most effective way of preventing the growth of a stultifying and liberty-destroying statism. By late 1920, as the onset of a severe recession produced calls for new market controls, the agitation for less government had become intermixed with agitation for new governmental services that would assist in developing the potential inherent in the private sector's associational activities.

## The Selection of a New President

For promoters of the "new individualism," the ideal president would have been Herbert Hoover, and in early 1920 a short-lived Hoover boomlet did develop. Among the politicians who controlled the Republican party machinery, however, Hoover had relatively little support. The leading candidates were General Leonard Wood, Governor Frank Lowden of Illinois, and Senator Hiram Johnson of California. The problem was that none of them could put together a convention majority, and in this situation the initiative passed to a small group of senatorial and business leaders who hoped to nominate a dependable and controllable party regular. On the evening of June 11, with the convention adjourned overnight, the group decided to support Senator Warren G. Harding of Ohio, a man whose chief qualification seemed to be his good relationships with all party factions. He became the compro-

The Democratic National Convention, San Francisco, California, in 1920. *(UPI/Bettmann)*

mise candidate and on the tenth ballot received the nomination. For vice-president, Harding's supporters had picked Senator Irvine Lenroot of Wisconsin. But the convention refused to go along. It chose instead Governor Calvin Coolidge of Massachusetts, the man who had won public fame crushing the Boston police strike.

The Democratic convention, meeting in San Francisco on June 28, also turned into a deadlock with neither former secretary of the treasury William Gibbs McAdoo nor Attorney General A. Mitchell Palmer able to secure the nomination. On the forty-fourth ballot the Democrats nominated James M. Cox, the governor of Ohio and the candidate with the closest ties to the party's urban and anti-Prohibition elements. Cox's running mate was Franklin D. Roosevelt of New York, who was at the time serving as assistant secretary of the Navy and was a strong League of Nations supporter.

During the campaign Cox and Roosevelt urged ratification of the Versailles Treaty and warned that a victory for Harding would mean the end of progressivism in domestic politics. Harding straddled the

League issue, encouraging both irreconcilables and reservationists to believe that his victory could serve their cause. He also appealed to the longing for domestic peace, for "normalcy," as he put it, rather than "nostrums." Campaigning against Wilson rather than Cox, Harding won over a number of groups that had come to blame Wilson and his works for their difficulties. In particular, the Democrats lost the support of the farming, ethnic, and independent blocs that had reelected Wilson in 1916. When the votes were counted, Harding had won a lopsided victory. Cox carried only eleven states—the Democratic "solid South"—for an electoral count of 127 to Harding's 404, and in the popular vote Harding received 16,152,200 votes (some 61 percent of the total) to Cox's 9,147,353 (35 percent). Eugene Debs, running on the Socialist party ticket even though he was still in federal prison for obstructing the war effort, polled a surprising 919,799 (3.5 percent). In the congressional races the Republicans ended up with a majority of 309 to 132 in the House of Representatives and 59 to 37 in the Senate.

Hopes of reestablishing a reform coalition, obtaining ratification of the Versailles Treaty, and installing the peacetime management envisioned in 1918 had all been shattered. Nor did the times seem propitious for a new flowering of civic virtue. Only weeks before, in what became known as the Black Sox scandal, an indictment of eight Chicago White Sox baseball players for allegedly throwing the 1919 World Series had tainted severely the very sport supposed to embody the nation's virtues. Yet the kind of managerial progressivism evident in the postwar designs for a new individualism did not depend on continued Democratic control of the presidency. It also had its Republican supporters. And under the auspices of such administrators as Herbert Hoover, Henry C. Wallace, and Charles Evans Hughes, a new effort to resurrect and perpetuate portions of the war apparatus would soon be under way.

CHAPTER 4

# In Search of Peace
# and Prosperity
## 1921–1924

 Historians have long looked on the presidency of Warren G. Harding as a major debacle. "Normalcy," they have explained in great detail, really meant the transfer of government to corrupt officials, incompetents, and rapacious special interests. Often missing from their accounts is the fact that the Harding era also came close to combining full employment and rising living standards with stable prices and international peace. For all the scandals, the new administration presided over a series of developments that made the American economy the envy of much of the world, and for all its commitments to small government, national tariff walls, and anti-foreignism, it offered a base for those seeking to reestablish major features of the war system and to organize a Republican alternative to Wilsonian internationalism. In part the story of America from 1921 to 1924 was one of political pilfering and continuing xenophobia accompanied by retreats into weaker government, special (as opposed to public) interest consciousness, and a diminished sense of international obligation. But it was one as well of new managerial designs foreshadowing the modern capitalism of a later era.

## The President and the Policymakers

The new president was not among the people who had helped to build the war organizations or enunciate managerial goals and values. Born near Blooming Grove, Ohio, in 1865, Harding had risen in life as owner and editor of the *Marion Star* and as an effective practitioner of local politics and small-town amenities. In a career that carried him from the state legislature to the U.S. Senate to the White House, he had become noted chiefly for his affability and party loyalty, his knack for promoting harmony, and his capacity for saying little yet impressing people with how he said it. His understanding of the world outside Ohio politics was minimal, and in the White House he continued to operate as an Ohio politician and small-town socializer. "God, I can't be an ingrate," he is supposed to have said. And in practice, the friends, associates, and supporters to whom he felt grateful received ample rewards. Men from his circle in Marion were appointed to such positions as comptroller of the currency, director of the Mint, and superintendent of federal prisons. Men to whom he had taken a liking were responsible for subsequent scandals in the Veterans' Bureau and the Alien Property Office, and in what turned out to be two of his most disastrous appointments he elevated close personal friends to cabinet positions. As attorney general he chose his longtime political manager, Harry M. Daugherty, and as secretary of the interior his closest friend in the Senate, Albert B. Fall of New Mexico.

Having taken care of friends and supporters, however, Harding was willing to delegate economic and diplomatic policymaking to the "superior minds" who understood such matters. Thus his cabinet came to include four of the strongest cabinet-level officers in the nation's history. Andrew Mellon, wealthy head of a financial empire and master of corporate finance, became secretary of the Treasury. Charles Evans Hughes, the Republican presidential nominee in 1916 and the nation's most eminent lawyer, became secretary of state. Henry C. Wallace, Iowa farm editor and a major figure in farm politics, became secretary of agriculture. And Herbert Hoover, the wartime food administrator and the nation's most eminent engineer, became secretary of commerce and set out to turn that department into a vast research and consulting service for economic decision makers.

Three of the "big four" had ties to Republican progressivism and had shared some of the earlier hopes for developing cooperative harmony under expert leadership. Hughes, Wallace, and Hoover had all been appointed in the face of opposition from party conservatives, and as administrators they envisioned a positive role for government going beyond that prescribed in Republican orthodoxy. Properly staffed and delimited, they argued, government could serve as a catalyzer and coordinator of cooperative endeavors, a gatherer and clearinghouse of needed information, and a consulting service for groups in need of organizational and technical expertise.

As constituted, then, the new administration contained influential spokesmen for a view of government drawn from the war experience. Yet limiting what the new administrators could do were a number of constraints and obstacles. They could not ignore the pressures for tax reduction and old-style protectionism. They faced uncooperative congressional blocs and administrative agencies. Power systems abroad, especially in Japan, Russia, and France, were annoyingly resistant to their designs for world order. And their positions depended on a president who was inclined to defer to the "best minds" yet reluctant to accept measures that were politically damaging or did too much violence to his small-town value system.

Policy was based on the balances struck between these opposing forces; not surprisingly, it contained a number of inconsistencies. Government shrinking advanced hand in hand with national protectionism, new programs of internal improvement, and new measures of farm relief. Yet there was movement toward the kind of managerial tools and aids that Hoover, Hughes, and Wallace envisioned—enough movement, indeed, to lend credibility to claims that permanent peace and prosperity were in train and that ways had been found to realize the dreams of the Progressive Era while avoiding the evils feared by conservatives. In part the continued weakness of reform statism can be explained in terms of an altered mood and greater political fragmentation. But also involved was a widespread belief that the "best minds" of the time were committed to progressive ends and were successfully developing superior tools for attaining them.

## The Search for International Stability

As Americans looked out on the world in 1921, they tended to see a compound of error and depravity that was partly responsible for worsening economic conditions in the United States. Europe, in particular, was accused by political leaders of misusing America's postwar aid and of now seeking to avoid the consequences through emigration, export dumping, and debt cancellation. The nation, many Americans were persuaded, had to defend itself. The result, when Congress met in special session, was quick action on two measures previously vetoed by President Wilson. In May, Harding signed both the Emergency Quota Act, cutting immigration some 60 percent, and the Emergency Tariff, which raised agricultural duties, embargoed other products, and provided new protection against foreign dumping. In addition, government leaders promised that taxpayers would be protected from Europeans' efforts to escape just debts or to bail themselves out through new raids on the American treasury.

Within the new administration, however, these protectionist impulses collided with a business internationalism seeking export expansion and wider opportunities abroad. America, it was argued, could not prosper if denied access to world markets and resources or if forced to wall itself off from an unstable and unprosperous world. And America did have the capacity to change things. Properly organized and assisted, its financial, industrial, and technical communities could form links with similar groups abroad, reduce the economic "politicization" that lay at the root of the difficulty, and put idle resources to productive use. The need was for a diplomacy that would help American business expand, and it was this kind of diplomacy that Hughes and Hoover sought to provide. Through conferences and negotiations they set out to reduce the perceived political obstacles. Through fact-gathering agencies and commissions of experts they sought to create shared values and keep decision makers enlightened. And through other conferences and consultations they promoted new units of public-private collaboration. The world they hoped to create was much like that envisioned in progressive and Wilsonian diplomacy, but their perceptions of how it could be created and the kinds of tools that would be most effective were not the same.

In 1920 both Hughes and Hoover had urged American membership in a delimited version of the League of Nations. But this, they now concluded, had become politically impossible. The most that could be hoped for was a series of separate measures linking the United States to the best features of the Versailles Treaty, and in a series of skillful diplomatic moves Hughes successfully forged such links. The Treaty of Berlin, ratified in October 1921, normalized German-American relations on the basis of the Versailles settlement. Similar treaties did the same for relations with Austria and Hungary. And beginning in 1922 the United States moved, through unofficial observers and conduits, to develop a system of cooperation and consultation with League agencies. In addition, Hughes pushed for American entry into the World Court, but this failed to win Senate approval.

While forging links to the Versailles system, Hughes also moved to "depoliticize" the Far East and reduce what the president called "the crushing burdens of military and naval establishments." In July 1921 the United States took the initiative in inviting the major powers and such other nations as had interests in the Far East to a conference in Washington, D.C. And there on November 12, in a keynote address that made banner headlines, Hughes not only discussed the need for transforming rivalry into cooperation but also set forth specific proposals for scrapping ships and maintaining fixed naval ratios. In thirty-five minutes, noted the English journalist Colonel Repington, the secretary of state sank "more ships than all the admirals of the world have sunk in a cycle of centuries."

Hughes's proposals bore fruit. By the time the conference adjourned in February 1922, it had produced three major treaties and several lesser ones. First of all, a naval limitations treaty pledged the five leading naval powers—the United States, Great Britain, Japan, Italy, and France—to halt the construction of capital ships (battleships over 10,000 tons) for ten years and to bring their holdings of such ships into a fixed ratio of $5:5:3:1.67:1.67$. This would mean 525,000 tons each for Britain and the United States, 315,000 for Japan, and 175,000 each for France and Italy. At French insistence, however, the provisions would not apply to smaller vessels, and at Japanese insistence the United States and Britain promised not to fortify their outlying island possessions in the western Pacific. Second, the Four Power Treaty ended the existing Anglo-Japanese alliance and substituted an agreement under which the British, Japanese, French, and Americans pledged themselves to respect each other's Pacific possessions and to consult in case of controversy. Third, the Nine Power Treaty pledged all the nations at the conference to respect Chinese sovereignty and to refrain from seeking special privileges in China. Finally, in a series of supplementary treaties, agreements were reached on limiting the use of submarines and poison gas, on cable rights and Chinese tariffs, and on the withdrawal of Japanese forces from Siberia and Shantung. In Hughes's eyes the new treaty system provided a framework for peaceful relations and economic cooperation in the Far East, and for a time it seemed that Japan might indeed become a cooperating partner in implementing American goals.

While building the new treaty system, American policymakers also worked to remove other political obstacles to development. Another series of negotiations aimed at isolating and ostracizing Soviet Russia, the assumption being that the communist system there must soon collapse. Still another sought to reduce British restrictionism in the Near East. And in Latin America attempts were made to replace gunboat diplomacy with a subtler management designed to install and sustain cooperative governments. For Santo Domingo this meant the ending of military government and the gradual withdrawal of American marines —the last of whom left in 1924. For Cuba it meant the withdrawal of a military mission that had overseen new elections in early 1921. For Nicaragua it meant preparations for ending still another military mission, and for Colombia it meant ratification of a treaty under which the country received compensation for its loss of Panama. The year 1923 also brought U.S. recognition of Mexico's revolutionary government, after the Mexicans had agreed to settle American territorial claims and to respect previous land grants. And out of protracted negotiations in 1922 and 1923 came an American-supported system for stabilizing

Central America, primarily through arms limitations, international tribunals, and economic development programs. The hemispheric goal of the United States, so Hughes declared, was a framework within which the American republics could work together to build a common prosperity, and by 1924 he believed that major segments of that framework had been put in place.

Meanwhile, Hughes and Hoover were also organizing and seeking to use new units of public-private collaboration. The nation's export industries were now organized and linked to expanding governmental services, an interdepartmental committee on foreign loans began working with banking leaders to guide the movement of American capital abroad, and a revitalized banking consortium became the vehicle through which foreign investments were expected to modernize China. In addition, Hoover sought to deal with the monopolistic pricing of foreign cartels by mobilizing and working through consortia of oil producers, rubber and coffee importers, and communications developers. Hoping that famine relief would serve both humanitarian and antibolshevist ends, Hoover resurrected his postwar relief organization and used it to conduct a private and ostensibly apolitical program that fed approximately 10 million starving Russians.

Such initiatives were accompanied by continuing efforts to organize an "apolitical" revival of the European economy. The key to this, it was believed, lay in revising World War I reparations, and by 1922 both Hughes and Hoover were proposing a committee of private financial experts to determine Germany's "capacity to pay." At first the French balked. They proceeded instead to occupy the Ruhr industrial district and to attempt to collect reparations by force. But when the Germans reacted with work stoppages and slowdowns financed by an inflationary expansion of their currency, France yielded to American and British pressures and acquiesced in the appointment of two expert committees, the more important of which was headed by the American banker Charles G. Dawes. Out of this, in 1924, came the Dawes Plan, adjusting reparations to accord with economic conditions and arranging for an infusion of capital, mostly from American investors, to restabilize Germany's currency. Hailed at the time as both a "scientific" and a "business" solution, the plan laid the foundation for the American-financed German boom of the middle and late 1920s.

As American policymakers moved to solve the German problem, they were also seeking to depoliticize other areas of policymaking. In 1922 Hoover, Hughes, and Mellon became the key members of the World War Foreign Debt Commission. Although the law creating the agency restricted its powers, Congress later acceded to a series of funding agreements that disregarded such restrictions and attempted to adjust interest rates and terms according to a scientific capacity-to-pay principle. Similarly, the Tariff of 1922 combined higher schedules with a flexibility provision under which the president, assisted by informed experts, could adjust rates to meet changing economic conditions. At the time it was not foreseen that virtually all such adjustments, except for inconsequential items, would be upward. In addition, Hughes attempted without success, in 1924, to prevent a racist ban on immigration by Asians. The unnecessary insult to Japan, he argued, would undo much of the work of the Washington conference. But in this field Congress was unwilling to delegate policymaking to administrative experts. Its only concession was to allow another expert commission, again with Hoover as a member, to work out the details of a new quota system that was to reflect the "national origins" of the American people.

As Republican diplomacy took shape, then, it made important concessions to the resurgent demands for isolationism, protection from foreign exports and emigrants, and unilateral action by the United States. Further restraining the major policymakers were their own attitudes toward political tools, military interventions, and entangling commitments. Yet these same policymakers also believed that American prosperity required a stable and prosperous world, and this they were seeking through the creation of new ordering mechanisms in the international arena. Through measures like the Washington Treaties, the Dawes Plan and European debt agreements, the China consortium, the informal links to the League of Nations, and the altered diplomacy for Latin America, they hoped to build the world order that their America required.

## The Old Individualism and the New

If Republican foreign policy was a curious mixture of the old and the new, the same was also true of Republican economic policy. In this field the Harding administration had inherited both a worsening recession and an ongoing debate over how to deal with it. Some participants believed that the proper response of government was the classic one of retrenchment and property protection, the theory being that this would allow natural economic processes to liquidate past errors and create the conditions required for further growth. But others thought that the government could and should play a positive role, especially through actions that would help enlightened managers to expedite the readjustment process and avoid much of the suffering, waste, and disorder that had accompanied the workings of the business cycle in the past.

For those stressing governmental retrenchment, Andrew Mellon became the chief spokesman. It was Mellon who supervised the installation of a new budget and accounting system ordering federal expenditures. And under the nation's first budget directors, Charles G. Dawes and Herbert Lord, economy measures did reduce federal spending by more than 20 percent. This allowed Mellon to argue for tax cuts, and in the revenue measures of 1921 and 1924 he succeeded in securing the kinds of reductions he believed capable of stimulating new business growth. Although defenders of the graduated income tax blocked parts of his program, the surtax applicable to the highest income bracket was reduced from 65 to 40 percent.

In addition, efforts were made to reduce areas of public enterprise that had developed during the war. Government ships were offered to private companies on generous terms, and when there were few takers, Harding tried unsuccessfully to get Congress to provide still greater incentives. The War Finance Corporation was given a new lease on life in 1921, but its functions were confined to aiding rural banks and helping to mobilize farm credit. And attempts were made to dispose of the governmental power and nitrate facilities at Muscle Shoals on the Tennessee River. These failed only after an offer by Henry Ford encountered unexpectedly strong resistance from public power advocates and rival business interests.

When men like Mellon, Dawes, and Attorney General Daugherty were permitted to make policy, the Harding administration also leaned toward crushing labor efforts to block what were perceived as natural economic readjustments. In 1921 it used federal troops to restore order in the coal fields of West Virginia. A year later it encouraged state action to break a national coal strike. And when government-backed wage cuts produced the national railway strike of 1922, Attorney General Daugherty obtained a sweeping court injunction prohibiting all strike activity.

At times the administration also lent encouragement to the resurgent open-shop movement; and when the courts restricted organizational rights and labor weapons, the administration opposed the legislative relief that labor leaders sought. Repeatedly, when union action was the issue, administration spokesmen talked of recovery and progress through the restoration of traditional individualism, the underlying assumption being that this restoration was most needed with labor.

Even as these actions were taken, however, such administrators as Hoover and Wallace were advocating and seeking to promote a new and more cooperative individualism. The economic difficulties, as they perceived them, were due less to swollen government or violated property rights than to misinformation, inadequate foresight, and poor organization. The remedy lay in cooperative structures that would correct these weaknesses. With Harding's acquiescence and occasional support, both Hoover and Wallace moved to transform their departments into agencies chiefly concerned with building and servicing such structures.

Hoover, in particular, proceeded to reestablish major elements of the wartime standardization, statistical, and conservation programs, again relying on industrial agreements and entrusting much of the administration to trade associations. Such programs, he argued, would allow industry to reduce costs and stimulate new investment without putting workers through an economic wringer. He also organized a program of managerial reform linked to the engineering studies that he had helped to launch in 1920. He established new agencies to help organize such disorderly areas as housing, transportation, radio, and bituminous coal. And moving into the labor and welfare fields, he became not only a promoter of labor-management collaboration and private welfare programs but also a key figure in devising new mediation machinery, pressuring the steel industry into adopting an eight-hour day, and organizing the first federal efforts to deal with unemployment. Out of the unemployment conference of late 1921 came both an organization for mobilizing local and private relief and agencies that attempted to expand construction activities and develop the kind of business planning that would bring future stability. Recommended as well was a program of public works planning designed to offset private fluctuations, but this failed to win congressional approval.

Meanwhile, sometimes in the face of Hoover's opposition, Wallace was establishing similar agencies in the Department of Agriculture. There the new Bureau of Agricultural Economics under Henry C. Taylor became the tool that was to provide agribusiness with better information, greater foresight, and needed organizational expertise. Also convened, in January 1922, was an agricultural conference designed to link public and private action and commit both to "sane solutions." Drawing support from both the Harding administration and a congressional farm bloc, Wallace pressed for new farm legislation. Between 1921 and 1923, measures were passed empowering his department to regulate various kinds of agricultural intermediaries, exempting farm marketing associations from the antitrust laws, and establishing new farm credit institutions. When he moved toward solutions with a larger governmental component, however, Wallace was unable to carry either the administration or the Congress with him. In 1924, as farm distress persisted, he endorsed the controversial McNary-Haugen bill, a measure calling for federal price supports and the dumping of agricultural surpluses abroad, but his endorsement was not enough to overcome congressional opposition.

What Hoover and Wallace accomplished was also attempted by other administrators, some of whom had a degree of success. Under William B. Greeley, for example, the Forest Service initiated an extensive array of cooperative action programs. Under Stephen Mather the Park Service formed a close alliance with transportation and recreational groups and continued to expand its domain. Under Thomas MacDonald the Bureau of Public Roads became another arena of deference to managerial and technical expertise in the making of policy choices. And under H. Foster Bain the Bureau of Mines became a promoter of cooperative conservation and safety programs. Plans for a department that would work with personnel managers and labor associations, however, failed to win sufficient support, and so did proposals for welfare and education departments that might help the providers of social services to order and rationalize their activities. Not all was retrenchment in these spheres. There were additions like the new grant-in-aid programs for vocational rehabilitation and maternal and child health care, and a series of national conferences and campaigns helped to bring a version of scientific management and business-like coordination into the field of social work. But there was nothing to compare with the Hoover and Wallace operations.

What was happening at the federal level had its counterparts at the state and local levels. At the time, the states and cities were still doing about 75 percent of all public spending. Alongside their rapidly expanding highway, educational, and civic improvement programs and their more moderately expanding social services, they too were spawning cooperative structures and administrative networks that linked their operations to the bureaucracies and associations of the private sector. There were, to be sure, exceptions to these patterns — governments that remained locked in a politics of rural nostalgia or venal bossism, or conversely, governments that were occasionally more responsive to antiestablishment rebels or humanitarian reformers than to modernizing organizational elites. But the main thrust of change was toward structures resembling those being built by Hoover and Wallace at the national level. "Good government" had come to be equated not only with honesty and economy but with the provision of managerial and technical aids, the creation of rationalizing mechanisms, and the support of social work concerned with developing and managing human resources. One result, as Professor James Lieby put it, would be "a decade of administrative improvement, perhaps the most effective and promising in the history of the United States."

As the New Era organization builders proceeded, they insisted that their programs were making "individualism" workable under modern conditions and thereby reducing irrational pressures for big government and other forms of collectivism. But they were sometimes challenged. Some conservatives, such as Raymond Pearl, grumbled that an administration elected to get the government out of business was now "doing more interfering with business than any other administration that we have had in peace times." Some liberals saw new exercises in trust building and government-supported exploitation. And within the government, the organization builders encountered opposition not only from economizers and standpatters but from defenders of the antitrust laws as well. Hoover, in particular, became involved in a running conflict with the Justice Department and the Federal Trade Commission and as a result of antitrust decisions was forced to back away from informational exchanges and other trade association programs that could be used to facilitate price-fixing. It was not until 1925 that the Supreme Court upheld his interpretation that the programs under attack could also make possible a more intelligent competition.

Had economic distress persisted, the programs of Hoover and likeminded administrators might well have been discredited and the way paved for larger elements of governmental coercion. Indeed, where distress did persist, as in agriculture and certain industries, the drift by 1924 was toward solutions featuring some form of government-backed cartelization. But through most areas of the economy the years 1922 and 1923 brought rapid recovery. Unemployment, which had reached an estimated 12 percent in 1921, dwindled to less than 4 percent. Output climbed nearly 50 percent, and from 1923 on the nation experienced a happy combination of rising productivity and income, stable prices, and nearly full utilization of resources. These developments supported claims that the "best minds" had indeed organized recovery and were in the process of organizing permanent prosperity, and the result was to be a further growth of Hooverian programs and the subsequent elevation of the "Great Engineer" to the White House.

## Ethnocultural Issues

As Harding's "best minds" sought to organize peace and prosperity, his administration faced new political disturbances generated by ethnocultural conflict. Emerging from the wartime loyalty organizations and the postwar crusades against "un-Americanism" was a set of pressure groups bent on restoring an older status system and erecting defenses against "contaminants" of the national life. In effect, nativism, racism, and social reaction had managed to cloak themselves in the garb of nationalism, and around the political efforts of these "100 percent Americans" and the counterefforts of their opponents much of the period's political activity revolved. At the national level the central issues were immigration controls, minority rights, freedom of expression, and the extent to which prohibition should be retained and enforced.

In part the impetus behind immigration control was pressure for economic protection. Yet by itself this could not have produced the legislation of the period; nor could it account for the type of quota system that was established. Also involved were heightened concerns about America's being undermined by alien cultures, races, and ideologies. The two together swept aside business efforts to maintain a flow of cheap labor and overcame the objections of citizens concerned with respect for America abroad. In 1924 the Johnson-Reed Act replaced emergency curbs with permanent legislation aimed primarily at restricting immigration perceived to be less assimilable. Under it there would be no quotas for the Western Hemisphere, largely because these were strongly opposed by southwestern agricultural interests. But Asians were to be excluded completely, and immigration from Europe was not to exceed fixed annual quotas for each nationality. Initially these were set at 2 percent of the foreign-born of that nationality resident in the United States in 1890. But in permanent form, as finally calculated and implemented in 1929, the quotas were to apportion an annual maximum of 150,000 so as to reflect proportionately the national derivations of America's population in 1920. The effect, as intended, was to reduce drastically the number of immigrants from southern and eastern Europe. The number admitted in 1925 was only one-seventh the number in 1924, and the proportion that this constituted of the total European immigration fell from 44 to 16 percent.

The triumph of immigration restriction, however, did not mean administration support for all the causes being pushed by "100 percent Americans." Harding showed no interest, for example, in reviving the red hunt, as some of his political associates were urging him to do. He gave no encouragement to proposals for peacetime sedition laws but proceeded instead to pardon socialist leader Eugene Debs and other victims of the earlier repression. Harding also refused to support "lily-white" politics or the reaction against feminism, going out of his way instead to chide southerners for their discriminatory practices, urging passage of a federal antilynching law, and appointing women to federal

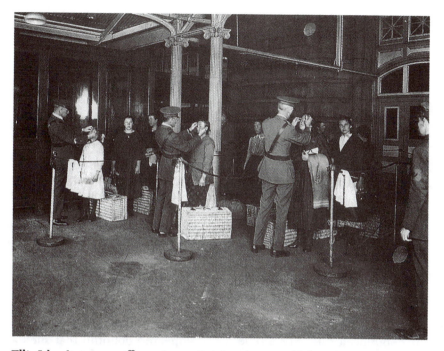

Ellis Island customs officers inspecting immigrants. *(Culver Pictures, Inc.)*

positions. During his administration, Mabel Willebrandt became assistant attorney general; Mary Anderson, Grace Abbott, and Louise Stanley were appointed to head federal bureaus; and Lucille Anderson became the first woman to enter the diplomatic service. Nor were the prohibitionists satisfied. They complained constantly about the lack of enforcement zeal on the part of the president and such cabinet members as Andrew Mellon and Secretary of War John Weeks.

Yet Harding and his associates were far from ardent champions of minority rights or cultural pluralism. Their disagreement was mostly with the extremist elements of the "Americanizers," not with the group's underlying assumptions. Along with their refusal to support such elements went reassurances to Americanizers of more moderate temperament. The freeing of political prisoners, for example, was accompanied by new calls for registration of the foreign-born and continued efforts to depict anticapitalist ideologies as un-American and psychopathic. The defense of minority rights was accompanied by toleration for lily-white operations, refusal to move against the terrorism of the Ku Klux Klan, and advice to blacks not to seek an "unattainable" social equality. The support for women's causes never extended to reforms threatening the domestic ideal or to such legislation as the proposed Equal Rights Amendment. And skepticism about Prohibition did not mean that the "dry" organizations lacked influence in the Harding administration. Indeed, the Prohibition Unit under Roy Haynes seemed to function more as an extension of the Anti-Saloon League than as an arm of the presidency.

Neither the "100 percent Americans" nor their opponents were fully satisfied with this mixture of policies. Yet it did placate those of moderate thought, and given the nature of America's party structure, it was difficult for the unplacated to challenge such policies in the electoral arena. Third parties seemed exercises in futility. And when the 100 percenters and their opponents both sought to capture the Democratic party and use it for their purposes, the result was intraparty warfare that virtually ensured continued Republican ascendancy.

## Political Alignments and National Scandals

By 1923 a mixture of political skill and good fortune seemed to be converting the anti-Wilson coalition of 1920 into continuing support for Republican rule. For a time it had appeared doubtful that such a conversion would take place. In early 1922 a number of discontented farm, labor, and reform elements had organized the Conference for Progressive Political Action, a move that seemed to foreshadow the kind of Republican party split that had enabled Wilson to win the election of 1912. And in the congressional and state elections of 1922 the Republicans suffered heavy reverses. But after the elections of 1922, economic protest rapidly faded, defused, so it seemed, by a combination of returning prosperity, antiradical rhetoric, and public acceptance of the claims of Hooverian administrators and their business allies. Although ethnocultural conflict remained intense, most of its potential for political mischief was being successfully shunted into the Democratic party. Politically, the policy mix of the Harding administration had become a going concern, and it would remain so for the rest of the decade.

What threatened to make Harding a political liability was not discontent with his policies. It was the famous "Harding scandals," involving corrupt activities by a number of his appointees and associates. As revealed by investigations in 1923 and 1924, this corruption had become particularly pronounced in the administration of veterans' benefits, oil reserves, alien property, and law enforcement. And for a time it was not clear that the president's sudden death in August 1923 would be sufficient to save his party from the feared political consequences.

One major set of scandals involved the Veterans' Bureau, the agency that Harding had entrusted to the political adventurer Charles R. Forbes. Between 1921 and 1923, subsequent investigations revealed, Forbes and his associates were engaged in systematically defrauding the government, primarily through accepting payments to approve padded construction contracts and arrange sales of government property at a fraction of its cost. In all, it was estimated, their activities cost the taxpayers some $200 million. Yet when Harding caught wind of what was going on, his anger quickly gave way to concern that the activities not be disclosed. After confronting Forbes and allegedly choking a confession out of him, Harding agreed that the miscreant should go abroad and resign. It was not until later, after Harding's death and after the Senate had investigated, that Forbes was finally prosecuted and sent to prison.

A second major set of scandals involved the Justice Department. Attorney General Daugherty allowed his close friend and confidant, Jesse Smith, to drift into extensive influence peddling, selling not only jobs, pardons, and permits but also protection for bootleggers, wartime profiteers, and tax evaders. In May 1923, when the president learned something of these activities and exposure seemed imminent, Smith committed suicide in Daugherty's Washington apartment. Nothing further came out at the time. But after Harding's death, an investigation uncovered much of the story. In March 1924, President Coolidge demanded and got Daugherty's resignation.

The third major agency involved was the Office of Alien Property Custodian, headed by a former congressman and war hero, Thomas W. Miller. At the time of his appointment Miller seemed the epitome of rectitude. But when approached by Jesse Smith and other political fixers, he proved to be corruptible. In September 1921, in return for a payment of $50,000, he decided that German shares in the American Metal Company had been wrongly confiscated and transferred the property to a bogus claimant. For this he was eventually sent to jail. And when it was found that $50,000 of the sum paid to Smith had been deposited in a bank account shared by Daugherty, the former attorney general was also indicted. At the trial Daugherty declined to testify on the ground that his personal relations with the president had been such as to make it impossible for him to do so. He was commonly considered as guilty as Miller, but after two juries failed to convict him, the charges were dropped.

Finally, there was the Teapot Dome scandal, which involved Secretary of the Interior Albert Fall. This had its beginnings in May 1921, when Fall succeeded in getting responsibility for the naval oil reserves at Elk Hills, California, and Teapot Dome, Wyoming, transferred from the Navy Department to the Interior. He then proceeded, secretly and without competitive bids, to lease the reserves to Edward Doheny of the Pan-American Oil Company and Harry Sinclair of the Sinclair Consolidated Oil Corporation. This was necessary, he would later argue, to prevent the loss of oil to adjacent wells and to secure storage facilities necessary for national security. His anticonservation attitudes and designs, however, had already aroused the ire of such conservationists as Gifford Pinchot and Harry Slattery. Out of their probings had come the launching of a senatorial investigation headed by Senator Thomas J. Walsh that would reveal that Fall received extensive favors at the time the leases were made. In conjunction with the lease on Elk Hills, Doheny had given him $100,000, allegedly as a loan but without security or specifications for repayment. And in conjunction with the lease on Teapot Dome, Sinclair had given him $223,000 in government bonds, $85,000 in cash, and some livestock for his New Mexico ranch. Eventually the government would win its suit to cancel the leases, and Fall would finally be convicted and sentenced to a year in prison and a fine of $100,000.

That Harding knew of Fall's activities seems doubtful. But clearly he knew enough about other acts of corruption to make his last days in office a time of deep worry and concern. Being president, he told Senator Frank Brandegee, was "hell." There was no other word to describe it. And to the newspaperman William Allen White, Harding expressed similar sentiments. "I have no trouble with my enemies," he declared. "But my damn friends, my God-damn friends, White, they're the ones that keep me walking the floor nights."

In July 1923, then, as he set out on a trip to Alaska, the president was already deeply depressed and worried. In Alaska the depression deepened, and in Seattle, where he stopped on his return trip, he nearly collapsed on the speech platform. He then went on to San Francisco, where he took to bed with what was diagnosed as bronchial pneumonia. And there, on August 2, 1923, he suffered a coronary thrombosis and died. At the time the nation was shocked and grieved, but the revelations that followed quickly deflated Harding's reputation. Rumors spread that he had committed suicide or had been poisoned by his wife or his doctor, and in a flood of exposés the public learned about his drinking, gambling, and sexual peccadilloes. In one of the most sensational of these, his former mistress offered details about how he made love to her in a White House clothes closet and had fathered her illegitimate child.

As Harding's reputation declined, Republican politicians worked actively to dissociate themselves from Harding the man and to blame him rather than the party for the misconduct that had occurred. Their goal was to retain power while escaping political punishment. Their success in doing so can be attributed partly to public apathy and marginal involvement of Democrats in the oil scandals, but it is perhaps most fully explained by the fact that Harding's successor was Vice-President Calvin Coolidge. Not only did the new president move to take the scandals out of partisan politics, primarily by appointing special prosecutors from each party and guaranteeing them a free hand, but he was also able, through his personality and demeanor, to provide a reassuring sense of austerity, rectitude, and fundamental morality. In what seems an amazingly short time, he was able to repair whatever damage the Republican party had suffered.

## The Consolidation of Republican Ascendancy

Although Harding and Coolidge were both from rural villages, the two men were quite dissimilar. Where Harding had been affable, extroverted, and easygoing, Coolidge was almost a caricature of rural New England reserve. Born and reared in the farming village of Plymouth Notch, Vermont, he had risen in Massachusetts politics through shrewd appeals to such virtues as thrift, caution, honesty, and taciturnity. Once in the White House, he became a symbol of integrity and simplicity in an age of organization, extravagance, and threatening change. Sophisticated urbanites might poke fun at his dour sobriety and eccentric mannerisms. But for many Americans he became a reassuring presence and almost a folk hero.

In political outlook Coolidge tended toward what Herbert Hoover called "real conservatism." His major concerns were with reducing federal expenditures, lowering taxes, and blocking liberal legislative initiatives. Not surprisingly, Mellon's influence on public policy tended to increase under Coolidge and that of more activist administrators tended to diminish. This change, however, was essentially an adjustment within an ongoing set of policies, not a change in direction. Nor were dissident groups in Congress able to force any major policy alterations. Their only significant success in 1924 was in passing a veterans' benefit measure over the president's veto. Under it veterans of World War I were to receive "deferred compensation" in the form of paid-up life insurance maturing in twenty years.

Coolidge's major goal, once the scandals had been "depoliticized," was the mobilization of a political base for the coming presidential election. In doing this he was aided in particular by his New England business connections, his surprisingly good relations with the national press, and the success of his secretary, C. Bascom Slemp, in rounding up southern delegates. Symptomatic of the Coolidge takeover of the party machinery was the elevation of Boston industrialist William M. Butler to the post of Republican national chairman. As the takeover proceeded, it became apparent that the Coolidge forces would dominate the Republican convention that met in Cleveland on June 10, 1924. There, on the first and only ballot, Coolidge received 1,065 of the 1,109 votes cast. As his running mate the Republicans finally decided on Chicago banker Charles G. Dawes, implementer of the federal budget system and author of the Dawes Plan.

On June 24 the Democrats gathered in New York's Madison Square Garden for what would be their most divisive convention since 1896. Arrayed on one side were elements of the party controlled by defenders of rural values, Prohibition, and "100 percent Americanism." Their candidate was the former secretary of the treasury and war administrator William Gibbs McAdoo. Arrayed on the other side were elements controlled by urban political machines and ethnic groups, opponents of the liquor law, and defenders of a heterogeneous America. They supported Governor Alfred E. Smith of New York, a man who had risen from city slums through the Tammany Hall organization. For sixteen days, amid fierce platform fights and ballot after ballot, the convention provided evidence of how deep ethnocultural conflict could run. Finally both Smith and McAdoo agreed to withdraw, and on the 103rd ballot the weary, exasperated delegates nominated John W. Davis, a conservative corporation lawyer who had served as solicitor general in the Wilson administration. To assuage rural elements, the convention then chose Govenor Charles W. Bryan of Nebraska, brother of William Jennings Bryan, as Davis's running mate.

Also in the field in 1924 was a third party, made up of Republican insurgents and the groups that had formed the Conference for Progressive Political Action in 1922. Meeting in Cleveland on July 4, these groups formed the Progressive party, nominated Senator Robert M. La Follette of Wisconsin, and adopted a platform calling for nationalization of key industries and a variety of political reforms. Some hoped that the new party could become the American counterpart of the Labour party in Britain; others, that it could at least prevent the consolidation of Republican ascendancy. But in operation it was to do neither. It proved short-lived, and its ability to pull Republicans away from Coolidge was more than offset by the repellent effects of its "un-American" image.

Indeed, Republican campaign strategy seemed aimed chiefly at promoting this image and spelling out the dire consequences that could stem from voting for La Follette. The choice, so Republican oratory declared, was "Coolidge or chaos." And as the campaign progressed, it became clear that most of the defections to La Follette were coming from Democratic rather than Republican ranks. On November 4, Coolidge polled 15,725,016 votes to only 8,385,586 for Davis and 4,822,856 for La Follette. In the electoral college this translated into 382 for Coolidge, 136 for Davis, and 13 for La Follette. The president had scored a solid victory, and in Congress the Republicans reestablished large majorities. In the new Congress they would control 56 seats in the Senate and 247 in the House of Representatives.

In part Coolidge's victory can be attributed to the divisions among his opponents and their inability to stir up the kind of mass discontent that could have challenged Republican rule. Yet these divisions and inabilities were related not only to improving economic conditions but also to Republican success in coopting the political center, defusing the kinds of tensions that tore the Democrats apart, and fusing traditional Republicanism with a managerial ideology especially attractive to America's expanding organizational elites. The victorious coalition of 1920 had become a going concern with its ascendancy now consolidated and with little prospect that it could be defeated without major changes in the political and economic environment.

# CHAPTER 5

# Toward a New Economy and a Higher Self-government

## 1922–1928

As the American economy recovered from the economic hardships of 1921, it entered on a pattern of development that made it the envy of much of the civilized world. In essence, it became the first industrial economy geared to the production of consumer durables and cultural fare for the masses, and as such it was widely hailed as a new kind of economy, a "people's capitalism" seeking profits through volume production and in the process healing social divisions and creating an uplifting abundance. The Americans, it was said, had learned how to build a technically advanced economy that was both increasingly efficient and increasingly attuned to popular needs. They had learned how to link the great functional groups of society—workers, investors, and consumers —into an interdependent community in which each was concerned with the interests of all. And marvel of marvels, they had been able to do these things while retaining the benefits of a private property system, individual initiative, and a carefully delimited government.

It was, of course, too good to be true. The self-disciplining arrangements believed capable of accomplishing such feats proved unable to check the massive economic contraction that got under way after 1929, and the impact of frustrated expectations was quickly felt in the political arena. Yet the failures should not obscure the considerable economic achievements of the 1920s. Nor should they obscure the extent to which the arrangements and designs of the era foreshadowed the kind of modern capitalism that would be hailed as successful in the 1950s. Long depicted as the Indian summer of an outmoded and passing economic order, the period from 1922 through 1928 really stands as a kind of premature spring for the capitalist adaptations that were to come.

## Technology and Management

Taken as a whole, the industrial statistics for the 1920s tell a story of amazing success. From 1922 to 1928 the index of industrial production climbed 70 percent. Gross national product (GNP), measured in constant dollars, rose nearly 40 percent, per capita income about 30 percent. Unemployment largely disappeared while wholesale and retail price levels remained stable, and as the tools of production became increasingly efficient, output per factory worker-hour climbed nearly 75 percent. The expanded product was being allocated in such a way as to widen the gap between rich and poor. But the share going to blue- and white-collar workers was enough to produce the world's first excursion into mass affluence. The real earnings of employed wage earners increased about 22 percent, at a time when the average workweek shrank about 4 percent. And for the first time in world history, numerous people were able to acquire complicated pieces of machinery and electronic devices, afford higher education and extended leisure for their children, and participate in activities once reserved for the wealthy few.

Behind this unheard-of mass affluence lay a new capacity to produce standardized goods at low per-unit costs. The period witnessed the rapid spread of the manufacturing techniques pioneered by Henry Ford and then used in war production: the marriage of machine-produced interchangeable parts with a moving assembly line that coordinated the efficient performance of numerous simplified tasks. It also saw the rapid introduction of scientific work management as pioneered by Frederick W. Taylor and his disciples. Their systems of shop organization, task analysis, worker motivation, and engineering control were now bringing gains in efficiency to numerous work sites. In addition, the 1920s witnessed the first major growth of systematic research into industrial methods. As still another part of what was being called the "technological revolution," the period witnessed a phenomenal growth in the use of mechanical power as a substitute for human or animal muscle. Along with improvements in steam-powered machinery came the extensive introduction of electric motors and internal combustion engines.

Also contributing to the new productive ability was the rapid growth of personnel work aimed at creating cooperative and production-oriented work forces. From the war experience had come a faith in personnel management, both as a way to curb undesirable labor organization and as a tool for increasing productivity. Contented, right-thinking, and relatively secure workers, a new group of managerial specialists had come to believe, were not merely socially desirable but also essential to mass production systems using modern techniques. And operating now through a new array of corporate personnel departments, these specialists were busy with efforts to engineer the kind of labor that was needed. They were developing scientific selection and motivation procedures, initiating new kinds of educational activity, and setting up programs aimed at giving workers a sense of participation and a stake in company welfare. Initially, they also challenged the power of factory foremen and their supervisors. But in most firms they had to settle for leaving this power intact and seeking to develop a "new kind of foremanship" committed to implementing their designs.

Along with revolutionary technologies and willing workers, the kind of economy being developed in the 1920s also required willing and able consumers. To some extent, these too were being engineered through the operations of a new group of business specialists. Advertising, its power greatly enhanced by new means of mass communication, was being used to change spending habits and create demand for new

President Warren Harding *(center, seated)* with some of the nation's business leaders. *(Left to right)* Henry Ford, Thomas A. Edison, Harvey S. Firestone, and *(standing)* George Christian. *(UPI/Bettmann)*

and fashionable products. Marketing organizations were being refocused to stress the rapid turnover of a limited stock of items. Frequent style and model changes were being used to render inherently durable goods obsolete. Business leaders accepted and approved increased incomes for wage earners, and the rapid development of consumer credit helped to supplement mass purchasing power. A relative rarity before the 1920s, consumer credit became a major new form of financial activity that allowed consumers to mortgage their future earnings, buy expensive durables for which they would never have the full purchase price at one time, and hope that continuing economic growth would take care of the debt burden.

Structural changes in the labor market also contributed to mass consumption. A growing number of jobs left more time and energy for leisure and for the consumption that could accompany it. A growing number offered little challenge and few satisfactions, leading their holders to seek status and recompense through consumption. And the family, with more women employed outside the home and more of these holding white-collar and quasi-professional jobs, became a prime customer for household appliances, nonfamily child care, and expanded educational, cultural, and recreational facilities.

Organizationally, then, Americans were moving toward a new kind of peacetime economy, and although profit seeking was a major motive force, it was hardly the whole story. Also involved was a value system that regarded profits made through such operations to be of greater merit and social value than profits made by other means. It seems at least possible that the power of American business might have yielded even greater profits had it been used to reduce wages, suppress invention, or sustain high profit margins on limited flows of luxury goods — all techniques that were widely adopted in Europe. But the power was difficult to mobilize for such purposes, chiefly, it seems, because a growing segment of America's corporate managers regarded them as antisocial or self-defeating and believed that profits could be made in socially beneficial ways. America was not without its wage reducers, invention suppressors, and high-profit-margin monopolists, but these groups tended to be seen as remnants of an unenlightened past or as abusers of the social trusteeship that property management was becoming.

In part this set of managerial attitudes had been fostered by prewar progressivism and the war experience. For a time profit making of a certain kind had gone hand in hand with social service, much as the prewar business clubs and professionalizers of business had insisted that it could. It was perhaps natural for those who had reaped this double reward to seek arrangements that would continue to provide it.

There was more involved, however. There were not only changes in the attitudes of individuals but changes in the kind of person who was directing corporate enterprise and making business policy. Coming into management were a growing number of people who had acquired the vision of a new capitalism at business or professional schools, and allowing such people to take charge were structural changes that reduced the policy input of shareholders and bankers. As the ownership of large corporations became increasingly diluted, the accountability of management to the stockholders became more myth than reality. Once managers had acquired the ability to generate new capital internally, through the withholding of corporate profits, their dependence on the great investment banks that had dominated an earlier period was substantially reduced. Increasingly, in such dominant firms as General Electric, General Motors, International Harvester, and U.S. Steel, managerial accountability was to other managers rather than to owners or financiers, and it was managerial perceptions and ideals that shaped the use of corporate property and the purposes for which corporate power could be mobilized.

This is not to say that all managers behaved according to the ideal. Behind the mask of the socially responsible manager there also appeared a new breed of corporate plunderers intent on enriching themselves through raids on company treasuries and misrepresentation of business prospects. Professional accountability, such as it was, could not prevent this, and as subsequently magnified through investigations born of the Great Depression, it would do much to discredit the managerial images of the 1920s. In the public mind, the decade would be remembered for the financial and speculative abuses of such people as Samuel Insull, Charles Mitchell, M.J. Meehan, and "Sell 'em Ben" Smith. But if there was a gap between ideal and reality, the two were not polar opposites. The American economy was the first to reassemble much of the war system and gear it to the mass consumption of durable goods and cultural artifacts. Though this can be partly explained by the peculiarities of American technologies, markets, and resources, a key factor may well have been the managerial professionalism of the makers of business policy.

## Economic Growth and Maladjustments

Of the new industries being developed in the 1920s, the most spectacular was the automobile. The breakthrough had come with Henry Ford's mass-produced, inexpensive Model T, and through elaborations and improvements on the Ford system the industry continued to combine extraordinary gains in productivity with steadily mounting sales. Worker-hours per unit of output declined steadily, falling on the average more than 7 percent a year. Sales rose from about 1.5 million vehicles in 1921 to over 5 million in 1929, when nearly 60 percent of all American families owned an automobile. More than any other, the industry became the showpiece of the new capitalism. Although some historians now question whether "automobility" really improved the quality of mass life, there were few doubters at the time. The industry was widely regarded as a progressive social force, fulfilling a long-standing popular dream and helping in the process to heal social divisions and satisfy social needs.

Growth extended to a number of ancillary areas. An expanding automobile industry meant rapidly increasing demand for steel, petroleum, glass, rubber, lacquers, and machine tools. It meant rapid growth for service industries catering to automobile users and, less directly, a new stimulus to real estate development, especially in suburban and vacation areas. Since governmental bodies were generally responsive to the industry and its customers — a fact reflected both in state road appropriations and in generous grants-in-aid for federal highways — there were rapid increases as well in expenditures on roadways, traffic control, and highway amenities. America was not only producing automobiles for the masses but also reshaping its economy and society to accommodate their mass use, and this involved immense new capital expendutures.

Although the coming of mass automobility was the greatest generator of new growth, it was by no means the only one. Another was the rapidly expanding use of electrical power, both by industry and by the growing number of families who were now acquiring electricity in their homes. In 1928 this did not include many farm families, but it did encompass approximately two-thirds of all families in the nation, and many of these had acquired electric irons, vacuum cleaners, washing machines, and other appliances. By that time approximately 70 percent of all factory machine equipment was also being run by electric power. Together these developments had brought sales of power and equipment that were nearly three times as large as in 1919.

Two other growth areas of major significance were motion pictures and radio. These now became the great purveyors of commercialized mass entertainment, for which the demand proved exceptionally expansive. In 1922 some 40 million movie tickets were being sold weekly. Seven years later, after the development of a system featuring "star" actors and the introduction of sound, weekly attendance at the nation's 23,000 movie theaters was approaching 100 million. The saga of radio was even more impressive. Bursting on the scene in 1920, when station KDKA began operating in Pittsburgh, the industry developed quickly, with far-reaching effects on popular life. By 1929 about 40 percent of all American families had acquired receiving sets, and nearly 800 broadcasting stations, organized into two major and two minor networks, were in operation. A telephone polling system had also been developed to measure the audiences being reached, and this was used to determine the value of airtime sold to commercial sponsors.

Americans in the 1920s were also making major additions to their educational institutions, especially at the high school and college levels. They were expanding their health care and social service system, especially in the private sector. They were altering their habits in ways that meant prosperity for the tobacco, cosmetics, soft drink, synthetic fiber, and commercial recreation industries. And for a time their demand for new or better housing, enhanced by new methods of mortgage financing, produced rapid growth in the construction and building materials industries. Part of the expansion too was the new aviation industry, a development of the war that continued to depend on various governmental subsidies. Although its expansion was limited, the feats of aviators and airplane builders were much publicized, and by 1929 the nation had an airmail system and fledgling air passenger and transport services.

To some extent such growth industries merely absorbed resources that were being freed by increasing efficiency elsewhere. But to some extent as well they grew by displacing older industries. The result for such fields as bituminous coal, cotton textiles, railroads and railroad equipment, horse-drawn conveyances, and the older agricultural staples was shrinking demand. Since some of these industries had great difficulty in solving the problems that this created, the period also witnessed the emergence of a number of "sick" industries characterized by overcapacity, low returns, irrational economic behavior, and bitter confrontations between management and labor.

Four industries were most prominent on the sick list. One was the mining of bituminous coal, an industry that suffered now from a combination of shrinking demand, wartime overexpansion, technological backwardness, and bitter but unsuccessful struggles to maintain wartime wage rates. During the decade of the 1920s it became the subject of numerous investigations and much legislative and engineering consideration, but solutions for its problems never seemed to emerge.

A second industry in much the same trouble was cotton textiles. Shrinking demand and overcapacity put strong pressures on profit and wage rates. Excursions into cooperative advertising, export promotion, and production restraints seemed unable to relieve these problems, and the result was accelerated movement of textile manufacturers from the Northeast to the South, bitter resistance to all efforts to unionize southern workers, and the persistence of substandard wages and meager or nonexistent profit margins.

The third industry in trouble was railroading. A heritage of over-capitalization and mismanagement, unimaginative regulation, and relatively powerful labor unions made it difficult either to meet the competition from newer forms of transportation or to adjust capacity to shrinking demand.

Finally, there was the depressed shipping industry, losing out not to newer forms of transportation but to more efficient or more heavily subsidized foreign fleets. A few shipping operators grew wealthy on government money, but most workers in the industry were not participants in the upward movement of income and living standards.

Exhibiting many of the characteristics of the sick industries was the nation's agricultural sector. On the one hand, it was a major participant in the "technological revolution," a fact attested by the rise of a machine technology built around tractors and trucks, by striking advances in managerial practices and plant productivity, and by the growing use of systematic research and capital-intensive methods. Yet with the exception of such areas as citrus, dairy, and truck farming, agriculture seemed incapable of solving its marketing problems. For most agricultural products the markets proved unexpandable, at least with the tools that farmers were able to develop. They could neither recapture the markets they had once had in Europe nor expand domestic markets enough to compensate for the loss. And since the population movement out of agriculture was not large enough to restore balance to the system, most of the country's farmers continued to suffer from market gluts and prices that did not cover fixed costs.

Economic rationality seemed to call for massive agricultural disinvestment and a greatly enlarged exodus of marginal producers. But hopes of market revival, attachments to farming as a way of life, and the sharecropping system still in effect in much of the rural South made the lot of would-be rationalizers exceedingly frustrating. Net farm income rose from about $6 billion in 1922 to about $8 billion in 1929, but per capita income remained substantially below what it had been in 1919, and the disparity between farm and nonfarm incomes continued to widen. In 1929 the average income per person on farms was $223 as against an average of $870 for those not on farms.

There were also sectors of industrial labor that did not share in the growing affluence. One was the large pool of unskilled or casual workers that was now being constantly replenished by displaced farmers and farm workers, many of them blacks leaving the rural

South. Such workers were in weak bargaining positions and were largely unaffected by the new company welfare and employee management programs. They filled low-paying jobs, especially in segments of the construction and food processing industries and other fields with high intermittency and seasonality, and their wages and working conditions showed little improvement. They remained at the fixed lower end of a wage-and-condition scale characterized by increasingly large differentials. In addition, in the sick industries workers were suffering from the effects of displacement and market pressures. For irregularly employed coal miners, textile workers stranded in New England towns, and similar groups, conditions tended to deteriorate rather than improve.

Finally, the kind of growth taking place was not without its costs in resource despoliation and community destruction, declining business independence and worker autonomy, and the reduction of skilled artisans to machine tenders and service employees. Many Americans were worse off in terms of the air they breathed, the water they used, the outdoors they enjoyed, and the communal relationships that gave their lives meaning. Many were compelled to purchase their places in the consumer culture at the expense of declining work satisfaction and less control over their labor. And many were shunted into jobs offering few material rewards or any others. The notion, moreover, that poverty was about to disappear was clearly in error. In 1929 some 6 million families had incomes below $1,000 a year, and neither the growth nor the social action of the period had done much to alter the pattern of rewards and barriers that kept them at this level.

In places the new economy exhibited glaring gaps between promise and reality, gaps that could potentially lead to mass protest and political upheaval. Perhaps the remarkable thing about the period was how little of this potential became actuality. For some people an older rationale for inaction took on new life: the gaps were attributed to individual failures and became the fault of the sufferers themselves. For others there was the new faith that problems could be resolved by widening the area or professional management. These planners sought not to overthrow the organizers and administrators of growth but rather to borrow their methods and secure their cooperation in reorganizing the economy's poorly functioning areas.

## Private Bureaucracies and Associational Activities

Since the turn of the century, social theorists both in the United States and abroad had drawn distinctions between the trusts and combines of monopoly capitalism and modern managerial corporations that could evolve into a neutral technocracy administering orderly growth and progress. Such conceptions formed one variant of the "new liberalism" advanced in the prewar period and the postwar debates; during the 1920s they were widely accepted in both academic and governmental circles. The direction of the great corporation, it was noted, was passing to growth-minded and system-conscious professional managers. So directed, the argument ran, such organizations no longer threatened liberal and democratic values. On the contrary, their productive and marketing power became a great liberating force. Their leadership in their respective industries worked to socialize and professionalize business behavior, and their responsiveness to popular and national needs was really greater than that shown by political parties or governmental bureaucracies. Business leaders recognized their dependence on and obligations to the various functional groups of the national community —to laborers, customers, and the public as well as to investors. They were developing, it was claimed, institutions through which they could remain responsive to all these constituencies.

Such images did not lead to repeal of the antitrust laws, but they were undoubtedly a major factor in bringing reinterpretations that turned their antimerger and anticoncentration provisions into little more than dead letters. Under court rulings of the period, a new merger and consolidation movement became legal; since this was widely accepted as socially beneficial, legislators made little effort to halt it. Between 1920 and 1928 approximately 1,200 manufacturing and mining mergers took place, accounting for the disappearance of nearly 6,000 firms. In utilities a similar process accounted for the disappearance of over 4,000 firms, and in distribution and finance there was a rapid growth of chain and branch systems. Vertical combination also made great strides, creating large, integrated firms that produced their own raw materials and operated distributive outlets.

To administer these operations the new managers developed elaborate private bureaucracies. Under central offices engaged in planning and appraisal, the managers established specialized functional departments concerned not only with production and marketing but also with personnel work, public and political relations, and product development. Some units, most notably General Motors, Du Pont, and Sears, Roebuck and Company, also amounted to federations of enterprises, centrally coordinated yet including quasi-autonomous product and territorial subunits. Being developed, moreover, as extensions of the corporate structures were a variety of company labor associations, educational institutes, better-business bodies, and social action programs.

That this expanding private bureaucracy was adequately constrained and operating in the public interest was a central theme in business advertising and promotion. Americans, it was said, owed their prosperity and progressiveness to a system that had avoided the pitfalls of statism, by developing ordering mechanisms in the private sector. But the disparity between claim and reality could not be entirely hidden. Critics continued to uncover cases in which high profit margins and gross inefficiencies were being sustained through price fixing. They uncovered other cases in which corporate power was being used to deny or suppress civil liberties, and by 1928 they were finding much to criticize in the organizational arrangements of the electric power industry. There corporate organizers had created complex pyramids of holding companies, occasionally to ensure better coordination or greater efficiency but much more often as devices for bleeding the operating companies of funds, evading the control of public utilities commissions, and defrauding investors.

Meanwhile, as corporate bureaucracies expanded, those administering trade and industrial associations also underwent rapid growth and development. The antitrust laws continued to be an obstacle. There was as yet no "rule of reason" stipulating that reasonable restraint of competition by cartels was legal and in the public interest, but new court rulings did sanction a kind of "cooperative competition," and "cooperative competitors" were being organized to oppose common enemies, mitigate "destructive competition" among themselves, and provide a common informational and moral base for decision making. By 1929 there were about 2,000 national trade associations, spanning nearly every industry and trade and engaged in activities that ranged from annual conventions and trade publications to elaborate programs of statistical dissemination, trade promotion, political lobbying, labor management, waste elimination, and trade practice control. Especially elaborate were the programs of the new "institutes" formed in the late 1920s. Though the full-fledged war system failed to reappear, the new bureaucracy did include many of the former war administrators, featured links to government through a committee system resembling that of the war years, and worked with government officials, as during the war, to formulate such publicly approved industrial codes and agreements as those supplementing the work of the American Petroleum Institute, the Motion Picture Producers and Distributors of America, and the National Fertilizer Association. As an association of associations, moreover, the Chamber of Commerce continued to serve as a harmonizer and informational clearinghouse and to provide a mechanism through which associational cooperation could be mobilized and deployed.

In a few areas association officials preached the kind of antimodernism that characterized small-business and artisanal associations in Europe. But generally they saw themselves as advancers of a superior kind of modernization, one that could bring the advantages of corporate consolidation and scientific management without sacrificing the advantages of entrepreneurial independence. This vision they articulated through association organs, governmental supporters, and professional organizations. It served both as camouflage for associations that were really extensions of the corporate bureaucracy and as an impetus to organization in industries that were unable or reluctant to participate in the consolidation movement. The coal, textile, and construction industries all tried to solve their problems through new excursions into association building, producing such bodies as the National Coal Association, the Cotton Textile Institute, and the American Construction Council. Similarly, under the auspices of the American Farm Bureau Federation and allied groups, agribusiness tried to develop cooperative marketing associations that could restore order and prosperity to the agricultural sector. In 1922 farmers obtained antitrust exemptions for such marketing combines, and though many of them quickly became disillusioned and turned to governmental relief schemes, others kept trying to work out a form of the "association idea" that would allow use of corporate methods for agrarian ends.

Still another extension of this associational bureaucracy also took shape in the troubled labor sector. There unionism and collective bargaining continued to suffer major setbacks. They were under attack both by organized advocates of "individual bargaining" and by corporate administrators seeking to engineer cooperative work forces. As one defeat followed another, total union membership declined from about 5 million to less than 3.5 million. Yet even as this occurred, other organizers moved in and sought with some success to build labor associations imbued with managerial values and receptive to managerial leadership. By 1929 such organizers had installed about 500 employee representation plans, each involving the creation of one or more company labor associations. They had become important features of such firms as Standard Oil, International Harvester, American Telephone and Telegraph (AT&T), and Goodyear Tire and Rubber. Even as they grew, moreover, corporate types had also taken over large sections of the remaining union apparatus and were using it to advance the idea of "copartnership" in the promotion of growth and productivity.

At the time, many observers hailed such developments as constituting a truly progressive system destined to supplant both the adversary proceedings of collective bargaining and the atomism of individual action. At last, they argued, the associative impulses of workers were being guided into constructive rather than antisocial channels. But subsequent developments would reveal that the foundations beneath these forms of association were exceedingly shaky. In too many cases what purported to be a productive partnership generating and sharing new wealth was in reality a device for denying associative rights, extracting more work for the same pay, or enlisting labor support for market-rigging operations. Unlike some segments of the expanding private bureaucracy, that in the labor field would be largely supplanted by a new and different kind of growth in the 1930s.

## The Quest for Macroeconomic Tools

As the new capitalism organized itself in the 1920s, some thought was given to overall coordination of the results. The painful fluctuations and dysfunctions of the immediate postwar period had left vivid memories, and from 1921 on, a number of economic leaders and former war administrators continued to offer designs for preventing similar disruptions in the future. The new economy, some argued, required forms of business and labor security that weakened or destroyed its capacity for automatic self-adjustment. But this did not mean that such an economy was doomed to ever more destructive breakdowns and purges. Nor did it mean that avoiding this fate required ever increasing areas of statist control and management. It was possible to devise nonstatist machinery that could keep the economy in balance and correct such imbalances and problems as did develop.

One kind of machinery that continued to have its advocates was an economic council system through which the leaders of the major industries and functional blocs would coordinate their activities, discern developing problems, and organize remedial action. As some saw it, the American economy could benefit from a less formal equivalent of the economic parliaments being organized or advocated in Europe. But for most the more relevant model was the wartime Council of National Defense with its functional representatives, its public-private collaboration, and its capacity to organize new action agencies as new problems arose. This was apparent in the proposals made by groups associated with the National Civic Federation, the Chamber of Commerce, the American Federation of Labor, and the Department of Commerce. On several occasions some form of economic advisory council, either attached to the Commerce Department or established as a private institution, seemed on the verge of taking shape. That it did not do so testified less to an absence of formative efforts than to persisting conflict, pluralism, and anticorporatism in the changing business order.

What did develop, serving as a kind of substitute for the envisioned council system, was a series of quasi-official "advisories" endorsed by committees of functional representatives and offered as guides and

stimulants to organizational action. Out of the unemployment conference in 1921 came an organizing committee for such operations, acting
both to arrange scientific surveys of the situation and to form the
representative bodies that would endorse the findings and stimulate
remedial action. Despite the fact that a number of the committee's
efforts were stillborn, it did arrange two major and several minor
productions. In 1923 its Business Cycle Committee, chaired by Owen
D. Young of General Electric, endorsed the latest scientific wisdom on
business fluctuations and urged stabilizing actions, especially programs
to improve the informational base of decision makers and reduce their
susceptibility to speculative enthusiasm and panicky retrenchment.
Lesser "advisories" followed, and in 1927 the machinery of the 1923
study was reassembled to survey recent developments and stimulate a
new round of corrective action. Under the direction of the economist
Wesley C. Mitchell, it eventually produced a voluminous report titled
*Recent Economic Changes in the United States.*

The Business Cycle Committee and its supporters also recommended special stabilizers to head off incipient booms and busts. Unemployment insurance and wage maintenance, it was recognized,
might prevent unbalancing swings in consumer spending. Countercyclical monetary actions might correct irrational demands for capital.
Proper management of exports might offset market disturbances at
home, and construction reserves might be built up and released in ways
that would maintain a stable flow of investment expenditures. The
recommenders drew the line, however, at proposals for erecting such
stabilizers in the public sector. Governmental spenders and managers,
they insisted, tended inherently toward irrationality and wastefulness.
Their sphere must be kept to a minimum, and though this minimum
should be managed with a view toward preserving economic equilib-
rium, the major stabilizing responsibility should be with the "higher
self-government" taking shape outside the state. More precisely, it lay
in a cooperative system of unemployment insurance and employment
stabilization, banking and export fraternities organized to act cooperatively in the public interest, and quasi-private councils through which
construction expenditures could be shaped into a countercyclical tool.

Viewed through the experience of the 1930s, such stabilizers as
were actually developed seemed weak indeed. The great majority of
firms did not install unemployment insurance or other forms of employment stabilization. The cooperative mechanisms through which
organized wage payers, bankers, and exporters were to act as macroeconomic stabilizers proved extremely fragile when put to the test. And
the prime instrument through which construction activities were to be
converted into an economic balance wheel, the Hoover-sponsored

American Construction Council that Franklin D. Roosevelt helped to found in 1922 and continued to head for the next six years, proved to be little more than a paper organization. Yet as of 1928 the strength of the tools needed was not readily apparent. Advances at the firm and industrial levels, it was widely believed, were creating a new economy less susceptible to booms and busts, more sensitive to danger signals, and more amenable, should it become necessary, to the kind of corrective action taken by the unemployment conference in 1921. Although hope continued for stronger coordinating and stabilizing mechanisms, a number of people involved in the quest for macroeconomic tools seemed to think that their search had been successful.

## Roots of the Coming Crisis

Beneath the surface indications of stability, however, the economy of 1928 was already in deep trouble. Markets for the new mass production industries—for automobiles, appliances, radios, and similar items —were already becoming saturated. The call for capital in these industries and ancillary fields was slackening. And new areas of spending that could take up the slack were failing to develop. Investors were not moving to develop large new growth industries, partly perhaps because the pattern of income distribution and consumer debt was now such as to make market creation difficult. Exports, too, were not readily expandable with the tools at hand; construction demand had not been deferred as the proponents of reserves had advocated, and the compensation that could come from public-sector expansion was narrowly limited by taxpayer resistance and commitments to retiring public debts and holding governmental activities to a minimum. The new economy, in short, had not really developed the mechanisms that could turn the new kind of growth into a continuing process, and its failure to do so would soon become apparent.

Nor was the economy resistant to major contractions. The "balance wheels" that were supposed to prevent disruption during economic slowdowns were not equal to the task and were indeed more than offset by potential depressants that relatively minor declines in demand could trigger into action. The banking system, despite some reforms, still contained many weak and overextended units and still lacked the means to keep the failure of such units from causing irrational bank runs and a general monetary contraction. A large segment of the corporate structure, especially public utilities, was such that even slight shocks could mean enormous losses for investors and further contractions in investment spending. Much of the market for consumer durables rested on spending and lending behavior that could be thrown into reverse with relative ease. And much of the new organizational machinery, once its operators became convinced that it lacked the power to regulate demand, could be turned into engines for idling resources and making the price and wage cuts characteristic of earlier liquidations exceedingly difficult. Even limited blows might turn a slowing of growth into economic breakdown, and three developments were already under way that would eventually deliver such blows.

The first would be the bursting of a massive stock speculation bubble that was already out of control by the end of 1928. New informational services, it became clear, had not made the financial investment system immune to speculative fever. An early bout of it had produced a boom in Florida real estate which, in 1926, had collapsed without seeming to affect general growth trends. But the new fever that was spreading in 1927 and 1928 would prove much more damaging. More and more Americans seemed willing to credit the unrealistic optimism of securities promoters, ignore traditional measures of value, and bid against each other for shares in corporate growth. Many were willing to finance such acquisitions by borrowing money at high rates of interest, and the monetary authorities, more concerned with international gold movements than with domestic credit use, were slow to move and ineffective when they did. By the end of the year the economy seemed destined to suffer the consequences of a major exercise in speculative folly.

The two other blows that would follow the stock market crash were being prepared abroad, the consequences of unsolved international problems. One was to come from the dumping of agricultural surpluses that were being accumulated by national price maintenance agencies. By 1928 such programs had become the typical response to continuing market gluts in agricultural goods. A number of nations had adopted them, and when they reached their limits, as most would do in 1930, the result would be a major blow to American economic expectations.

The third blow would come from the collapse of the international exchange system erected under the Dawes Plan and the war debt settlements. This sytem depended on a continued outpouring of American capital to help Europeans meet their trade deficits and debt obligations. When the mechanisms that produced this outpouring failed, as they did after 1929, the result would be a proliferation of trade barriers, rapid shrinkage of world trade, and a European panic that would trigger further contractions in the United States.

The movement toward a new economy, then, was about to encounter major obstacles that would make a temporary mockery of its formulas for a people's capitalism and a higher self-government. The

New Era system would soon be an economy in crisis, with a quarter of its work force unemployed and much of its production capacity idle. The crisis, it now seems clear, was less the product of outmoded ideas and institutions than of institutions that foreshadowed the future but could not bear the weight being put on them. Although badly discredited for a time, much of the organizational apparatus would survive. And what would follow, at least in its major outlines, was alteration aimed not at scrapping this apparatus but at filling organizational gaps, reinforcing it with the power of the state, and organizing governmental balance wheels to replace the private ones that had failed.

CHAPTER 6

# The Associative Vision at Home and Abroad
## 1925–1928

 In June 1925, three months after Calvin Coolidge's second inaugural, Herbert Hoover journeyed to Oskaloosa, Iowa, to speak to the graduating class of William Penn College. It was a ritual that might have been given over to the usual platitudes. But Hoover chose instead to expound a theory of national progress and of how governmental activity could foster it. America, he said, had long shown an instinct for the kind of community action that could resolve social problems and prevent the growth of stultifying bureaucratization. This peculiar genius had enabled it to conquer a continent and become the world's leading industrial nation, and this same genius was now developing forms of "associational action" that would allow progress to continue along a "new scientific and economic frontier." The great concern of true progressives was that this development might be halted. It might succumb to unenlightened selfishness, to destructive forms of statist intervention, or to a "vast syndicalism" that captured the state and used it for class purposes. The job of progressive government, he continued, was both to guard against these eventualities and to stimulate progressive forms of cooperative organization. Its ultimate aim should be a "partnership" of responsible and interdependent social groups acting together to stretch "an enlarged vision of neighborly relations" over "the nation as a whole."

Hoover spoke for only one segment of the Republican administration, of course. His vision of governmental activism was not shared by such conservatives as Andrew Mellon and Calvin Coolidge. Nor did his perceptions of progressive organization agree with those of critics in the antitrust agencies and conflict-oriented areas of the federal bu-

83

reaucracy. Yet the vision he set forth was clearly a major force in shaping public policy between 1925 and 1928. Activities that could be fitted into it acquired a capacity for survival and growth. Those that could not were vulnerable to cutbacks, abolition, or redirection. The result, despite Coolidge's emphasis on economy and inactivity, was not really a reduction in governmental expenditures and activities. While pruning took place on one side, the organizers of associational action were creating a kind of "associative state" reliant on private structures but partly financed by public funds. These additions outweighed retrenchment elsewhere, and many Americans accepted them as a superior kind of national progressivism meeting social needs that could not be satisfied by the bureaucratic and "class legislation" proposals emanating from Congress.

## Building the Associative State

At the center of governmental activism was a dynamic and expanding Commerce Department, reaching out now to draw other areas of the federal bureaucracy within its orbit and halt activities that challenged its own perceptions of the public interest. Initially Hoover had operated alongside and sometimes in conflict with Hughes and Wallace. But after 1924, with Wallace dead and Hughes returning to private life, Commerce burst out of earlier jurisdictional boundaries and sought to function as a "ministry of reconstruction" concerned with all phases of economic organization and decision making. As early as 1922, Hoover had turned what remained of the Labor Department into a cooperative satellite. Subsequently he attached much of the Interior Department, annexing such bureaus as Mines and Patents and shaping policy for most of the others. At the same time he succeeded in making Commerce a dominant force in shaping international economic relations, encroaching in many areas on the traditional jurisdiction of the State Department. Similarly, after Wallace's death in October 1924, he was successful in installing William Jardine, a man who agreed with his prescriptions for farm relief, as the new secretary of agriculture. Under Jardine the Department of Agriculture ceased to be a major center of anti-Hooverism; it purged those who had been guilty of such behavior and became a member of the Hoover team.

In addition, the Hoover organization moved with considerable success to revamp the antitrust and regulatory agencies, not, so it claimed, to permit antisocial behavior but rather to halt destructive organization wrecking and encourage fruitful forms of cooperative action. Under the post-1924 attorneys general, Harlan Stone and John Sargent, the Antitrust Division lent its blessing to a variety of associational activities previously considered illegal. Its job, as interpreted by the new antitrust chief, William Donovan, was one of helping constructive cooperationists to avoid legal difficulties. Similarly, the Federal Trade Commission underwent a major transformation. Under the chairmanship of William Humphrey, whom Coolidge appointed in 1925, it drastically reduced its investigatory activities, began negotiating more informal settlements, and started sponsoring trade practice conferences at which private leaders and FTC officials agreed on codes of ethical behavior for numerous industries. In theory the commission was still carrying out its mandate to eliminate unfair methods of competition. But it was now doing so by devolving its power on private bureaucracies and allowing them to define what was fair and what was unfair.

Adding such agencies as the Interstate Commerce Commission and the Federal Reserve Board to the Commerce-led team proved more difficult. Plans for a new kind of ICC, which would help the railroads to reorganize themselves into an efficient and responsive national system, failed to materialize. And Federal Reserve policy, as developed by Benjamin Strong of the New York Federal Reserve Bank, was much more concerned with reestablishing an international gold standard than with organizational and managerial reform. It strongly resisted Hoover's repeated efforts to develop new credit controls. Yet both the ICC and the FRB did seek to regulate by devolving power and responsibility on private groups, and work with these groups, it was assumed, would eventually bring their "regulators" into the larger "cooperative system."

New regulators, in the meantime, were being added not as independent entities or agents of popular action but as parts of the Commerce-led system. New controls over the Alaskan salmon industry, for example, were entrusted to Hoover's Bureau of Fisheries and used to implement conservation measures long urged by the canners' association. A "model" labor mediation system for the railroad industry (set up under the Railway Labor Act of 1926) emerged from Commerce-led efforts to develop mechanisms that both labor and management would support. New safety and operational standards in the aviation field became the responsibility of Hoover's Aeronautics Branch and its outcropping of collaborative associations. And in radio, a frequency allocation system developed by the Commerce Department finally received statutory sanction and became the basis for ordering access to that new resource. In each case the aim was to reinforce private ordering mechanisms with governmental power or approval, and in each this was accepted as necessary for further development of progressive organization and practice.

The promise, however, was that this union of public and private power could be held to a manageable minimum or would be needed for only a temporary period. The real faith of the Hooverites was not in statist coercion but rather in publicly endorsed agreements that had an approved yet extralegal status and would therefore lend quasi-official standing and protection to private compliance efforts. It was through such agreements, they believed, that a fruitful balance between order and liberty could be achieved, and by 1928 they were pointing proudly to three bodies of agreement that had allegedly done so. One consisted of publicly endorsed pledges to refrain from antisocial employment practices, the most cited examples here being the steel industry's agreement on an eight-hour day and joint commitments elsewhere to safety and factory standards. The second consisted of more than 100 federally approved standardization and conservation agreements, each credited with helping to build the new mass consumption economy or to curb waste of resources. The third consisted of more than fifty trade practice codes, certified by the FTC as specifying unfair methods of competition and spelling out the obligations of the ethical and socially responsible competitor. Together, it was said, these represented a new triumph for the American way, and together they constituted both the implementation of wartime lessons and the foundation for a new and superior socioeconomic order.

As of 1928, Hoover seemed convinced that the major threats to this developing associational action were being effectively contained. It was not until later that he became much concerned with the market riggers, corporate plunderers, and protectors of inefficiency who were operating behind the associational façade. State-approved associational action, he continued to believe, was helping to check big government and class-oriented "syndicalism," not to move the nation toward them. His chief concerns were with agriculture, the sick industries, and electrical power, areas where, as he saw it, failure to develop healthy forms of association and public-private cooperation had allowed state coercionists to gain political followings. Yet even in these areas he could find relatively little to worry about. Congressional attempts to legislate statist solutions had been turned back, and time had been gained for reeducation and for the building of truly progressive forms of collective action.

## Containing Congressional Initiatives

Of the statist solutions that Hoover worked to block, the most prominent and in his eyes the most threatening was the one embodied in the McNary-Haugen bill and supported by a movement generally designated as McNary-Haugenism. Sponsored by Senator Charles McNary of Oregon and Representative Gilbert Haugen of Iowa, the bill would allegedly make the tariff effective for farmers. Under it a federal agency would support and protect domestic farm prices, seeking to give such goods the "fair exchange" or "parity" value they had sold for in the prewar period. This agency would then dispose of accumulated surpluses abroad, taking losses on such transactions, and would finance its operations by assessing "equalization fees" against farm producers. The scheme had first appeared in 1922, in a pamphlet by former war administrators George Peek and Hugh Johnson. It had subsequently won the support of Secretary of Agriculture Wallace, the American Farm Bureau Federation, and a number of business leaders. Though it had gone down to defeat in 1924, its supporters had not given up. Peek proceeded to build a powerful legislative lobby, and a collapse of cotton prices in 1926 brought growing support in the southern as well as the western states.

In 1927 and again in 1928, advocates of McNary-Haugenism developed enough strength to put their program through Congress. But on each occasion President Coolidge imposed a veto that could not be overridden. Relying heavily on memoranda supplied by the Commerce Department, he condemned the scheme as class and bureaucratic legislation that would have disastrous effects on private initiative, constructive cooperation, and U.S. relations with other nations. The real answer, said Coolidge, was further encouragement to educational services and cooperative marketing. Apparently without much enthusiasm, he lent his support to the Hoover-Jardine plan to assist such organization with federal credits. This was a proposal that Hoover had been refining since the early 1920s. It could, he argued, fill the organizational gap responsible for farm difficulties and such phenomena as McNary-Haugenism, and even though farm leaders were in no mood to listen in 1927 and 1928, Hoover seemed convinced that they soon would be.

Movements analogous to McNary-Haugenism also developed in some of the sick industries. There, as in agriculture, schemes appeared for state-supported cartels or for using governmental power to put a floor under prices and wages, and in Congress this was reflected in proposals for antitrust revision, fair trade laws, and special price and wage controls for such industries as bituminous coal. Unlike the McNary-Haugen bill, though, such measures never came close to displacing Hoover's operations or to confronting the president with legislation that he felt compelled to veto. The only sick industry to be the subject of new legislative action was shipping, and there the enhanced subsidies and new credits followed the administration's prescriptions as to appropriate and necessary governmental action.

Tax and welfare policy also continued to follow administration prescriptions, although in these areas they came more from Andrew Mellon than from Herbert Hoover. In 1926 congressional defenders of graduated income and estate taxes were unable to prevent further reductions, one being a drop in the maximum surtax from 40 to 20 percent. And having failed to establish the constitutionality of federal child labor and minimum wage laws, the advocates of welfare statism largely withdrew from the federal arena and concentrated what energies they could still muster on the state level. In their present weakness they could not even save the limited funding for infant and maternity health that had been established under the Sheppard-Towner Act of 1921. In 1927 the program was extended for another two years, but only on condition that it would then be phased out.

In most fields proposals for government-operated enterprise had even less congressional support. Yet in one area this was not the case. By 1926 the abuses of private power and fertilizer companies, coupled with the failure to find acceptable lessees for the wartime developments at Muscle Shoals, on the Tennessee River, had opened the way to limited "experiments in socialism." A growing bloc of congressmen, led by Senator George Norris of Nebraska, came to support federal expansion and operation of the Muscle Shoals facilities. In May 1928, despite strong opposition from the power lobby and the Coolidge administration, Congress passed a measure under which a federal corporation would develop the Tennessee valley, produce large quantities of cheap power, and work out a "yardstick" for measuring the fairness of private power rates. As with the McNary-Haugen bill, the president's veto became the instrument of containment. With Congress adjourned, he took no action on the measure (using a tactic known as the pocket veto) and passed the issue on to his successor.

On the river development question as a whole, however, the administration's stand was not entirely negative. The American solution, so Hoover's Commerce secretariat kept insisting, lay neither in Norris's "socialism" nor in an unregulated and haphazard system of private exploitation. It lay rather in a "partnership" of federal, local, and private agencies, all working together to apply engineering expertise and implement cooperatively developed regional and national plans. Hoover articulated this notion in a series of "superpower" conferences, in agitation for a national waterway plan, and in protracted negotiations on the development of the Colorado and Columbia river basins and a Saint Lawrence seaway.

Coolidge, moreover, did eventually accept an enlarged sphere of federal responsibility and signed two major developmental measures into law. One authorized an extensive flood control program for the

Mississippi River, the aim being to prevent future floods from having the disastrous effects of one that occurred in 1927. The other implemented an interstate compact dividing the waters of the Colorado River and authorized federal construction of a huge Boulder Canyon dam and an accompanying water delivery system. Under the compromise finally adopted, the federal government was also to install and operate a hydroelectric power plant but was to sell power wholesale to a specified group of private and municipal distributors.

For the most part, then, congressional initiatives that challenged administration prescriptions were effectively contained. Members of Congress who held different visions of government and different perceptions of progressive organization were able to win substantial followings. But what they could produce in the way of new laws and programs was either negated by presidential veto or reshaped to fit the administration's definitions of what was American and progressive. As of 1928 the Hooverian views on these matters remained dominant.

## Ethnocultural Tensions and Issues

Though ethnocultural tensions remained high, they were now producing remarkably few eruptions in either Congress or the administration. In this area, to be sure, there was little philosophizing about the emergence of a new and superior synthesis. But many Americans preferred the situation that existed to the changes that various groups were advocating, and it was people of this view who were making national policy.

On the matter of immigration, for example, majority sentiment supported the central features of the legislation enacted in 1924. Although a number of ethnic minorities continued to criticize the ethnocentric and racist ideas reflected in the quota system, they were unable to influence many legislators. And though organizations espousing "100 percent Americanism" continued to propose measures to reduce foreign influences, they had no success in bringing about legislative action. The only protesters with much impact were the German and Scandinavian ethnic groups, who wanted to retain the 1924 quotas and prevent the implementation of those based on "national origins." The changeover, they argued, would necessarily be based on arbitrary determinations and would most affect would-be immigrants from Germany and the Scandinavian countries, people who had made and would make good Americans. They strongly supported the one-year postponements passed by Congress in 1927 and 1928, and given Hoover's sympathy with their position, they had hopes of making the postponement permanent in 1929.

Congressional and administrative responses to Americans dissatisfied with the existing status of minority rights were also minimal.
Although battles over feminism, cultural freedom, and the civil liberties of "un-Americans" continued in local governments and the federal
courts, there was little support for altering decisions through national
action. To the protests of the black minority against racial discrimination, the responses were limited to those that would not arouse fears of
a new "black reconstruction" or challenge the legitimacy of the southern establishment and its institutions. They consisted only of a few
additional appointments to federal offices, a slight increase in the support for black educational institutions, some improvement in civil service job opportunities, and an occasional rhetorical gesture.

Perhaps the most unstable of the accommodations that had
emerged by 1925 was that in regard to Prohibition. A kind of balance
had been struck, one that allowed prohibitionist ideals to be embodied
in federal law while tolerating lax enforcement, continued drinking,
and massive bootlegging. Yet even as Coolidge backed away from
actions that could upset this balance, the stage was being set for new
and fiercer battles over the issue. Gaining strength from 1925 on was a

For those who believed that Prohibition bred crime and corruption, the St.
Valentine's Day Massacre, February 14, 1929 in Chicago, Illinois, proved the
point. *(Brown Brothers)*

repeal movement led by the Association against the Prohibition Amendment, supported by many urban Democrats, and financed by some of the nation's wealthiest men. This movement was advancing new counterimages that depicted Prohibition not as a liberating and progressive reform but as a repressive denial of cultural and individual freedom, a breeder of crime and corruption, and a burdensome imposition on the nation's taxpayers. Increasingly, social drinking was now being associated not with the moral evils and un-American behavior of the old-time saloon but with fashionable living and liberated comportment, the assertion of individual and minority rights, and the romance of adventurous youth, the emerging independent woman, and the workingman's club. If such counterimages should prevail, even a Prohibition that did little prohibiting would soon be in jeopardy.

The response of the Anti-Saloon League and its allies was mounting alarm and heightened fanaticism rather than concessions seeking to deflate the repeal movement. Proposals for partial repeal of Prohibition or for redefining intoxicating beverages so as to exclude beer and wine were denounced as compromises with evils. The new lifestyles, despite their popular appeal, were condemned as degenerate, immoral, and un-American. And in prohibitionist circles the political success of Alfred E. Smith, culminating in his capture of the Democratic party machinery in 1928, became a resurgence of evil forces threatening to undo what had been accomplished through a century of effort. Bent on defeating Smith, dry leaders organized Democrats for Hoover and in the wake of Smith's defeat pushed for vigorous action against law-breakers and people who condoned or excused their behavior.

Indeed, Smith's nomination and Hoover's willingness to become the candidate of the anti-Smith forces had the effect of reopening the congressional and administrative arenas to the kind of ethnocultural warfare that Coolidge had avoided. The years after 1928 would bring a severe test not only for Hoover's economic prescriptions but also for his assumption that he could satisfy the Hoover Democrats without doing severe political damage to himself and his party.

## The International Scene

Also to be tested after 1928 were the Republican formulas for international order. To a later generation these would seem to bear part of the responsibility for worldwide depression and the coming of a second world war. Yet as the Coolidge era drew to a close, the world seemed to be moving in conjunction with American interests and dreams. Reporting to Congress in December 1928, Coolidge could note the prevalence of peace and goodwill, coming, he said, from mutual understanding and from "the knowledge that the problems which a short time ago appeared so ominous are yielding to the touch of manifest friendship." And according to Secretary of State Frank B. Kellogg, the irascible but generally competent lawyer-politician who succeeded Hughes in 1925, the actions of the period had laid the foundations for what could be a new era of permanent peace.

To the Hughes system of the early 1920s the post-1924 policymakers sought to make three major additions, two of which failed to win acceptance. One was American membership in the World Court, strongly endorsed by both Coolidge and Kellogg but finally blocked by Senate reservations that the court members found unacceptable. The other countries objected in particular to allowing the United States to block advisory opinions in cases where it had or claimed to have an interest, and as of 1928 the efforts of Elihu Root and a League of Nations committee to reach an acceptable compromise on this issue had not yet borne fruit. The other attempted addition was extension of the Washington naval limitations system to include smaller vessels. In 1927, responding to a growing concern about international rivalry in cruiser construction, President Coolidge called for a naval disarmament conference to meet in Geneva and complete the work begun in Washington. His call was accepted by Britain and Japan, but from the beginning the negotiations went badly and were under constant attack from nationalistic and big navy groups in each country. After six weeks of deliberation, the conferees conceded failure and disbanded without a new limitations agreement.

The addition that did win approval and become part of the American design for permanent peace was the Kellogg-Briand Peace Pact, signed in Paris in August 1928 and eventually subscribed to by most of the nations of the world. In part this was an outgrowth of pacifist idealism, especially of the post-1921 movement for outlawing war as an instrument of national policy. But also involved was Kellogg's determination to guide the movement into constructive channels and prevent the French from using it to involve the United States in their security system. His response to Aristide Briand's proposal for outlawing warfare between France and the United States was to urge a multilateral pact that committed all signatories to renounce aggressive war as a legitimate tool for advancing national interests. This was the conception that prevailed; it won Kellogg the Novel Peace Prize. The pact would later be criticized as little more than an "international kiss," but a good many New Era diplomats seemed convinced that it could help to deter aggressive militarism and strengthen the other ordering mechanisms that America had helped to establish.

While lauding the creative balance between nationalism and internationalism, New Era statesmen also assumed that the measures taken to promote European recovery from the war had been effective. American capital was now flowing into Europe, especially into Germany. In fact, Americans bought about 2.5 billion in German securities during the years 1924–1928. With the proceeds from such purchases and loans, Europeans were not only making reparations and debt payments but also modernizing and developing their economies. Only a few Americans at the time seemed aware of how unstable the resulting structure was, especially in view of the protectionism still practiced by the leading industrial nations and the fact that the remaining international debt burdens (around $625 million a year for Germany and a funded total of $11,671,400,000 owed by European nations to the United States) constantly threatened the currency systems of the nations involved. On occasion, Herbert Hoover, Owen D. Young, and Dawes Plan administrator S. Parker Gilbert did issue warnings. But neither they nor others in positions of power were willing to support such remedies as state or state-controlled lending, full cancellation of the debts, or an end to protective tariffs. The result was a European economy that became more and more dependent on a continued outflow of American capital that had little prospect of being sustained indefinitely.

During this same period American efforts to stabilize East Asia were also encountering major difficulties. In Japan anti-Americanism again became a major force, apparent particularly in protests over American immigration policies and a reassertion of Japan's "special interests" in China. China, moreover, was undergoing new upheavals, manifested in civil war, violence against foreigners, and bitter conflict between the left and right wings of a rising nationalist movement. At Nanking in 1927 nationalist soldiers slaughtered a number of foreigners, and American gunboats helped to restore order. Yet in spite of these developments, much of the optimism of the earlier period persisted, and American goals, it was thought, were still realizable. In 1928 two forces in the area were believed to be enhancing the chances of realization. One was the continuing influence of Japanese moderates, an influence that the United States might strengthen through constructive diplomacy. The other was the new nationalist government that had finally won recognition in China and with which the United States reached agreements settling the Nanking claims and recognizing China's tariff autonomy. Chiang Kai-shek, so a number of American diplomats had come to believe, was the leader of the moderate and progressive elements in China, and these could become the vehicle for containing radicalism and imperialism and achieving the kind of East Asia the United States desired.

Policymakers also seemed convinced that Western imperialism was being liberalized and steered into constructive channels. In the Near East the struggle against "closed doors" had finally brought a multinational consortium allowing American firms a share in oil development and permitting future entry through a subleasing system. Elsewhere the efforts to make colonialism pay through price-raising cartels supported by governmental power seemed to be in retreat. Against these the Commerce Department had waged a series of campaigns, seeking in particular to mobilize and bring pressure through American buyers, lenders, and competitors. The world, so it was thought, was being nudged away from exploitive and warbreeding imperialism toward the kind of "cooperative competition" that could bring orderly progress. Few people could foresee the intensified economic nationalism and anticolonial upheavals that would really characterize the 1930s.

Beneath the surface, developments were under way that would eventually lead to a worldwide depression, another world war, and revolutionary upheaval in the underdeveloped world. But as the architects of America's post-1921 diplomacy surveyed their work in 1928, they did not consider any of these things at all likely. On the contrary, they saw themselves as having found ways to attain the benefits of international order and progress without giving up those that derived from national independence and individual enterprise.

## The Pan-American Vision

Meanwhile, efforts were continuing to build a new pan-Americanism. Although Hughes was no longer secretary of state, his designs for improved peacekeeping machinery and the phasing out of gunboat diplomacy were still in place and apparently on the way to fuller realization. The new Central American system seemed to vindicate itself when cooperative action restored order in Honduras, and in August 1925 American marines left Nicaragua. Nor had the Commerce Department abandoned its vision of an ever larger market created through the joint activities of American capitalists, trained economic experts, and cooperative Latins. Under its auspices business contacts continued to be systematically organized, uniform standards and laws promoted, and pressure brought against operations considered economically unsound.

In late 1925, however, two developments inaugurated a train of events that would severely test the Hughes and Hoover policies. One was the outbreak of civil war in Nicaragua, touched off by Emiliano Chamorro's seizure of government power and continuing even after the United States had helped to force Chamorro out and install Adolfo Díaz as his successor. By the end of 1926 a rival government under

Juan Sacasa held substantial areas of the country, and as fighting intensified, pressure for American military intervention was building. The
other development was a resurgence of revolutionary nationalism in
Mexico. There a new administration under Plutarco Calles scrapped
agreements reached in 1923, sponsored new legislation requiring foreign oil companies to exchange their holdings for long-term leases,
launched a bloody anticlerical campaign, and offered recognition and
aid to the Nicaraguan rebels. To a number of Americans, the Mexican
Revolution seemed to have got out of hand again, and by early 1927
there were calls for armed intervention in Mexico as well as Nicaragua.

Coolidge turned a deaf ear to the clamor for war with Mexico,
especially after the Senate voted unanimously in favor of peaceful
arbitration. But Nicaragua was another matter. There the president
yielded to pressures for intervention, sending in a force of 5,000 marines to support the Díaz government and in the process arousing a
storm of criticism in both the United States and Latin America. The
whole vision of pan-Americanism seemed in jeopardy, revealed, so its
critics declared, as a façade for exploitive imperialism backed when
necessary by armed force. If pan-Americanism was to be saved, this
relapse into gunboat diplomacy had to be liquidated. The result, in
April 1927, was a special pacification mission, headed by Henry L.
Stimson, once Taft's secretary of war. In May, Stimson succeeded in
persuading the warring factions to lay down their arms, allow Díaz to
complete his term, and accept the results of an American-supervised
election in 1928. Only one small rebel band, under Augusto Sandino,
held out against this arrangement, and once the election was held and
José Moncada, military commander of the rebel forces, was installed as
president, most of the marines were again withdrawn.

Meanwhile, the Mexican problem also seemed to be moving toward
resolution. In September 1927, Coolidge replaced Ambassador James
Sheffield with Dwight W. Morrow, a House of Morgan partner with
unusual persuasive and diplomatic skills. Some three months later Morrow persuaded America's hero aviator, Charles A. Lindbergh, to make
a goodwill flight to Mexico City. Taking advantage of the subsequent
cordiality, Morrow was able to arrange face-saving formulas that allowed foreign companies to retain subsoil rights acquired prior to
1917, mitigated or postponed actions against American landowners,
and brought a truce in the battle between church and state. His diplomacy achieved no permanent resolution of the tensions between the
new pan-Americanism and Mexico's revolutionary nationalism, but, as
historian John D. Hicks has noted, Morrow did demonstrate that "with
tact and patience the peace could be kept."

Thanks to the work of Stimson and Morrow, the way seemed open
to further development of the envisioned pan-Americanism, and in late

1928 three actions seemed to indicate that further progress was being made. In November President-elect Herbert Hoover began a lengthy goodwill tour of Latin American nations, articulating his hopes for greater hemispheric cooperation. In December the Pan-American Conference on Conciliation and Arbitration assembled in Washington, eventually producing new agreements and agencies for handling international disputes. And in the same month Undersecretary of State J. Reuben Clark finished a policy memorandum repudiating the Roosevelt Corollary to the Monroe Doctrine and declaring that the doctrine did not justify American police actions in Latin America. Intervention, it said, might be justified on other grounds, but the Monroe Doctrine stated "a case of the United States versus Europe," not "the United States versus Latin America." Although not published until 1930, at which time the diplomatic establishment showed a reluctance to embrace it as "official policy," the memorandum was nevertheless a milestone in the retreat from interventionism. To the surprise of many observers, this retreat would survive the subsequent economic breakdown. Despite renewed pressures for armed intervention and the collection of debts by force, the Hoover administration would not relapse into a new round of gunboat diplomacy and military occupations.

Continuing commitments to nonintervention, however, would not mean realization of the vision's other aspects. Despite claims to the contrary, the proponents of pan-Americanism had not developed machinery that could sustain the flow of American capital into the region or ensure that it would be used there for productive purposes. As subsequent investigations would reveal, the financing operations involved large elements of misrepresentation and economic malpractice. As in Europe, a shaky structure was being built that could not withstand a decline in American capital exports, and the eventual result would be a Latin America forced into wholesale debt repudiation and general economic contraction, torn by political upheaval and instability, and convinced that it had again been victimized by "Yankee imperialists."

In the end, whether in Latin America, Europe, East Asia, or the United States itself, the New Era formulas for orderly progress would fail the tests to which they were eventually subjected and would be labeled naïve and unperceptive or accused of being smokescreens for rapacious private interests. Yet their failure should not be permitted to obscure the genuine achievements of the policymakers seeking to apply them. Nor should failure obscure these formulas' often perceptive analysis of alternatives or their foreshadowing of later designs for orderly progress. The policymakers of the period were not merely reactive or negative; they were the heirs and transmitters of managerial visions that included embryonic forms of corporative planning, world community building, and "alliances for progress."

CHAPTER 7

# Alternatives to the Mainstream

Americans, a succession of historians have noted, have prided themselves on being a practical people, confident that they can solve problems as they arise. Yet, an equal number have noted, they have also been an intensely ideological people, raising liberal dogmas into a national philosophy. Along with tests of workability they have insisted on tests of "Americanness," ruling out support for anyone who has challenged the national philosophy itself. Only when arrangements have been perceived as meeting both these tests have they been relatively free from criticism and demands for reform.

Such was the case with the mixture of public and private activities that took shape in the 1920s. Many, but not all, observers viewed the New Era arrangements both as a flowering of American liberalism and as a huge practical success, and others believed them sufficiently effective and safe to be tolerable. It was from outside the mainstream that a variety of critics challenged the dominant perceptions, depicting a society mired in error and perversion and offering alternatives both to New Era Americanism and to the American system itself. They too were part of America in the 1920s, and segments of their part were to be of major significance for the decade that followed.

### Competing Visions of a New Liberalism

Of greatest significance, perhaps, were critics who envisioned a new liberalism yet denied that the New Era arrangements were bringing or could bring it into being. Modern technology, they believed, was capable of providing uplifting and liberating abundance, and the realization of this potential was compatible with and perhaps dependent on the retention of a capitalist economy and a liberal political order. But the notion that it could be done through capitalist syndicates and the machinery of private bureaucracies was to them both fanciful and dangerous. The task would require an enlightened governmental apparatus, using its power to obtain decisions that private organizations could not make, although just what this apparatus should consist of and just what decisions it should make and enforce were questions on which its proponents found it difficult to agree.

To some critics, for example, the major deficiency in the New Era arrangements was their inability to produce the spending decisions needed for sustained growth and continued progress. The technology pioneered by Henry Ford and the planning activities of the private sector were steps in the right direction, but ultimately they were incapable of curbing or correcting the destructive aspects of a maturing capitalism. This would require governmental power, specifically the transfer of a larger portion of the spending decisions to the public sector and the development there of an apparatus to ensure that they were made in the interests of the system as a whole. So said such unconventional economists as William T. Foster and Waddill Catchings, especially in the widely read works *Business without a Buyer* (1927) and *The Road to Plenty* (1928). And so said the founders of the Planned Prosperity League, which in 1929 presented a plan for construction reserves to be managed in the interests of overall economic stability. In particular, they urged commitments to a superhighway system and the gearing of its construction to a prosperity index.

A second vision of enlarged government came from people still committed to the "new freedom" ideology of the prewar period. The fatal flaw in the New Era arrangements, as they saw it, was the assumption that special interests could be enlightened or professionalized and thus turned into social interests. Releasing such interests from market discipline was in reality an invitation to social disaster, and under modern conditions, it was argued, the maintenance of this discipline could not be left to natural law or private action. It required a powerful government engaged in constant action against market riggers and in a constant process of taking over and operating sectors that were inherently monopolistic. Hence the first priority of the true progressive should be the rescue of the antitrust and regulatory agencies from their captors, and the second should be the building of governmental organizations with the ability to sustain market discipline and to conduct efficiently the enterprises in which release from such discipline was a social necessity.

Still another vision of enlarged government came from the heirs of the "new nationalism" and others convinced that a planning and welfare state could serve liberal ends. Like the antitrusters, such critics rejected the assumption that special interests could be enlightened or professionalized. Yet at the same time they regarded the notion of government-enforced market discipline as unworkable and anti-modern. The answer lay not in an apparatus that supported entrepreneurship but rather in one that would free scientific professionals from the grip of the pecuniary-minded and allow them to use their talents to serve public interests. The true founts of wisdom were such critics as the economists Thorstein Veblen and Simon Patten, not the jurist Louis Brandeis or Woodrow Wilson. And as the decade progressed, such theorists as John Dewey, Charles A. Beard, Stuart Chase, and Rexford G. Tugwell were sketching the outlines of a planning and welfare apparatus believed capable of speeding up and managing national progress. Such a vision also continued to appear in the pages of such liberal journals as the *New Republic* and the *Survey,* in some of the calls leading up to the Progressive party convention of 1924, and late in the decade in the formation of a League for Independent Political Action.

Operating in liberal circles as well were reformists who could accept the central coordinating mechanisms of the New Era political economy but wished to erect alongside of these a new set of governmental welfare structures. Much of what they believed necessary consisted not so much of a planning, antitrust, or managed spending apparatus as an enlarged public sector that would enforce fair labor standards, protect the weak from economic exploitation, provide public health and housing services, and operate new systems of health, unemployment, and old-age insurance. Real social welfare, they insisted, the kind essential to the realization of liberal goals in an industrial and urban age, could come only through a national system of public institutions, not through extensions of private philanthropy and local community action. Working through such organizations as the National Child Labor Committee, the American Association for Labor Legislation, and the American Association for Old Age Security, these reformists continued to develop designs for the envisioned institutions and to agitate for programs of implementation.

Another kind of new liberalism came from people opposed to governmental bureaucracies yet seemingly convinced that their own private bureaucracies and syndicates could employ governmental power as an instrument of national progress. Modern democracy, as these liberals saw it, must function not through an enlarged state but through corporative institutions resembling those of the war period. And unlike the people associated with the Hoover operations, they believed that the building of such institutions would require, for a time anyway, substantial grants of governmental power to those engaged in it. This view appeared in much of the agitation for the McNary-Haugen bills, and in business circles it continued to generate designs for a planning and welfare system administered through government-supported cartels. By 1929 these designs were coming particularly from the leaders of the National Civic Federation, from writers associated with *Forbes* magazine, and from minority elements in the Chamber of Commerce. In their more extreme form, they were also being set forth in the literature of the Committee on Industrial Coordination and in such books as Benjamin Javits's *Make Everybody Rich* (1929).

Finally, from still other quarters came visions of a new apparatus moving to end discriminatory social codes rather than economic disorders. The crucial defect in the American system, so these critics argued, was not in its political economy. It was in the unprogressive, unjust, and wasteful way in which minorities and women were allowed to participate. Until this defect was remedied—something that would require extensive state action against the discriminatory institutions that controlled access to jobs, housing, education, and social services —the system was in constant danger of degenerating into disorder and irrationalism. So said a variety of minority groups and feminist leaders. Moving beyond the concerns of particular groups, such politicians as David Walsh and Fiorello La Guardia envisioned a new America enriched by cultural diversity and equipped with institutions guaranteeing equitable treatment for all.

Outside the mainstream, then, liberals of various sorts continued to view the New Era arrangements as prescriptions for disaster rather than progress. Pointing to major flaws in the period's underlying assumptions, they set forth competing versions of a new liberalism. When post-1929 developments seemed to confirm their prognoses, their solutions would acquire greater credibility and growing public support.

## Alternatives on the Right

America, Herbert Hoover liked to say, was "a nation of progressives," quarreling not over liberal ends but the means to attain them, yet the America of the 1920s also had critics of another sort, people whose quarrel was not with an "old," "new," or "false" liberalism but with liberal thought and liberal ends themselves. Rejecting the visions born of the Enlightenment and adopted as part of the national philosophy, such critics offered alternatives aimed not at liberating the masses but at protecting society from them or eradicating their desire for individual fulfillment.

For some of these critics the great shortcoming of American society was its failure to develop aristocratic institutions capable of nurturing cultural creativity, protecting traditional wisdom, and restraining mass appetites. Promising beginnings along this line had been cut off by concessions to popular agitation and acquisitive materalism. The result was a society purportedly catering to its worst elements and stifling its members possessed of the greatest creativity and wisdom. Among some intellectuals this view caused deep despair, a conviction that escalating concessions to the masses must eventually destroy everything of real social value. Others spoke of a "saving remnant" that would withdraw into isolation and survive the barbarian onslaught. Still others held hope that America might now correct nearly two centuries of error. If the power of popular demagogues and aggrandizing bureaucracies could be curbed and held in check, a genuine aristocracy might emerge, gain social legitimacy, and establish institutions that would liberate the creative and the wise.

Where this aristocracy would come from was an open question. The most likely spot, a number of conservative critics believed, was the business elite that had survived the competitive tests of the past three decades. This survival, to be sure, had depended on the possession of certain undesirable qualities, among them "ruthless individualism" and an "eye for the main chance." But the survivors were also people of wisdom and ability, with demonstrated leadership qualities, a growing appreciation of the finer things of life, and increasing interest in developing the institutions that could nurture and train a genuine aristocracy. If they could be protected from populist impulses — and some organizers of antiradical and antibureaucratic groups hoped to provide such protection — evolution might well take care of the rest.

This dream, however, was not shared by all who hoped for the development of aristocratic institutions. The nation's business elite, as some saw it, had remained far too individualistic, divided, and mass-oriented to fill the role being outlined for it. It had internalized too much of the libertarian rhetoric being used to counter populist and working-class impulses. And for these reasons it had little potential for developing into the kind of aristocracy that conservative critics yearned for. If such an aristocracy was to emerge, it would have to come from other sectors of society.

To a few intellectuals, for example, the major hope of redemption lay in reviving and developing the kind of agrarian aristocracy that had once ruled the South. There, it was argued, the United States had once had the basis for a truly integrated society, built around an "innate code of obligations" and a "mutuality of interests." If Americans could only see how liberal fallacies and corporate capitalism had destroyed this hope for a wholesome and meaningful way of life, redemption from the fragmenting cleavages and social disorders of the modern era might begin. Such views were expressed by a number of conservatives, none more eloquent than a group of writers, literary critics, and historians associated with Vanderbilt University. In the work of these "southern agrarians," men like John Crowe Ransom, Allen Tate, and Donald Davidson, the institutions of the New Era were indicted not so much for their economic evils as for their psychological costs to the human organism. These critics gathered their indictments into a symposium under the militant title *I'll Take My Stand* (1930).

Envisioning still another kind of aristocracy were the "new humanists," led by such critics as Irving Babbitt, Paul Elmer More, Stuart P. Sherman, and Norman Foerster. For them the model was neither the antebellum South nor an emerging industrial gentry but rather the learned Puritan divines who had provided moral leadership in colonial New England. In the Puritan leaders, it was maintained, America had once had an elite capable both of disciplining itself and of devising machinery that could protect the wise and cultivated from mass bestiality. That elite had also possessed the reason and will necessary to discern the ethical absolutes underlying all moral progress. Hence the great task of genuine "humanists" should be that of exposing the heresies of the nineteenth century, upholding such standards and restraints as had survived, and thus paving the way for another aristocracy in the Puritan mold. As the decade ended, moreover, a few such critics seemed convinced that their remedy for the sorry condition of American civilization could actually be implemented. In a manifesto titled *Humanism and America* (1930), they argued that the nation's intellectual climate was now swinging back to an appreciation of permanent values and of a social order able to protect and sustain them.

Even more designs for a redemptive aristocracy were set forth in the America of the 1920s, designs whose formulators looked back to Hamiltonian federalism and religious authoritarianism or abroad to nations ruled by military, religious, and statist hierarchies. But promoters of these had neither the eloquence of the "southern agrarians" and "new humanists" nor a "cult of the commercially successful" on which to build. They received little attention, even among Americans who yearned for an aristocratic order, and these yearners never became more than a tiny minority within a larger conservative constellation. Much more attuned to American values were alternatives that idealized traditional middle-class life and looked to a resurgence of the older middle class for moral regeneration and social redemption. It was this middle-class "right," appealing especially to those with vested interests in traditional norms and relationships, that constituted the largest group of Americans who considered the New Era arrangements too liberal or too progressive.

## Between Fundamentalism and Fascism

At the core of middle-class rightism, as it appeared in the America of the 1920s, was an idealized community in which sturdy farmers, enterprising but community-spirited businesspeople, and industrious and cheerful workers lived side by side in peaceful and prosperous harmony. The members of this community recognized the mutuality of their interests, and in well-filled churches, character-building homes, and community service organizations they learned the fundamental truths that allowed them to live rewarding and moral lives. Having discovered a body of higher law, they needed little government. And having developed time-tested and unquestioned methods of allocating wealth and status, they enjoyed a community life free of envy, conflict, and resentment.

That America had ever contained such communities was dubious. But among middle-class rightists their existence in a golden past was an article of faith. America, they insisted, had once been a land in which adherence to social and economic fundamentals resulted in a rewarding and harmonious community life. And America, they also insisted, could become such a land once again. Given proper encouragement and protection and proper antidotes to the poisons that were weakening and corrupting society, the spirit and the community institutions of the golden age could regain their vitality and restore national virtue.

For some people, proper protection meant action against the very heart of the "new economy" of mass production and mass marketing. It meant protection of traditional crafts and occupations and especially of the livelihoods of traditional merchants and farmers. Many more seemed to assume that the real corrupter was not economic change but rather the modernist ideas, alien value systems, and imported social misfits that were fostering an "un-Americanism" incompatible with the attainment of social virtue. Hence the real remedy lay in even more stringent immigration measures; stronger curbs on subversive forms of association and expression; fuller protection for the traditional family, school, and church; and firmer defenses of the ethnic, racist, and sexist distinctions embedded in traditional social codes.

There was never full agreement among rightists. Some concentrated on one foe to the exclusion of others; some were more inclined toward statist measures than others; some were willing to sanction violent and illegal methods, while others were not; and some saw the need for action as pressing and imminent, while others favored a gradualist approach. There were also partisan differences and disagreements about the boundary between the American and the un-American. Yet rightist coalitions were able to bridge these divisions, win control of a variety of business, patriotic, and religious societies, put together such new vehicles as the Sentinels of the Republic and the American Vigilant Intelligence Federation, and in these ways exert political influence and keep their vision of an alternative America before the country.

For a time it even seemed that America was about to produce its own variant of the fascist and "radical right" movements that had arisen on the European continent. Marrying the doctrines of middle-class rightism to traditional bigotry and war-fostered vigilantism, the rapidly expanding Ku Klux Klan emerged as the most prominent manifestation of the traditionalist counterattack against modern ways. Between 1920 and 1925 this "invisible kingdom" grew from 2,000 mem-

A Ku Klux Klan gathering in 1921. *(UPI/Bettmann Newsphotos)*

bers to 2 million, attracting not only rural defenders of traditionalism but also substantial elements from the "older settlers" in the expanding cities. Although most of the Klan's leaders condemned European fascism as an alien ideology, commentators then and later were quick to note some striking similarities. As the historian George Mowry has pointed out, both movements were ideologically grounded in village or preindustrial ideals; both called in almost mystical terms for a return to the virtuous life of the past; both were intensely nationalistic, with a stress on folkish and racial purity; both attacked minorities as being of inferior or defective stock; and both condemned most aspects of the new urban culture, especially its polyglot racial mixtures, its intellectuality and leftist politics, and its new standards of moral behavior. Both, moreover, considered themselves the organized good of the community, and both saw the return to virtue as being achieved through an arduous struggle with pernicious and subversive influences.

At the peak of its strength, the Klan offered a chilling glimpse into New Era America's potential for fascism. It found and recruited a deeply troubled group of middle- and lower-middle-class Americans. It showed how appealing a distinctive garb (long white robes and conical, face-covering hats), supersecret rituals, and guarded open-air meetings could be to people yearning for a touch of the mysterious. It tapped the darker sides of nationalism, populism, and folkishness, combining its form of authoritarianism with calls for community revitalization and attacks on established elites considered to be enemies of the "people." In the name of popular virtue, the Klan challenged the basic concepts of human dignity and individual rights. For a time, moreover, it seemed to thrive on exposés of its extralegal and terroristic activities—a kind of vicarious participation in its direct methods of dealing with sinners, corrupters, and social enemies by beating, burning, and lynching.

America, however, was neither Italy nor Germany, where fascism was thriving. America lacked the surviving elements of an "old regime" that saw fascism as the road to restoration. It lacked the linkages between managerial bureaucracies and middle-class rightism that developed abroad. It lacked an intelligentsia willing to develop a respectable ideological cover. And it possessed what Germany and Italy did not: a set of deeply rooted commitments to a liberal polity and a politics of accommodation. Gradually, it became apparent that much of the Klan's growth was due less to underlying fascist proclivities than to a temporary acceptance of its claim that it represented genuine "Americanism," and from 1925 on, as this claim lost its credibility, the movement lost most of its membership and power.

What also hastened the organization's decline was its susceptibility to capture by politicians interested in using its ready-made "political machine" for their own purposes. In such states as Texas, Louisiana, Oklahoma, Kansas, Colorado, and Indiana, the Klan served as a vehicle through which politicians of less than savory character—people like Felix Robertson, Clarence J. Morley, and David C. Stephenson— elevated themselves into positions of power. Scandals followed, the most notorious of these revolving around sexual misbehavior, election frauds, and political graft in the state of Indiana, where the Klan chief was convicted of assault, rape, and kidnapping. As such behavior was disclosed, it accelerated the organization's mounting membership losses and growing tendency to disintegrate into warring factions. By 1930 membership had dwindled to an estimated 100,000.

Even as the Klan faded, however, a considerable group of Americans continued to see their homeland as a nation fallen from grace and corrupted by false ideals, foreign influences, and inferior human stock. In an array of rightist organizations the vision of restoring a golden age through a return to abandoned principles persisted. And in the 1930s the vision would gain new adherents, both from the victims of economic catastrophe and from citizens who saw redemption being blocked by another injection of poisonous un-Americanism.

## The Anticapitalist Left

Curiously, many of the rightist images of New Era America could also be found at the other end of the political spectrum. In leftist perceptions, too, the institutions being built by New Era capitalists and administrators were dehumanizing and incapable of meeting the need for a wholesome community life. But for the left, the basic source of corruption was neither a departure from tested fundamentals nor failure to fill institutional vacuums. It was rather the disintegrating and corrosive impact of capitalist acquisitiveness and institutionalized greed. On this central point the great bulk of the anticapitalist left accepted the teachings of Karl Marx and equated true progress with the coming of communal property and socialist institutions.

One variant of the Marxist solution had long stressed a gradualist strategy. It envisioned capitalist corruption gradually yielding to an expanding welfare state responsive to ever widening popular participation, the end result being the attainment of a socialist commonwealth. In Europe this had become the ideology of Social Democratic parties, and in America such a party had seemed to be taking shape during the quarter-century prior to 1917. The war, however, had brought divisions and repression. Though Socialist party membership had climbed again in early 1919 (reaching a peak of about 109,000), the subsequent impact of antiradicalism from without and antigradualism from within had left the Socialist Party of America a shambles. Having failed to capture the organization, the advocates of "revolutionary socialism" broke away to form the Communist and Communist Labor parties. Apostates of other kinds also left, and by 1921 Socialist party membership had dwindled to barely 13,000. In popular imagery, moreover, socialism had become solidly linked with "un-Americanism." Most Americans were convinced that the 915,000 votes cast for Eugene Debs in 1920 had been expressions of personal empathy or of concern for civil liberties, not votes for a socialist America.

In the mid-1920s the remnants of the Socialist party, under such leaders as Victor Berger and Morris Hillquit, continued to champion a gradualist strategy. In 1922 the party accepted an invitation to the Conference for Progressive Political Action, and in 1924 it supported Robert La Follette in the hope that his organization might develop into something comparable to the British Labour party. The Socialists also worked for the formation of state labor parties to which socialist units might attach themselves. But all initiatives seemed only to bring further decline. By 1928, when Norman Thomas became the party's presidential candidate, its membership had dwindled to less than 8,000, and it had become increasingly an organization of ministers and intellectuals rather than industrial workers. Outside of a few urban strongholds (such as Lower Manhattan, Milwaukee, and Reading, Pennsylvania), organized American socialism was hard put to bring a few civil liberties cases into court and keep the idea of social democracy alive among a few intellectuals and youth groups.

The other major variant of Marxism was that envisoning the attainment of the socialist commonwealth through violent revolution and a "dictatorship of the proletariat." Gradualism, Marxists of this sort argued, could never achieve the necessary transfers of power. These could come only by following the Russian example; for a time, especially in early 1919, their hopes were high that America was about to do so. Stimulated by news from abroad, the Marxists organized themselves as the Left Wing Section of the Socialist party, and by late 1919 the section had spawned separate Communist, Communist Labor, and Proletarian parties. Even after the repression that followed, these groups stuck with the Russian analogy. Their strategy was to "go underground" as radicals had done in czarist Russia, and by 1922 the Communist and Communist Labor parties both had underground organizations, each with an attached "open" party serving as its legal periscope.

From the beginning, organized American communism had been quick to send emissaries to the Soviet Union and surrender most of its autonomy to the Moscow-controlled Third International. It was under the International's tutelage that the separate organizations were finally joined in a single party and the underground policy abandoned, and it was from Moscow that the orders came for expelling such heretics as the Trotskyists (followers of Leon Trotsky) and Bukharinists (followers of Nikolai Bukharin), for shifting from "dual unionism" (building separate communist unions) to "boring from within" (infiltrating existing labor groups) and then back again, and for subordinating American considerations to the building of socialism in Russia. In theory such subservience was supposed to hasten the day when capitalism could be overthrown everywhere. But in operation it became another element that discredited the critiques and prescriptions emanating from the Communist apparatus. As of 1929 Communist efforts to develop a base in the labor unions and reform-minded political groups had failed miserably, and party membership had dwindled from 50,000 to less than 10,000.

Also populating the anticapitalist left at the time were a variety of syndicalist groups, mostly tiny remnants of the Industrial Workers of the World, the Syndicalist League of North America, and earlier flirtations with guild socialism. These groups had in common a vision of the syndicalist commonwealth, purged both of market capitalism and the political state and reorganized around the factories, mines, and other places of production. But ideas as to how the vision could be realized ranged from the notion of sabotage and mass protest culminating in a general strike to claims that worker councils or a new kind of productionist-minded unionism could be the instruments of transition.

In some quarters the syndicalist vision had also become fused with notions of a technocratic order run by production engineers and soviets (councils) of technicians. Technological advances and engineering methods, theorists of this sort argued, had put a liberating abundance within the reach of the American people. But this could not be attained in a system that remained subject to "sabotage" by capitalists, romantic delusions on the part of workers, and disruption by political adventurers. Its realization required an engineering directorate empowered to gear production and distribution to scientifically determined social needs. In time, it was believed, such a directorate would be established. It would come through a gradual expansion of the technostructure within the capitalist order, through a general strike of the technicians supported by workers' organizations, or through a breakdown of the existing system and an abdication of its ruling elites.

One center of such thinking was an organization known as the New Machine, founded by the management engineer H. L. Gantt. In the years from 1916 to 1919 it brought together a number of radical engineers and other technocratic theorists. Another center, appearing in the mid-1920s, was Charles Ferguson's Technarchy. But the group attracting the most attention was the one associated with the economist Thorstein Veblen. At the New School for Social Research, in New York City, Veblen had continued his analysis of business waste and "sabotage" and had begun exploring the possibilities of organizing engineers for the revolution, a project explained in his book *Engineers and the Price System* (1921). Among his associates were Howard Scott, Guido Marx, and Otto Beyer; for a time they organized and operated the Technical Alliance, which urged surveys of waste and conducted conferences on the engineer's social function. The group won few followers in the 1920s, but a number of its members would reemerge as leaders or supporters of the Technocracy movement that gained attention in 1932 and 1933.

Still another kind of anticapitalist radicalism envisioned a collectivist commonwealth to be attained through cooperative economic organization and collaboration between radicalized farm, labor, and consumer groups. It would build in particular on collectivist impulses of indigenous origins rather than seeking to implement European ideologies. In operation this meant that most of its support came from remnants of earlier agrarian radicalism. It was to such groups that the Farmer-Labor parties of 1920 and 1922 sought to appeal. It was as a champion of public enterprise in farm-related industries that the National Nonpartisan League emerged as a political force in the upper Midwest. Founded in 1916 by Arthur Townley, the league enrolled thousands of members in fourteen states; in North Dakota league-backed politicians even gained control and put through a program of state-operated banks, packing houses, elevators, flour mills, and insurance services. These enterprises, however, fared badly in the recession of 1920–1922, and thereafter the league's influence rapidly dwindled.

New Era America, then, was not without its anticapitalist left. Visions of a socialist or collectivist commonwealth continued to be offered as alternatives to the existing system, and theoreticians continued to debate the strategies best suited to realizing these visions. But in a nation enjoying rapid material gains and disposed to see departures from the national philosophy as subversive or pathological, such visions had minimal appeal. Neither the working class, depressed farmers, nor middle-class engineers and technicians could be turned into instruments for attacking capitalism. Nor did the disillusioned intellectuals of the period, disdainful though they were of the "new capitalism" and America's "business civilization," see much merit in socialist critiques and prescriptions. It was not until the early 1930s, when economic catastrophe seemed to lend credence to Marxian and Veblenian analysis, that a number of these intellectuals found the answers and formulas of the anticapitalist left both perceptive and persuasive.

What was true of the anticapitalist left was also true of the anti-democratic right, the quasi-fascist elements of the middle-class right, and the "new liberalisms" that tried to challenge antistatist traditions. Vocal though these radicals were in the 1920s, their formulas for a different America failed to mobilize the social groups and strata to which they were addressed. They would get a new chance when boom turned to bust and New Era formulas lost their credibility.

CHAPTER 8

# Social Rebels and Social Orderers

If American society in the 1920s resisted political radicalization, it was not a society without dislocations and concerns about social order. Throughout the period the growth of the "new economy" continued to disrupt existing institutions and patterns of life. It brought with it another wave of migration to the cities, this time mostly from the rural South and West rather than from Europe. It withdrew economic support from older forms of family, community, and religious life. It posed new problems that existing educational and welfare institutions found difficult to handle. And it created a social context in which rebellions against established ways could sustain themselves and force accommodations in the mechanisms being used to maintain order and stability. In the social sphere the decade was an "unsettling" one, productive of both social rebels and new kinds of social orderers. Or, as various historians have argued, it was a period during which social progressivism meant both liberation from traditional constraints and the constitution of social authorities steeped in wisdom drawn from a new priesthood of social scientists.

This is not to say that all Americans in the 1920s were affected by such social changes. Nor is it to deny that the changes were part of a continuum reaching back into the 1890s and forward into the 1960s. But a history of the 1920s that failed to discuss these changes would be hopelessly incomplete. Accompanying the postwar quest for an ordered and professionalized capitalism was a simultaneous and significant search for new forms of family, school, press, church, community, and the delivery system for social services.

## The Old Family and the New

In the society of nineteenth-century America the family had served as a major agency of socialization. Indeed, it had borne much of the respon-

111

sibility for shaping and buffering the individuals who competed for economic rewards. It had also been an institution with diverse and variant forms, but the dominant structure, especially among the nation's broad middle classes, had emphasized parental control, sexual discipline, and deference to the husband-father as family head and provider. This structure, the dominant culture held, was essential to social health and well-being, and outside the family, society had been arranged to uphold it. Rebels had found few alternatives available, and efforts to create alternatives had met stiff resistance.

By the 1920s, however, the supportive context in which the traditional family functioned had weakened considerably. Economic growth had provided alternatives for rebels against established roles. Mass communication and widespread mobility had heightened the awareness of such alternatives. And from society's standpoint the family had become less important. It provided less of the training needed for effective economic performance and less of the socialization on which stability and order depended. In the twentieth century, moreover, family heads were no longer invariably wise and benevolent wielders of institutional power. Their kind of wisdom had depreciated in value, and their authority was more frequently seen as working against the interests of society as a whole. In too many instances, a growing array of critics charged, that power was being used to block needed social adjustments, warp and repress individual personalities, or sustain exploitive, despotic, and morally repugnant relationships.

As societal supports weakened, rebellion had got under way. The prewar years had had their "liberation" movements, extolling the virtues of sexual freedom, sensual gratification, and parental permissiveness. Despite efforts to check the process, the years from 1919 to 1929 witnessed the growth of a youthful subculture embracing these counterestablishment ideals and equating them with modernity and sophistication. The colleges had their "flaming youth," kicking over parental traces and tasting hitherto forbidden pleasures. Both working-class and middle-class homes had their "problem children" and adolescents out of control. And under the impact of the new subculture, the rules and conventions that had once governed courting behavior and family formation were disintegrating. The chaperone all but disappeared from the scene, parental control over marriage decisions underwent a drastic decline, and respectable families condoned "necking" parties in the privacy of apartments and automobiles.

Also joining the rebellion against traditional patterns was the "new woman," no longer willing to play the roles of homemaker, subservient mate, and moral exemplar. The prewar years had also witnessed the birth of counterestablishment ideals concerning women, especially among the wing of the feminist movement concerned with amending oppressive social codes. By 1915 enough "new women" had appeared for the widely read critic H. L. Mencken to announce the arrival of the "American Flapper."

After the war, as the drive for woman suffrage succeeded and that for better economic protection faded, changes in demeanor and social behavior continued. More women and especially more wives sought and found roles outside the home. More women rebelled against masculine possessiveness and double moral standards. More were willing to sever the bonds of unhappy marriages, more practiced birth control and planned parenthood, and more engaged in the period's symbolic acts of liberation: they smoked cigarettes, went to speakeasies, talked openly and frankly about sexual subjects, and dressed in a style that combined short skirts and makeup with bobbed hair and a boyish figure. Although full equality with men was still a long way off, society was now tolerating behavior once regarded as insufferable.

One factor that helped to sustain such rebellions was the support they received from the arbiters of fashion and manners and the mass media. Through such support they became identified with sophistication, modernity, and personal liberty, all things that their opponents found difficult to attack. Reinforcing this support was that derived from the social sciences. If the traditionalists still invoked biblical authority and the "wisdom of the ages," the rebels had found Sigmund Freud, John B. Watson, and Havelock Ellis. Sexual and family relationships, they could argue, were contrived and culturally determined, not ordained by God or by an unchangeable human nature. They could be altered and molded to enhance human happiness, and those inherited from America's past were badly in need of alteration. They were survivals from an unenlightened age and generators of social dysfunctions, mental illness, and crabbed, unhappy, and maladjusted human beings.

Rebel success, however, did not mean the dissolution and disappearance of the family. Although liberationist logic might call for a postfamilial society of autonomous and "freely loving" individuals, free to bond with whomever they chose, there were limits as to how many such individuals the existing power structure would tolerate. Nor were most of the rebels themselves willing to pursue "liberation" to its logical ends. The need, as they and others perceived it, was not to abolish the family but to find modern forms of it that could accommodate the new freedoms within a framework that would allow the family's persisting social functions to be performed.

By 1930 two ideals were being offered as solutions to the problem. One was the "companionate" family, envisioned as abandoning the older patriarchal hierarchy in favor of a modern "partnership" held

together by shared activities and interests, emotional support and satisfying sexuality, and the magic of romantic and parental love. In such a
family, it was argued, the "new woman" and the potentially rebellious
child and adolescent could be given roles that combined enhanced
freedom and individuality with effective performance of the family as a
social unit in a changing society. The result, it was said, would benefit
not only women and children but men and the cause of social progress
as well. In practice, however, realizing the ideal would prove difficult,
and to the extent that it was realized, it tended to undermine the
emotional support and companionship that women had previously
found with members of their own sex. Later interpreters would see this
as an important factor in the weakening of the women's movement.

The other ideal was the "managerial" family, which as envisioned
would function as a domestic team tied together not only by affection
but also by up-to-date wisdom provided by trained experts in such
areas as child care, domestic relations, character building, and household management. It would operate, in essence, as part of an administrative network through which a "domestic science" might be applied
to family life. Such experts in the 1920s, inspired in part by visions that
had come out of the war experience, were rapidly expanding their
domains. Specialists in child nurture, juvenile delinquency, and exceptional children were all developing ways for their expertise to be institutionalized and applied. So were home economists, family rehabilita-
tors, youth leaders, and professional character builders. Claiming to
reflect the latest in scientific wisdom were a variety of manuals on
sexual techniques, marital relations, child psychology, family expenditures, and scientific housekeeping. In theory, this institutional growth
provided "helping hands," allowing the family team and its instrument
of implementation, the modern homemaker, to draw on outside resources to create a better product. But in practice, the tendency was for
the "helping hands" to become new centers of authority, bringing their
own values into family affairs and working for a family system that
could reinforce and complement the other institutions characteristic of
an emerging managerial order. This was especially true of the ideology
and prescriptions promoted by such agencies as the Agriculture Department's extension service and a Hoover-controlled organization
known as Better Homes in America.

Traditionalists continued to rail against these solutions. The only
real remedy for social ills, they insisted, was a return to the traditional
family structure with its supporting moral code and social arrangements. But that such a restoration could actually be brought about
became increasingly doubtful. Despite inherent problems the new
ideals and ordering mechanisms could mitigate the dislocations gener-

ated by economic change and mass mobility, and increasing numbers of Americans were accepting them, at least in part.

This acceptance, however, did not extend to even a majority of families. Such changes and conflicts, it should again be emphasized, were much more characteristic of the urban middle class than they were of Americans occupying the lower rungs of the social or economic ladder. For these groups the story of changing family structures revolved less around individualistic rebellion or bureaucratic impulses than around the impact of agricultural depression, uprooting migrations, and ghetto life on traditions already at variance with the dominant one. In some cases the change was toward structureless demoralization and disorganization resulting in a "free-floating" individualism that was regarded as pathological yet in some respects was strikingly similar to the "free-loving" associationism idealized by middle- and upper-class rebels. In other cases the change was toward a matrifocal structure in which a strong female figure with a dependable source of income became the stabilizing core and source of authority. In still others—indeed, in the great majority that have been studied by historians—the change was toward a household structure with elastic boundaries, taking in relatives, outsiders, and subfamilies as the need arose and proving amazingly adaptive to coping with the burdens of lower-class life and defending the subcultural traditions that were at variance with New Era ideals. Significantly, the penetration of companionate and managerial ordering mechanisms into family life made less headway and met with far greater resistance at lower income levels than it did in the middle ranges of the social structure.

## The Educational System

If family life in the 1920s was an "unsettled" area of social behavior, the same was also true of school life and educational relationships. Traditional educational patterns, like the traditional family structures, were losing societal support and being challenged by educational rebels and modernizers. They were unsuited, it was claimed, to modern citizenship, modern economic life, and modern pursuits of happiness, —a fact that had become strikingly evident during the mobilization for war. Despite stiff resistance from educational essentialists and fundamentalists who would stick with the basic subjects of traditional education, the American school system was being reshaped along lines that were expected to train modern citizens and workers.

For one thing, the system was being rapidly expanded, the reigning assumptions being that modern society needed more education and that more of it should come through the schools rather than other institutions. Enrollment in the public schools grew from 23,278,000 in 1920 to 28,329,000 a decade later; most of the expansion was at the secondary level, but some of it was via the addition of kindergartens and the extension of elementary education to children who had previously been denied much schooling. During the same period enrollment in institutions of higher learning nearly doubled, from 598,000 in 1920 to 1,101,000 in 1930. Expanding also was the part of the educational system devoted to the search for and production of new knowledge. Business, governmental, and foundation researchers were increasing, and so were scholar-teachers with combined instructional and research missions.

As the system grew, it was changing in other ways. Country schools were being merged for greater efficiency. Educational governance, despite resistance from school boards and trustees, was moving into the hands of technical specialists and professional administrators. Teachers were being required to meet higher professional standards and learn new and allegedly more scientific teaching methods. New measurements of efficiency and achievement were being developed and spread across the country through professional interaction and highly publicized educational surveys. And reflected now in numerous curricular reforms was the view that modern education should move beyond traditional goals and equip students with the social, political, and vocational skills needed for modern life. At all levels offerings were being broadened, vocational and citizenship training expanded, and traditional subjects remolded to meet changing needs.

In part, the changes were responses to altered patterns of educational demands by the citizenry and its representatives stemming partially from a continued concern about proper socialization of the lower classes. But also involved was the ideology of "progressive education" associated with the philosopher John Dewey and others who followed his lead. The function of education in a progressive society, Dewey had argued, was to create an enlightened and adaptable citizenry capable of making rational choices and adjusting to the social roles that continued progress required. It would make democracy in an industrial-urban age possible, both by unmasking the irrationalism in traditional arrangements and by providing the knowledge and training that individuals needed to participate in modern forms of cooperative action. It was to these dual missions of "liberation" and "resocialization" that the educational modernizers of the period claimed to be dedicated.

Keeping the two in tandem and in balance, however, was no easy task. Progressive education could, on the one hand, become an instrument of managerial manipulation used for antidemocratic purposes.

This possibility loomed especially large in the drive to supplant liberal with technical education and in such phenomena as the business-run Americanization programs, the vogue for bringing scientific managment to the schools, and the institutionalized partnership between corporate and academic researchers. As some critics saw it, an "educational trust" consisting of powerful administrators, experts, and business interests was already in the process of subverting the educational system that supported American democracy. On the other hand, there was the danger that the liberation from tradition that was envisioned would destroy older loyalties and identities without creating new ones to take their place and would thus produce disintegration and anarchy rather than progress. This possibility loomed large in the notions of an education built around myth destruction and responses to "felt needs" and natural curiosities expressed by children left to structure their own learning.

To educational traditionalists such dangers seemed to outweigh any possible benefits. Modernism, as they saw it, was pushing the school into areas where it did not belong, destroying its capacity for moral training and social integration, and undercutting popular authority as institutionalized in elected school boards. It was, they believed, a recipe for social disaster rather than social progress. Throughout the period they organized countermovements that when joined with other opponents of educational progressivism, particularly the Catholic parochial schools and the racially segregated system in the South, were capable of thwarting modernist projects. Schemes for a federal department or board that would promote modern education in the same way that the Department of Agriculture promoted modern farming failed to win the support needed for passage by Congress. And education continued to vary greatly from region to region and district to district. In amount and quality, the South continued to lag behind, and education for blacks remained particularly deficient there.

## The Provision of Public Information

The institutions through which public information was gathered and disseminated, such as the media, were also undergoing change and engendering debate in the 1920s. These, like traditional education, had once been used to reinforce village ideals or to service small educated elites. But from the 1880s on, this older system had gradually yielded to a "mass journalism" involving large corporate organizations, an emerging journalistic profession, and information tailored to meet growing popular demands. Such publishers as Joseph Pulitzer, William

Randolph Hearst, and S. S. McClure had developed mass circulation papers and magazines filled with popularized reportage and special features. Despite their dependence on advertising revenue, these publications had succeeded in establishing themselves as gatherers and dispensers of factual information. The potential for abuse, it was argued, was held in check by rising professional standards, acknowledged lines of demarcation between reportage and special pleading, and competing sources of information.

In the 1920s this system of mass journalism continued to expand and develop new offerings. The decade witnessed such successes as the tabloid, the news digest, and the syndicated feature. It witnessed the further growth of newspaper chains and cooperative services, and it became, to the dismay of some traditionalists, the age of the media figure and the "big story," with journalists linking millions of readers in shared vicarious experiences.

This pattern, moreover, was one that the new medium of radio followed rather than broke. There too the gathering and dissemination of public information was entrusted to organizations whose principal revenues came from advertisers. And there, as in newspaper journalism, the emphasis was on building and holding mass audiences, rationalizing operations through consolidation and cooperative activities, and arguing for a nongovernmental discipline grounded in professional obligations and rival information sources. Although federal licensing became necessary to achieve orderly use of the airwaves, radio journalism was neither nationalized nor subjected to any very stringent set of controls over quality or undue commercialization.

As mass journalism grew, two other developments were taking place. One was the rapid proliferation of specialized informational agencies, serving, for the most part, the nation's newly forming trade, professional, and special-interest communities. Not only was America in the 1920s informed through mass circulation media, but it also supported an expanding array of trade and professional journals, specialized informational exchanges, and organs addressed to limited and special publics.

The other development was a rapid expansion of the public relations (PR) apparatus that had first appeared in the prewar period and burst into full bloom under the war system. Staffed by press secretaries and publicity experts, this new institutional structure depicted itself as a bridge between wielders of power and a democratic citizenry. It existed, it was argued by such publicists as Edward Bernays and Ivy Lee, to enlighten public opinion and to help secure constructive social action. But critics saw it differently. The real purpose of PR, they insisted, was to manage informational flows in the interests of those who hired its services, and the people staffing it were best seen as hucksters or propagandists rather than true journalists.

As with progressive education, the champions of the media envisioned an evolution that would have both liberating and ordering effects. On the one hand, the media would work to overthrow traditional authority and unfetter people kept in ignorance of the outside world. On the other hand, it would facilitate a "new citizenship" and the formation of community ties and cooperative endeavors. Yet, as with education, the task of holding these two things in tandem was not easy. Liberation, it seemed to some, was opening the way for the mindless and socially destructive consumption of journalistic sensationalism. The search for a new order, others felt, could lead not to informed community action but to misinformed puppets manipulated by information managers.

As in the educational field, moreover, traditionalists doubted that the benefits of change outweighed the costs and the dangers. As the older standards and behavioral patterns crumbled, some traditionalists sought to reimpose them through a network of community censors. As small-town and local newspapers folded, some people urged that they be given special protection and encouragement. And as many modernizers reached for public support of their informational services, they encountered traditionalist charges that they were subverting free institutions and wasting the nation's resources. If modernizers had so far won most of the battles, it was by no means clear that they could keep doing so.

## Religious Life

If the schools and the press were unsettled areas in the 1920s, the most heated controversies seemed to revolve around religious modernism and its challenges to established teachings and values. As in other areas, the roots of this modernization reached well back into the nineteenth century, and by 1920 it had already altered much of the nation's religious life. Doctrines reconciling religious teaching with scientific evidence had gained widespread acceptance in mainstream Protestant denominations. Ministers had lost much of their traditional status and authority. And "creeping secularism" had found expression in a gospel of social and environmental reform, a conversion of churches to what critics considered mere recreational centers, and a tendency to downgrade the importance of religious experience. Being weakened, too, was the nation's informal Protestant establishment. Catholics, Jews, and skeptics were no longer staying in the roles to which the establishment had assigned them, and efforts to keep them there were losing societal support.

In the 1920s these alterations of American religious life continued to gain momentum. The teachings of such modernist theologians as Harry Emerson Fosdick, A. C. McGiffert, and Henry Preserved Smith gained further acceptance, especially among urban congregations and seminary students. The churches, like the schools and the press, underwent consolidation and the introduction of managerial and technical expertise. Worldly pursuits of happiness and the inroads of scientific materialism continued to encroach on religion's place in American life. Many religious leaders, having frankly embraced evolution and the introduction of scientific and historical methods into biblical study (the so-called higher criticism), abandoned theological explanation of the Bible for a version of the "social gospel" or some vision of an ethical world built around a "new humanism." In many quarters support for the traditional Protestant dominations also continued to weaken. Catholics, Jews, and unbelievers, it was argued, were entitled to their own beliefs and at the same time to full citizenship in the American republic, and only by recognizing these rights and working toward a pluralistic order based on mutual toleration and cooperation could the nation's religious system adapt to modern spiritual needs and sensibilities.

Religious modernizers, then, like their counterparts in the educational and informational fields, saw themselves as both liberators and orderers. Yet to the defenders of traditional religious practice they were subversives and heretics, denying God's dominion over human affairs, rejecting revealed truths, and undermining the foundations on which moral behavior rested. A militant antimodernism arose to fight the reformers, and the antimodernists were able to mount major counteroffensives that heightened religious tensions and conflicts.

One such counteroffensive was directed against the notion of a pluralistic order recognizing equality of status for non-Protestants. To substantial numbers of Americans, especially in the South and the Midwest, this kind of liberalism amounted to fundamental error, and they reacted by espousing militant forms of anti-Catholicism, anti-Semitism, and anti-intellectualism, joined, in many instances, with the doctrines of "100 percent Americanism." Anti-Catholics worked to close the parochial schools, uncover "papal plots" against American liberties, and bar Catholics from positions of political or social influence. Anti-Semites, including for a time Henry Ford and his *Dearborn Independent*, resurrected and spread baseless charges of an international Jewish conspiracy to control the world. Urged on by such newspapers as J. Frank Norris's *Searchlight*, religious militants set out to expose the atheists and unbelievers who had allegedly infiltrated into the nation's educational and intellectual institutions as teachers and leaders. Nor was this intolerance to be found only in lower- or middle-class groups. As non-Protestants sought access to the nation's elite colleges, clubs, services, and board rooms, they were met with more formalized barriers, often in the disguise of merit systems or tests of character. Even Harvard University established a Jewish quota, leading one Jew to label the institution an "intellectual Ku Klux Klan."

A second counteroffensive, building in the prewar years but now greatly intensified, was directed against modern science and modernist heresies within the Protestant camp. The biblical scriptures, so religious fundamentalists continued to insist, were to be interpreted literally. Any deviation from this was an attack on fundamental truth. Especially pernicious, as they saw it, was the Darwinian notion that humans had evolved from lower forms of animal life. In the early 1920s the fundamentalists campaigned to purge "atheistic evolutionists" from the churches and schools. Once William Jennings Bryan, the old spokesman for rural and evangelical America, had joined the crusade, it was carried to state legislatures and church governing bodies all across the country. Only in the South, however, primarily in what detractors called the "Bible Belt," did the cause develop strong popular support and have a measure of success. In North Carolina and Texas educational authorities forebade evolutionary teachings. And in Tennessee a purge of university professors was followed by an antievolution law; in 1925 it became illegal for instructors in the state's schools or colleges to teach any theory denying the biblical account of creation.

In the wake of this legislative action the American Civil Liberties Union offered to finance a constitutional test of the statute. So when John T. Scopes, a young high school teacher in Dayton, Tennessee, intentionally violated the law, the stage was set for one of the decade's great journalistic sensations, the "monkey trial." William Jennings Bryan was engaged for the prosecution. Clarence Darrow, the famed criminal trial lawyer and an avowed agnostic, joined the defense. The resulting clash was front-page news all over the world. In the end Scopes was found guilty (his sentence was later reversed on a technicality), and subsequently the antievolution law was upheld by the state supreme court. But the real climax came shortly after the verdict. On July 26, 1925, while still in Dayton, Bryan became ill and died — a victim, his followers said, of his strenuous efforts to defend the true Christian faith.

In the months that followed Bryan's death, the antievolutionists formed organizations and intensified their activities. Through such groups as the Bryan Bible League, the Bible Crusaders, and the Supreme Kingdom they brought pressure to bear on other legislatures

Clarence Darrow addressing the jury during the Scopes "monkey trial."
*(Brown Brothers)*

and worked for an antievolution amendment to the federal Constitution. But substantial success eluded them. By 1928 they had secured antievolution measures only in Mississippi and Arkansas, the latter acting through a popular initiative that bypassed the legislature. A year later the crusade was ebbing. Modernists and liberals were successfully holding the line, at least to the extent of blocking antimodernist efforts to dictate what should be taught in the nation's public schools.

As the decade ended, it seemed clear that America's religious traditionalists lacked the power to halt or reverse the developments associated with modernization. The real potential for greater order, it appeared, lay not in their efforts but in those of modernist theologians, religious pluralists, and formulators of a religious relativity attuned to constant change. Yet the power that they retained in American society was far from insignificant. If they could not restore the "old-time religion," they still provided alternatives for Americans disillusioned with modern life and its frightening uncertainties.

## Community Life and Welfare Services

Bemoaned as well in the 1920s, particularly by people from rural areas or small towns, was the loss of traditional community structures and established patterns of community life. In the past these had defined the status, obligations, and identity of many Americans. They no longer did so, and one response had been a variety of movements urging some form of "community restoration." These had constituted one aspect of prewar reform, and in the 1920s the idea continued to serve as the rallying cry of local merchants fighting the chain stores, farmers battling urban sin and monopolistic industries, and local establishments resisting further progress of the organizational revolution. America, these groups argued, must not destroy its "pillars of the community" and thereby become a land of communityless human atoms manipulated by communityless holders of power.

Similar warnings came from some academic sociologists. The disintegration of community life, they feared, could mean a permanent state of social "disorganization" and individual "anomie." Yet more than countering this view were perceptions of a community-minded people substituting modern forms of community life for those now on the decline. Occupational and interest groups, it was argued, were developing into functional communities equipped with wisdom and awareness grounded in the findings of social science. This was the argument of Owen Young in regard to the Electrical Manufacturer's Association, and similar arguments could be found in professional and business circles. Further, it was argued that even as the pillars of the older edifice gave way, mutually interdependent functional groups were fusing into new social units and erecting the framework for modern forms of community endeavor.

The decade, moreover, despite its reputation for individualism and self-centeredness, was one in which a variety of activities were carried on in the name of community. It was a period of expanding service clubs (Rotary and Kiwanis, in particular) engaged not only in after-dinner oratory but also in local and national projects, of an organized philanthropy consciously seeking modern substitutes for the vanishing processes of village life, of corporate managers seeking recognition as community trustees, and of real estate and suburban developers advertising themselves as "community builders." It was a period as well of "community development" operations, mostly under Chamber of Commerce auspices but with some encouragement from the Department of Commerce and other public agencies. And in the name of community welfare or civic betterment, it became an era of urban zoning laws, scattered experiments in community planning, and numerous exercises in bringing representatives of organizations and specialties together in community federations and councils. In the creation of these bodies, the Cleveland Welfare Federation became a widely copied model, and by some observers it was regarded as analogous to the trade associations in business.

Upon examination, too, social researchers usually found not a growing mass of aimless individuals but an ongoing and adaptive group life developing its own pressures and sanctions. The organization building of the period reflected not only managerial promotion but also new patterns of group loyalty, especially to the profession, the company, the trade, and the club. Factory labor, researchers at Western Electric found, did not consist of undifferentiated humans responding uniformly to changes in their environment. It consisted rather of informal worker groups of varying degrees of cohesion and autonomy. And despite the attack on ethnic loyalties, an attack carried on by modernizers and hypernationalists alike, ethnic-based communitarianism showed amazing resiliency. Far from dissipating, it became the basis for increased civic and political activism and for an ideology that equated the liberal dream with enhanced status and greater freedom for ethnic subcultures. Ethnicity, it seemed, might be a much more adaptive loyalty than once thought. It might find ways to survive and grow in a society that was replacing traditional arrangements with modern ones. Or it might continue to thrive in pockets of resistance to a modern order — in Appalachia and the Deep South, in parts of the rural Midwest and the Hispanic Southwest, in the Jewish Lower East Side and a variety of little Italies and Polonias, and in similar enclaves elsewhere.

Among black Americans there were also indications of greater community spirit and cohesion. Continued migration of black southerners to the North brought disorganization, explosive racial tensions, and all the miseries of life in the black ghettos of the big northern cities. Yet at the same time this population shift formed the basis for heightened racial solidarity among blacks in an expanding network of community programs. Mutual-aid societies and neighborhood improvement associations offered themselves as instruments of racial affirmation and progress. Programs for studying black history and culture aimed both at changing white attitudes and at fostering a more intense feeling of racial worth and pride.

Two phenomena of the 1920s reflected the developing potential for racial nationalism that went beyond efforts to attain full American citizenship. One was the search among black intellectuals for African roots and distinctive forms of black art and literature, a search most apparent in the cultural movement known as the "Harlem Renaissance." Centering in the Harlem district of New York City in the years from 1921 to 1929, the movement celebrated blackness and particularly the beauty, vigor, and honesty of life in the ghetto. The other was the mass appeal of Marcus Garvey's Universal Negro Improvement Association, a quasi-militaristic organization that preached a form of black Zionism and sought to organize a return to an African homeland. Founded in 1914 by a Jamaican immigrant who saw himself as the "Black Moses," the organization expanded rapidly in the wake of the race rioting of 1919. In the early 1920s it had hundreds of thousands of adherents and sympathizers, most of them drawn from the urban ghettos and most rejecting, at least temporarily, the integrationist goals of the older black leadership. Later the group would fade into obscurity, a victim of frustrated expectations, fraudulent promotion, and official repression. But its achievements between 1920 and 1925 revealed a potential for racial nationalism that could bring new vehicles of community action and community discipline into being.

Americans in the 1920s, then, were not only severing old community ties but forming new ones. And for a good many this meant that the "community," defined as a changing mixture of the old and the new ties, could retain its role as the chief developer and dispenser of social welfare services. If the older structures were no longer adequate, new structures were rising. Around them, provided that destructive community conflict could be avoided or contained, Americans could build a modern welfare system without giving up the benefits of community feeling and initiative. They were not faced with a choice between impersonal commercial services and the kind of impersonal and unfeeling statist bureaucracies that had been set up in Britain and Germany.

Occupying a central place in the envisioned welfare system was the rationalized community unit, bringing the leaders of specialized public and private agencies into a joint welfare council and entrusting the execution of council policy to a professional welfare expert. As noted previously, such arrangements represented the welfare sector's counterparts to trade and industrial associations. Through them, it was argued, the benefits of professional expertise and consolidated budgeting could be combined with the advantages of agency autonomy and voluntary action. As the decade progressed, a number of such units were formed. In some areas they developed as extensions of the earlier Charity Organization Societies or the war-born Community Chests. In others they grew out of community responses to emergency situations. In still others they were promoted by schools of social work or professional organizations of social workers. Under the Iowa Plan, for example, a projected scheme of organization initially adopted in 1913, the

State University Extension's Bureau of Social Welfare organized such community units in twenty-two Iowa counties.

Three other sets of institutions occupied important positions in the envisioned system. One was another structure of community welfare units, based not on the county or city or neighborhood but on the newly forming corporate, occupational, and ethnic communities. This was exemplified in such agencies as the newly established "employee service" departments at Goodyear and International Harvester, the welfare programs of the Amalgamated Clothing Workers, and the welfare centers created by the Federated Jewish Charities. As envisioned, this structure would supplement and intermesh with the geographically based units. The second was a set of coordinating and promotional organizations, working to foster more efficient intermeshing and action and helping communities to mobilize and expand their resources when confronted with emergency situations or new needs. In part these were to operate as permanent agencies. This was the idea, for example, behind such bodies as the National Council of Social Work, the American Association for Community Organization, and the Ohio Council of Social Agencies. In part they were to be reserve bodies, capable of springing into action to cope with emergency or special situations, much as the Committee on Civic and Emergency Measures had been created by the unemployment conference in 1921 or the President's Flood Relief Committee had been formed in 1927. Finally, filling out the picture, was an emerging set of special funding agencies, increasingly professionalized and allegedly capable of raising and managing funds on which straitened community units and other parts of the welfare apparatus could draw. Operating through a network of community foundations (again, the Cleveland Foundation was often the model) and organized appeals (both by community chests and such specialized national organizations as the Red Cross and the Salvation Army), this component of the system was supposed to minimize public funding and thus avoid the evils of "politicization."

As the decade ended, some critics had already labeled this "American solution" a pipe dream and a failure. Most of it, they claimed, was unrealizable, and the part that was realized had already demonstrated its inability to deal with wasted human potential, mass insecurity, and the persisting misery of the people at the bottom of America's social scale. As yet, however, such views were relatively rare and without much influence. Defenders of the solution could point to the expansion of welfare work, to encouraging developments in individual and corporate giving, and to what were cited as highly successful responses to the mass unemployment of 1921 and the catastrophic Mississippi flood of 1927. Most Americans seemed to believe that they had found a superior approach and that this approach was being implemented and was proving itself in practice.

In other respects, too, most Americans seemed confident that their society was closing the "institutional gap" opened by economic and technological change. If there were dislocations and rebellions, there was also movement toward a new order to be achieved through altered forms of the family, the school, the press, the church, the community, and the social service system. The New Era dream was of an intelligent and humane society rationally adapting to economic and technical progress while avoiding the twin perils of anarchy on the one side and statist politicization on the other. Although some critics branded this an impossible dream, doomed to collapse of its own contradictions, the American people as a whole were still caught up in it. It was not yet the "shattered dream" that historian Gene Smith would later describe.

# CHAPTER 9

# The Persistence of Unequal States

On August 11, 1928, some 60,000 persons gathered in Stanford University Stadium to witness Herbert Hoover's formal notification of the Republican party's nomination for the presidency. In the address that followed, Hoover discussed a variety of national problems, but his two major themes were ending poverty and achieving equality. "We in America today," he said, "are nearer to the final triumph over poverty than ever before in the history of any land." The poorhouse was vanishing, and the time was approaching when poverty, with its "grinding by under-nourishment, cold, . . . ignorance, and fear of old age," would be "banished from this nation." Nor would the institutions essential to realizing this "noblest of human aspirations" mean a retreat from the nation's egalitarian ideals. New Era America, Hoover stressed, was firmly committed to an "equality of opportunity" that entitled "every American — rich or poor, foreign- or native-born, irrespective of faith or color," and including "every boy and girl" — to attain "that position in life" merited by "ability and character." It had no place for "privi-leged classes or castes or groups who would hold opportunity as their prerogative." Nor could it allow them any place if it was to continue reaping "the gigantic harvest of national progress."

For Hoover and other New Era leaders, the institutional growth that had accompanied the emergence of organizational capitalism was producing not only abundance but social justice as well. Like the atomistic market of precorporate capitalism, the new machinery was seen as justly rewarding the socially deserving, and the rhetoric extoll-ing it was quick to deny that it involved discriminatory practices not based on individual merit. Yet just as an older American liberalism had found ways to accommodate and justify illiberal forms of social hierar-chy, the managerial liberalism of the New Era also found ways to

128

incorporate such hierarchies. Despite Hoover's claims, America in the 1920s remained in many ways a racist, sexist, class-bound, and inhumane society, and most of the potential for making it less so was being developed not in the new managerial order but through the actions of the people whose equality was still being denied.

## The Boundaries of Class

Class boundaries in New Era America were more flexible than those in Europe. "A significant proof," wrote Hoover in 1922, lay in the fact that "of the twelve men comprising the president, vice-president, and cabinet, nine have earned their own way in life without economic inheritance, and eight of them started with manual labor." In America's elites one could find new entrants who had risen from humble origins by dint of ability and ambition. In its mass culture could be found numerous experiences that were shared across class lines. Even as the growth of wage labor created the social base for class consciousness and conflict, these boundaries blurred in the diverse origins and makeup of the nation's burgeoning middle class.

Yet as the decade's most perceptive social analysts recognized, America in the 1920s was not a land without class boundaries and barriers. In their study of "Middletown" (Muncie, Indiana) in 1929, Robert and Helen Lynd found that the "crazy-quilt array" of nearly 400 occupations could actually be resolved into two kinds of activities, one characteristic of the working class, the other of the business class. Within each group, they conceded, one could find important behavioral and status variants. But it was the "division into working class and business class" that constituted "the outstanding cleavage in Middletown" and acted as a prime determinant of the quality of life there.

The Lynds also went on to provide a poignant and much quoted description of these differing qualities of life. Members of the business group typically lived on "a neatly paved, tree-bordered street" in a home with "a trim terraced yard," the latest in equipment, and an interior in which "everything from the bittersweet in the flower-holder . . . to the modern mahogany smoking table by the over-stuffed davenport" bespoke "correctness." But the "working man, coming home after his nine and a half hours on the job, walks up the frequently unpaved street, turns in at a bare yard littered with a rusty velocipede or worn-out automobile tires, opens a sagging door," and enters a living room from which "the whole house is visible—the kitchen with table and floor swarming with flies, . . . the bedrooms with soiled, heavy quilts falling off the beds, . . . the whole inte-

rior . . . musty with stale odors of food, clothing, and tobacco. . . . Rust spots the base-burner. A baby in wet, dirty clothes
crawls about the bare floor among the odd pieces of furniture."

According to the Lynds and other analysts, moreover, being born
on one side or the other of this class division was the most significant
cultural factor shaping the remainder of people's lives. It influenced
whom they would marry, what church they would attend, whether they
drove a Ford or a Buick, whether their daughters were admitted to the
desirable high school clubs, and "so on indefinitely throughout the
daily comings and goings of a Middletown man, woman, or child." On
one side of the line, the able and ambitious moved through doors of
opportunity opened partway by class-based privilege. On the other
side, they encountered class-based obstacles reflected in the society's
expectations, attitudes, and practices.

One way to square the Hooverian claims with the realities of Middletown was to deny that much ability or ambition existed on the
working class side of the divide. Such denials, backed by appeals to
cultural stereotypes and natural evolution, had helped to bridge the
gap between the ideal and reality in an earlier period. In New Era
America these notions of a working class that had achieved the position
in life merited by its "ability and character" persisted. It was all that
anyone could expect, some said, from a human stock that was biologi-
cally inferior, morally deficient, or culturally dysfunctional, and to a
remarkable degree such assumptions continued to operate in the ostensibly meritocratic structures now being built by credentialed experts.
These notions were reflected, for example, in the educational counsel-
ing and vocational guidance movements. In personnel work, the emphasis tended to be on reconciling workers to their proper place in an
allegedly scientific occupational structure, not on opening doors of
opportunity for people capable of holding higher positions.

Hoover's talk of ending poverty, moreover, tended to ignore an
American underclass that was not sharing in the period's economic
gains. In the South a lower class of sharecroppers and tenant farmers
remained both depressed and oppressed, suffering as it had in the past
from malnutrition, poor housing, hookworm, minimal social services,
and exploitive arrangements that bordered on peonage. In rural hinter-
lands elsewhere, in a variety of urban enclaves, in depressed mining
camps and textile towns, and in the spaces occupied by migrant farm
workers, itinerant hoboes, and floating industrial laborers, conditions
remained almost as bad. If the poorhouse was vanishing, the poor were
not, and the institutions Hoover praised could not really make them
vanish. On the contrary, the economic development that they promoted left much of the underclass untouched, and the persistence of

negative stereotypes of the poor within these institutions worked to narrow opportunities for escape from poverty.

What the lower classes thought about the persisting gap between ideal and reality has been difficult for historians to discern. But it seems clear that few accepted the negative stereotypes common in middle- and upper-class circles, that many took pride in the network of self-help activities grounded in their own institutions, and that a majority perceived of themselves not as proletarians but as worker-citizens who could expect to share in the benefits of economic and technological progress. These people harbored a widespread sense of abuse and injustice, coupled with negative images of the rich and powerful and considerable skepticism about managerial designs for a capitalist utopia. But they never coalesced into the strong class-based movements and parties that arose in Europe. Conspiring to keep them weak were the persisting legacies of antiradicalism and labor fragmentation, continuing faith in liberal prescriptions, and the reinforcement of managerial hierarchies through corporatist tendencies and a focus on aspirations away from work.

Still, some developments in the 1920s can be seen as helping to pave the way for more class-conscious labor actions in the 1930s. The militant strikes of 1919–1922, although mostly unsuccessful, left a residue of experience, attitudes, and potential leadership that permitted greater effectiveness in the mid-1930s. A tenacious network of labor research and educational agencies, featuring such institutions as Brookwood College, the Workers Education Bureau, and the journal *Labor Age*, continued to nourish ideas of working-class ability and virtue. In the communities of recent immigrants, where perceptions of ethnic and class barriers tended to fuse, deepening resentment led to ethnic working-class activism a decade later. A potential for class-based protest existed in the 1920s, and a general discrediting of managerial values and prestige in the 1930s would allow some of this potential to become manifest.

## Racial and Ethnic Barriers

Inequality in New Era America also reflected the persistence of racial as well as class barriers. For the nation's 11 million blacks and for smaller minorities of Mexican, Amerindian, and Asian descent, the color line continued to limit opportunities and to support pervasive patterns of economic subordination, social discrimination, political disfranchisement, and legal insecurity. Neither the older ideal of democratic citizenship nor the newer one of functional meritocracy would appear to have any place for such barriers. But as in the case of class, ways were found to smuggle them in as convenient indicators of "ability and character."

By 1930, despite continued migration to northern and western cities, nearly 80 percent of America's blacks still lived in the South and remained subject to discriminatory laws and social codes openly based on claims of white supremacy. Blacks, southern whites asserted, were by nature mentally and morally inferior, lacking in ambition, and either childlike or bestial in their inability to control their passions. Such characterizations remained entrenched in southern political discourse and hence continued to be invoked to justify legal and social sanctions intended to keep blacks in their place. Separate waiting rooms, railroad cars, schools, churches, restaurants, drinking fountains, and theater sections were all a matter of law. So were devices designed to keep blacks from voting or to perpetuate separate systems of justice. Reinforcing the color barrier were social conventions that required rituals expressive of unequal conditions (the back entry for blacks, for instance), barred displays of mutual respect (such as shaking hands or tipping hats), reserved desirable places and areas for whites, and tolerated terrorism as a means of enforcement. Even language served this purpose. For example, blacks were required to address whites formally, whereas southern whites ordinarily addressed blacks by their first names or by such terms as "boy," "girl," "aunty," or "uncle."

In the North the color line was somewhat less onerous. There, blacks could vote and expect better schools and better legal protection. But discrimination, particularly in jobs and housing, was still very much a part of their lives. A combination of employer prejudice, white worker hostility, and restricted opportunities for training kept most blacks in menial, unskilled, and low-paying jobs. And through a combination of restrictive covenants and informal exclusionary agreements, huge residential tracts were closed to blacks, thereby restricting their residential options to less desirable areas. The "black districts" of the South had their counterparts in the "black ghettos" of northern and western cities, although in the latter the opportunities for blacks to develop their own class divisions tended to be somewhat greater.

Northern industrial managers, moreover, tended to see white supremacy not as unfounded prejudice but as a building block of the new managerial order. Writing in *Industrial Management*, for example, Ralph Immel told his fellow professionals that blacks could be developed into "high grade" workers with a "faithfulness" exceeding "many white and especially alien workmen." But to do so, he said, managers must recognize that the race was incapable of "the highest development" and should not be placed in supervisory roles, that its "unreasoning, child-like optimism" and "natural laziness" could be enlisted in the search for easier and more efficient ways, and that it was best suited to work having a "natural rhythm" and allowing for spells of rest to sustain a "naturally buoyant nature." Invoked here were racist stereotypes resembling those invoked by white southerners. But the language was that of scientific modernism, citing as support the findings of physiologists and psychologists along with the experience of employers who had "made a distinct success" of "negro labor." For Immel and the managerial types he represented, race had become an indicator of "ability and character," and racial hierarchy had thus been incorporated into a world ordered by managerial expertise.

Other minorities, too, continued to suffer from barriers built into the organizational society and its modernizing processes. Mexican-Americans, particularly in the Southwest, were subjected to social discrimination, political disfranchisement, and color bars that denied them equitable access to jobs, housing, and social services. Native Americans continued to chafe under policies that left them to scratch out a meager existence on arid reservation lands. Japanese-Americans, particularly in the western coastal states, found that their employment opportunities were still primarily limited to agriculture, gardening, and household service. In theory, economic growth might work to undermine racism and the practices that it produced, but the growth actually taking place in New Era America was not doing so.

Other developments, however, can be seen as foreshadowing a time when greater racial equality would be achieved. In the white community, a number of people did recognize the gap between theory and practice and seek to narrow it through affiliation with such groups as the National Association for the Advancement of Colored People (NAACP), the Commission on Interracial Cooperation, the American Indian Defense Association, and the Indian Rights Association. In the courts and in Congress, occasional victories for minority rights were won, the most notable being defeats of further Indian land grabs and a 1927 decision (*Nixon v. Herndon*) overthrowing Texas's white primary law. Through well-publicized investigations, focusing particularly on atrocities against blacks and the shocking conditions on American Indian reservations, wide segments of the public were induced to express moral outrage. In the minority communities themselves, a growing sense of grievance found expression in the activism of such groups as the NAACP, the American Negro Labor Congress, the Society of American Indians, the League of United Latin American Citizens, and the Confederation of Mexican Workers Unions. Many members of minority communities still opted for acquiescent strategies of accommodation and survival. But others were undergoing a political awakening that would in time lead to effective assaults on racial barriers to advancement.

Also of significance for the future were divisions over the desirability of assimilation. For some members of minority communities, especially among educated elites seeking opportunity and established ones craving respectability, the ideal was to acquire "white ways" and be accepted in the dominant culture on terms equal to those of whites. But for many others the ideal was a separate race-based culture that would be recognized as an equal worthy of respect and would provide the racial community with a much needed sense of identity, pride, security, and empowerment. The latter found expression in the "New Negro," Harlem Renaissance, and Negro History movements, in the new critiques of the assault on Indian tribalism, and at a more popular level in such phenomena as "race" recordings, gospel blues, and the appeal of the "Black Zionism" preached by Marcus Garvey's Universal Negro Improvement Association. This new sense of pride foreshadowed future movements envisioning "nations within a nation" and sparked fierce exchanges, setting the pattern for future clashes between integrationists and separatists. To the leaders of the NAACP, for example, Garvey was "either a lunatic or a traitor." But to admirers he "made black people proud of their race" and "taught them that black is beautiful."

Still another barrier to equality of opportunity in New Era America was based on ethnicity. As of 1930 white immigrants and their children still made up over 30 percent of the American population and constituted over half of the people living in the nation's twenty largest cities. Ethnic communities, arising through willing association but also to avoid nativist prejudice, remained very much a part of the American scene. Ethnic-based discrimination, grounded in a mixture of cultural stereotypes and pseudoscience and directed especially against the "new immigrants" from southern and eastern Europe, continued to affect access to occupations, housing, education, and social services. Moreover, birth into an ethnic enclave still had the power to define major aspects of social life. It could and often did provide a sense of security, rootedness, and communal support. But it also foreclosed choices concerning school, church, occupation, holidays, friends, clubs, residence, and marriage partner.

Much of the resentment generated by ethnic-based discrimination would be mobilized into political and labor activism only in the 1930s. But the 1920s did witness political awakenings among ethnic groups similar to those occurring among racial minorities. Some groups rose to defend threatened institutions, especially Catholic parochial schools, religious rites, and foreign-language media. Some mobilized to reject claims that they were unassimilable or of inferior human stock. As in the case of racial groups, however, this rejection was accompanied by ambivalence about the desirability of assimilation. Attitudes spanned the spectrum from "Anglo-conformity" at one end through "melting pot" notions and pluralistic ideals to cultural isolationism and nationalism at the other end; the strength of each particular stance varied from group to group, and differences between generations were often especially pronounced. In these respects, too, the period set patterns that would persist in the future.

## The Construction of Gender Roles

The other persisting barrier to equality of opportunity in New Era America operated through the construction of gender roles that disadvantaged women regardless of "ability and character." Suffrage had been won and the older boundaries of "woman's sphere" had been expanded, blurred, or perforated. But the assault on the exclusionary preserves of "men's work," "male space," and "masculine behavior" would stall in the 1920s, partly, it seems, because of a resurgent antifeminism and partly because of definitions of the "new woman" that were embraced as improvements on the female condition yet served to solidify and sanction a continuing state of male privilege. Gains there were, but as of 1930 the renegotiation of gender roles envisioned by the prewar feminist movement seemed farther away than ever.

Most outspoken in their demands for full equality were the radical feminists associated with the National Woman's Party (NWP) under the leadership of Alice Paul. Drawing on social research done at the University of Chicago, Stanford, and Columbia, they argued that there was little distinction between the sexes in mind or psyche, that full equal rights were therefore justified, and that this would benefit both women and society at large. Their vehicle for attaining the goal was the Equal Rights Amendment, introduced in Congress in 1923. But in developing support for it, they had little success. They faced not only opposition from antifeminists, who were convinced that American women had already acquired all the equality that was good for them, but also from social feminists for whom the ERA was a threat to protective social legislation; from the League of Women Voters, now stressing participation in "men's parties"; and from a younger generation more concerned with scrapping the double moral standard. During the 1920s the ERA was never reported from committee, and endorsement of Hoover in 1928 brought only further disappointment. His statements about equality of opportunity for "every boy and girl," so the leaders of

Suffragists picketing the Metropolitan Opera House in New York City in March of 1919. *(Left to right)* Mrs. Ella Thompson, Mrs. Alex Shields, Miss Alice Paul, and Mrs. Wilma Keans. *(UPI/Bettmann)*

the NWP believed, could be translated into support for the ERA. But in office, Hoover refused to endorse the measure.

For the social feminists of the period the road to greater equality lay not through a sex-blind legal structure but through special legislation that would recognize female vulnerabilities and provide suitable protection and assistance. In their vision of the "new woman," the unexploited female industrial worker, the respected and socially conscious professional, and the woman reformer working to make the "national household" more "homelike" were still the central ideals. This view continued to dominate such organizations as the National Consumers' League and the Women's Trade Union League; to be expounded by such prominent women as Jane Addams, Florence Kelley, and Mary Anderson; and to define the "women's issues" pushed by the Women's Joint Congressional Committee. When it came to securing legislation, the social feminists could count far more setbacks than victories. Their power, they found, was limited not only by conservative opposition but also by persistent efforts to smear them as "reds," continuing attacks from radical feminists, and unexpected defections on the part of women's professional groups. But they could and did take credit for the maternity and infancy aid program established under the Sheppard-Towner Act, they were successful in retaining much of the earlier protective legislation and sustaining the work of the Women's and Children's bureaus, and in their agitation for social reform they helped to shape legislation that would eventually be enacted in the 1930s.

The flaw in social feminism, its feminist critics claimed, was its concession of essential differences that could be used to justify continuing patterns of male dominance and female subordination. In New Era America, the assertion of such differences did lend support to an occupational structure that remained highly discriminatory. The "new economic woman" was moving into jobs and careers outside the home, and increasingly these were in the factory, office, or store rather than in agriculture or domestic service. Between 1920 and 1930 the number of gainfully employed women grew from 8 million to nearly 11 million, and as of 1930 one in four was married. But 86 percent still toiled in ten relatively low-paying occupations; women's pay averaged only 55 percent of men's; and much of American society still held that married women "belonged" in the home, that those working outside it were endangering society for the sake of "pin money," and that paid work for women should serve primarily as a "way station to marriage" and be compensated accordingly. The professions, moreover, continued to shunt women into lower-rewarded "feminized" specialties, and in the clerical field, now seen as an area of opportunity for young women with high school educations, female roles remained closely analogous to their traditionally separate and unequal roles in the home. The period did have its breakthroughs, most notably in the acclaim that it gave to women sports stars and aviators (especially Amelia Earhart) and in its pioneering figures in such areas as government service, educational administration, business management, religious leadership, and cultural production. But in none of these areas did sex cease to be a major determinant of occupational opportunity.

For a few "material feminists," a realistic program for promoting equality would require the "socialization" of housework and child care in ways that would lead to "feminist homes" and remove the major burdens preventing women from competing on equal terms with men. But most women's groups, including the radicals affiliated with the National Women's Party, distanced themselves from such prescriptions. Home economists, especially those who wanted to bring scientific management to the home, offered an alternative more in line with New Era managerialism. In their version of the "modern home," as promoted in particular by the Better Homes organization attached to the Department of Commerce, housework would be transformed and rendered less burdensome through rationalization and mechanization. At the same time, the home would acquire new managerial functions as an institution through which expert knowledge could be put to work in the causes of human, economic, and community development. As a "scientific manager" in this new managerial home, the "modern American woman" would find equality compatible with continued national progress. As critics pointed out, she would also remain a dependent, both on her husband and on the experts whose "science" she would apply, but such criticisms did not prevent the ideal from being used to counter the pressures for reforming the occupational structure.

Other versions of the "new woman" also obscured and thus helped to perpetuate inequalities grounded in gender role construction. The flapper became the epitome of liberated comportment, a veritable pioneer in asserting new rights in regard to sex, dress, manners, and other forms of female expressiveness. But in doing so she made feminism seem old-fashioned, undercut or called into question earlier bonding among women, and defined femininity in a way that could be and was used to justify denial of equality in other areas. The "Mrs. Consumer" promoted in the period's commercial culture expanded "woman's sphere" in the realms of consumption and status symbolism but in doing so only reinforced the role of "male provider" as justification for other inequalities. And the "companionate wife," even as she gained new rights within the marriage contract and a new recognition of women's sexual and emotional needs, found that she was more dependent on marriage than her husband and that responsibility for its success fell primarily on her shoulders. Paradoxically, moreover, the evolving dating system combined freedom for women with greater dependence on the male as provider and controller. Unmarried women could move courtship into exciting public places and escape the controlling supervision of home, community, and chaperone. But the new rules and rituals made it clear that dating was now taking place in "man's sphere," with men as the hosts and providers and with women obligated to behave in ways that earned further invitations and more spending.

Still another development combining limited gains for female freedom with a reaffirmation of male authority was the course taken by the birth control movement. Once hailed as an "opening wedge" in a revolution that would bring women full independence, birth control now moved into the middle-class mainstream as part of the ideal of an emotionally fulfilling marriage. In efforts to bring it to the lower classes, Margaret Sanger and her associates joined forces with male medical professionals, agreed that birth control clinics should be under their watchful control, and urged passage of "doctors only" bills that would give physicians a monopoly over the dissemination of contraceptive information. Helping to reinforce this conservative bent, moreover, was Sanger's wooing of eugenicists intent on stopping the further "multiplication of the unfit." From these people she secured the kind of scientific respectability and monetary support that she had never had from the political left. But their emphasis on woman as breeder was a far cry from her earlier arguments for feminine freedom and opportunity.

As the nation moved through the 1920s, then, the dreams of prewar feminists still remained far from realized. American women at the time enjoyed new freedoms and embraced new attitudes. Most enjoyed higher living standards, and many were major contributors not only to the changes that modernizers associated with national progress but also to the overthrow of Victorian gender ideology and the articulation of ideas that would come into their own a half century later. But the decade's managerial liberalism found ways to incorporate a continuing pattern of separate and unequal spheres, primarily by building them into its roles for the "modern woman" and marginalizing alternatives. Despite Hoover's claims, gender-based discrimination remained a persisting facet of the New Economic Era.

## Unequal States and Liberal Ideals

Indeed, Hoover was clearly mistaken in both his assertion that America had achieved equality of opportunity and his claim that the central institutions of New Era America were firmly committed to it. On the contrary, discriminatory differentiation by class, race, ethnicity, and gender was being built into modernizing models and changing occupational and social structures, partly as concessions to the resistance of antimodernists and partly through appeals to a pseudoscience that could justify denials of opportunity in the language of scientific modernism and evolutionary progress. The gap between ideal and reality remained wide, and the notion that pushing for rationality and efficiency could close it was not being borne out in practice. But asserting that the victims of discrimination lacked "ability and character" and that this had been demonstrated by both science and history made it possible to argue otherwise.

Still, if opportunity was being denied, the liberal ideal of equality of opportunity remained a national objective to which the victims of discriminatory practices could appeal in the name of justice and fairness. By invoking the ideal and exposing the gap between theory and practice, they could argue that the preservers of class, racial, ethnic, and gender privilege were the true "un-Americans." In the New Era of the 1920s they did continue to make these arguments, to form organizations for advancing them, and to help prepare the way for reforms and changes of attitude that would eventually reduce the gap between ideal and reality. For a few, liberalism and capitalism themselves became the enemies blocking any real attainment of social justice. But for most, the goal was better realization of liberal ideals, not the abandonment of these ideals as national objectives.

# CHAPTER 10

# Intellectual and Cultural Pursuits in a Modernizing Age

For students of American culture the decade of the 1920s has had a powerful fascination. It was a time, it was once thought, when an established cultural and epistemological consensus broke asunder and gave way to clashing conceptions advanced by rival cultural and intellectual elites. Although recent research has tended to push the occurrence of this phenomenon back into the prewar period, those cleavages deepened and intensified in the 1920s. The sciences became battlegrounds between an older scientific absolutism and the new champions of relativity, indeterminacy, and empirical problem solving. High culture, as expressed in literature and art, tended not only to attack scientific and popular values but also to develop deep schisms over what constituted literary and artistic excellence. Popular culture, as reflected in mass tastes and mass consumption of cultural products, not only followed paths that alienated the nation's cultural elites but also came to embrace differing and competing responses to mass anxieties and aspirations. If there was a unifying pattern to the period's cultural pursuits, it lay in the common stimulus provided by economic and institutional change. The responses to this stimulus were divergent and dissonant.

For better or worse, the cleavages and disjunctures of this period have remained enduring features of twentieth-century American culture. They were not, it seems, merely manifestations of a chaotic and irresponsible interlude sandwiched between the decline of one cultural consensus and the rise of another. They indicated instead a passage into the modern cultural condition. For understanding that condition, the intellectual and cultural history of the 1920s can be highly instructive.

## Scientists and Scientific Endeavor

For American scientists the years from 1917 to 1929 were years of expanding opportunity and numerous achievements. The war period had brought increased support for nationally approved research, and the postwar decade — even though it turned back efforts to retain the war system — did bring a new willingness to channel corporate, public, and endowment funds into support for scientific endeavor. Science, the New Era leaders kept saying, was the "new frontier," capable of generating innovations that would keep America open, growing, and progressive. And as support grew, the "new pioneers" were making discoveries that New Era society was putting to practical use. Their achievements could be seen in such science-based industries as chemicals and electronics, in prodigious feats of production and marketing, and in the new tools and insights available to doctors, lawyers, teachers, managers, and social workers.

Such achievements in applied science were also accompanied by impressive advances in basic scientific knowledge. In physics a variety of experiments and observations confirmed the theoretical constructs of Albert Einstein, Louis de Broglie, and Werner Heisenberg. Much of the physical world, it was shown, followed the principles of relativity and quantum mechanics rather than those associated with Isaac Newton. In chemistry similar advances took place, especially in the understanding of chemical processes and their manipulation to create new materials. In biology the decade witnessed not only new insights into the needs of healthy organisms but also a fuller understanding of how new species evolved and how hereditary traits were transmitted. And in psychology, where the study was now giving way to the laboratory or controlled observation, the body of data unexplainable by older theories of innate drives and human rationality was growing. Much of it seemed to support some combination of the theories advanced by John B. Watson and Sigmund Freud, theories that stressed the causal role of environmental conditioning or of an irrational subconsciousness rather than the older determinants.

In the social sciences, too, the period was one of intellectual excitement, methodological innovation, and renewed convictions that a true "science of society" was possible. It could not be built, the innovators argued, through deductive reasoning from self-evident truths. There were no such "truths" that could be accepted as first premises. But trained investigators could assemble aggregations of empirical data, subject these to rigorous analysis, and arrive at an ever fuller understanding of how operating societies worked. Such were the beliefs underlying a new wave of research activities, and as the decade progressed all the social sciences were affected. A "new sociology," centered especially at the University of Chicago, specialized in factual surveys, team observations of community life, and ecological investigations of the city. "Institutional economics," developed by such economists as Wesley Mitchell, John R. Commons, and John M. Clark, turned from classical theory to historical reconstruction and detailed institutional analyses. A "new realism" in political and legal studies focused on such phenomena as judicial and voting behavior, interest group interaction, popular stereotypes, and political propaganda. Anthropology jettisoned unilinear theories of cultural development and began reconstructing cultures as independent, self-fulfilling, and equally valuable wholes. And a "new history," pioneered by such historians as James Harvey Robinson and Carleton J. Hayes, stressed social and scientific developments as the keys to understanding modern processes of historical change.

Like the businessmen, engineers, and social workers, New Era scientists and social scientists also sought to rationalize their activities and make them more efficient and productive. They established the wartime National Research Council on a permanent basis and in 1923 added the Social Science Research Council as another rationalizing body. They preached "cooperative individualism" in which research teams and professional orders would play key roles. A number of them worked to build institutions that could reach the general public and the holders of power and turn them into supportive components of the envisioned system. From their efforts, for example, came a Science Service designed to popularize scientific developments and foster scientific-mindedness, an array of advisory committees for public and private agencies, and a national committee devoted to fostering scientific-mindedness among corporate givers and foundation executives. The assumption, especially among such enthusiasts as Robert A. Millikan and George Ellery Hale, was that efficient and productive science, rationally organized and properly justified, could serve not only as the new agent of national progress but also as the instrument through which cultural fragmentation could be halted and reversed.

This dream, however, remained largely unrealized. Despite the work of the rationalizers, American science retained much of its prewar pluralism and segmentation. If anything, the walls between disciplines tended to harden, and methodological and epistemological battles grew more intense. Despite efforts at cultural reintegration, the sense of estrangement between scientific endeavor and the values held in other sectors of American society seemed to deepen and intensify. In popular culture scientists were seen not only as pioneers but also as ivory tower innocents, keepers of strange mysteries, and potentially dangerous to democratic institutions and public morals. In business circles they were seen more as a resource to be used and controlled than as a model of social virtue. In literary and artistic circles they were frequently depicted as cold and alienating, more machine than human. And within the scientific community such misunderstanding and lack of appreciation reinforced perceptions of an outer world that was basically hostile or at best indifferent to the values and qualities of mind that were essential to continued human progress.

The sense of estrangement was also intensified by the continuing battle over evolutionary theory and by scientific discoveries that seemed to undermine widely held beliefs. From physics, especially that built around Einstein's theories of relativity, came the startling proposition that the average person could never hope to understand the physical world in which he or she lived. It was comprehensible only to the few minds capable of mastering a rarefied mathematics, and their conclusions would have to be accepted on their authority. From psychology and the social sciences came a similar proposition, that only a few were truly capable of understanding human and social problems. Most people could never do so and were therefore incapable of making sound decisions or wise policy choices. From articulate minorities in a variety of disciplines came challenges to the whole conception of natural and human progress. The growth of science, it now appeared, might mean not only the decline of religion but also a crisis for the liberal postulates that underlay American governance; the result in some quarters was strong resistance to inquiries that did not recognize other sources of truth and confine themselves to socially approved areas.

Even as this resistance developed, moreover, other discoveries were undermining the claim that scientists were themselves capable of discerning and understanding reality objectively. Ironically, physics was now disclosing a universe that was indeterminate, at least at the atomic level. It was suggesting that nature itself was irrational and could never be entirely known, even by trained scientific minds. In the social sciences, the weapons previously used to attack traditional wisdom were now being turned against that claiming a scientific basis. Perceptions of social reality, it was argued, were inevitably conditioned by the experience and perspective of the perceiver. Scientists, like other people, perceived different realities and built consensuses through social pressures against the heretical, and like others they still lacked the key that could eventually unlock all the mysteries of human behavior.

As the 1920s drew to a close, then, scientific endeavor still occupied an uneasy place in American society. It was hailed as the new fount of progress, given more support than during any previous peacetime period, and lauded for its advances along a new frontier. Yet to the dismay of early enthusiasts, its findings frequently ran counter to established cultural axioms, its practitioners often behaved in ways that confused and alienated nonscientists, and its claims to possess a true power of revelation were undercut by exposure of its methodological and epistemological limitations. Its prestige and achievements were such that it could resist efforts to make it wholly subservient to commercial, political, or religious endeavors. But they were not such that science could become the core of a new cultural consensus or the apex of a new social order.

## The Literary and Artistic Elite

The position of science in New Era America had its counterparts in the isolation and fragmentation of other forms of intellectual endeavor. Increasingly the literature and art of the nation's cultural elite was not the literature and art appreciated by the masses or by other elites. And increasingly this was seen less as a gap between vanguard and followers and more as a condition imposed by the very nature of literary and artistic endeavor. Once writers and artists had believed themselves capable of changing or reinforcing national values, and for a time the modernist rebellion against genteel standards had been waged in the name of mass liberation and social uplift. But as the decade progressed, "modernism" in high culture frequently ran directly counter to "modernization" in the economic, social, and political sectors. The modernist movement not only attacked traditional values but also expressed marked revulsion against mass culture and rationalized organizational society. It became associated not with democratic reform or technocratic rationalization but rather with sensitive individuals repelled by traditional society yet unable to find satisfying and respected places in a world of mass production and bureaucratic structures.

In traditionalist circles this kind of modernism was still denounced as immoral and socially subversive. But by the mid-1920s efforts to ban or repress it were losing strength. If New Era leaders questioned its value, they seemed willing to tolerate it; and if appreciation of its output was limited, there was enough to allow a tolerated activity to grow and prosper. Recognition abroad raised its status at home, especially among people anxious to overcome America's reputation for cultural backwardness. One result of enhanced appreciation and status was a new complex of supporting institutions. By the end of the decade the modernists had their own art galleries, museums, and publishers, their own outlets for experimental theater and music, their own array of judges and interpreters, and their own forms of association and community support. Their institutional base was small when compared with what it would become in the 1950s and 1960s, but it was of sufficient strength to survive the assaults of a wave of antimodernists and cultural redeemers in the 1930s and 1940s.

During the 1920s, moreover, such support did seem to release wellsprings of insight, energy, and creativity. It brought substantial freedom not only from the aesthetic canons of the past but from mass tastes, political movements, and idiosyncratic patrons as well. Taking advantage of the opportunities that this provided, American writers and artists embraced an exciting experimentalism and left behind them a body of work remarkable in both quantity and quality. Incorporated in it were breakthroughs to new forms and subjects, new perceptions of the human and artistic predicament, and a multifaceted search for new standards, purposes, and identities.

For the American novel the decade was one of exceptional richness. Literary naturalism flourished as Darwinian determinism was reinforced by the findings of the new psychology; the result was such novels as Theodore Dreiser's *American Tragedy* (1925). For an emerging group of younger writers, a group that Gertrude Stein characterized as the "lost generation," the 1920s were years of successful experimentation with new forms and new material. Such writers as Ernest Hemingway, Sinclair Lewis, F. Scott Fitzgerald, and James Branch Cabell developed fresh and highly influential styles in which spare, taut sentences, skillfully crafted dialogue, and satirical symbolism were central features. They and others also cracked most remaining taboos on subject matter and discovered new social types and new kinds of human experience worthy of extended scrutiny. They wrote of individuals scarred or destroyed by the war experience, of the hypocrisy and smugness of small-town life and business boosterism, of degenerate elites and doomed pleasure seekers, and above all, it seemed, of people who realized the hollowness of human dreams and strove restlessly to make their peace with this disturbing insight.

One side of such writing set forth a searing critique of the era's dominant values. Another exposed and ridiculed people who believed that redemption could come through political reform, material gains, or shifts in social leadership. Yet taken as a whole, the novels of the 1920s were neither completely negative nor entirely devoid of values. They can also be studied, as the intellectual historian Roderick Nash has pointed out, as manifestations of a pervasive search for alternative values. Some novelists tried to find these in an idyllic primitivism, but the majority offered such "modern" solutions as a naturalistic morality, a retreat into bohemian countercultures or knowing laughter, or an existential affirmation of unbending struggle in the face of inevitable failure. Beneath the bitter satire and iconoclasm of H. L. Mencken, editor of the *American Mercury* and high priest of literary innovation, lay a quest for new standards of excellence and civilization. Behind the nihilistic despair expressed in the works of Hemingway and Fitzgerald lay the outlines of an existential heroism, achieved not by attaining glory or suffering martyrdom but by grace and courage in the face of impending doom.

Despite modernist victories, traditionalism remained alive and productive in the 1920s, stimulated, it seemed, to new levels of achievement. It was represented now by the New Humanists and Southern Agrarians, by newly emerging groups of folk-minded regionalists, and by such established novelists as Edith Wharton, Willa Cather, and Ellen Glasgow. And from it came another stream of literature that combined criticism of New Era values with assertions of alternatives. For the most part, however, the alternatives offered in such writing were drawn from the American past rather than the liberated imagination. They came embodied not in existential rebels or creators of a new morality but in portraits of people who had remained anchored to moral absolutes, had recognized and lived by traditional wisdom and established folkways, and had built the agrarian-oriented and allegedly more wholesome societies of the Middle Border and the South.

American literature in the 1920s, then, was not devoid of positive values. Nor was it characterized by complete rejection of national history and traditions. Yet its value systems and symbols were incapable of becoming the nuclei of a new cultural consensus. And its creators and defenders, whether of the modernist or traditionalist variety, disdained efforts to fashion high art from the technical achievements, social visions, and popular triumphs of the New Era. In the mass media a new set of heroes appeared, taming the techno-organizational revolution and turning it to beneficent ends. But such themes did not attract talent of the first order, and the decade ended without a major novel built around these feats and their performers.

What was true of prose writing was also largely true of other areas of artistic endeavor. In poetry and drama, for example, the decade witnessed similar modernist breakthroughs, characterized by experimentalism, exploitation of new themes and subjects, and innovations in form and structure. Among its artistic triumphs were the grim tragedies of Eugene O'Neill, the theatrical realism of such playwrights as Maxwell Anderson and Laurence Stallings, the intellectual poetry of T. S. Eliot and Ezra Pound, and the unconventional verse of such rebels as Robinson Jeffers, E. E. Cummings, and Edna St. Vincent Millay. Yet it was a decade as well of a more traditional kind of creativity, a decade when Stephen Vincent Benét tried to capture the national heritage in epic poetry, when the southern "Fugitives" offered romanticized images of their region's past, and when Robert Frost lit "poetic bonfires" illuminating mysteries in New England settings. By 1930 modernists and their opponents could both look back on an era of remarkable creativity. But again both groups seemed repelled by New Era goals and visions. Only in Carl Sandburg's affirmations of national vitality or in Hart Crane's *Bridge* (1930), written as a refutation of Eliot's *Waste Land*, was there anything approaching a celebration of the courage, faith, and skill that had wrought technological and industrial marvels.

In painting the pattern was much the same. Coming to fruition now were two aspects of the prewar revolt against academic painting, one being the seamy realism of the "Ash Can" school of painters and others associated with them, the other an abstract modernism embracing and building on a variety of European movements. In the first category such painters as John Sloan, George Bellows, and Edward Hopper left a vivid pictorial record of the darker and drabber side of American life. In the second were the cubist works of Charles Sheeler and Joseph Stella, the expressionism of Georgia O'Keeffe and Stuart Davis, and the efforts of such artists as John Marin and Max Weber to capture moods and emotions on canvas. Yet modernist triumphs did not prevent good traditional work from being done. Nor did they prevent the beginnings of a folkish regionalism portraying the dignity and strength of rural traditions. It was during the late 1920s that such regionalists as John Stuart Curry, Thomas Hart Benton, and Grant Wood began the kind of work usually associated with the 1930s.

As in the literary arts, painters in the 1920s explored humanity's animalistic urges and subterranean psyche, its existence in an unfeeling and decaying social order, and its embracing in the past of more wholesome ways of life. But like the writers, only a few sought to maintain the earlier linkages between art and reformist or radical politics; still fewer sought to capture on canvas the vitality, achievements, and visions of New Era industrialism. The European movements proclaiming an aesthetic of the factory or an erotic vitalism of the machine — movements that were in part inspired by European perceptions of Frederick W. Taylor's scientific management and Henry Ford's assembly line — failed to attract American talent of the first order. And though cubists like Joseph Stella and Niles Spencer did seek aesthetic inspiration in the dynamism and engineering feats of modern America, they tended to be exceptions with few imitators or followers.

Nor was the pattern substantially different in the musical arts. Here, as in literature and painting, the period became one of exciting experimentation with new forms and themes, some of which was hailed as providing a foundation for an independent American music. Such modernist composers as Aaron Copland, Henry Cowell, and Roy Harris became musical pioneers, both in developing freer forms and in using native themes, and with assistance from friendly publishers and conductors, they succeeded in finding a place in the repertoires of established performing groups. During the same period Charles Ives composed works for which he would later be recognized as America's most accomplished and original composer. Composers like Deems Taylor, Howard Hanson, and Ernest Bloch struck closer to the classical approach, but even they began to exploit themes drawn from American history and experience. Yet declaring independence from European tutelage and Victorian constraints did not, as some enthusiasts had hoped, bring music that all Americans would find meaningful, enjoyable, and expressive of their collective life. On the contrary, the gap between "serious" music and the popular variety seemed to widen. Such bridges as were attempted, as in the efforts to join the polyrhythms of jazz to symphonic forms, were spans not to the dominant forms and central images of popular music but to the innovative and primitivistic portions that liberated intellectuals found appealing.

Seen in perspective, then, the period was one during which cultural innovators won a substantial measure of the freedom for which they had been agitating. Old constraints weakened, impulses toward political control faded, and institutions that valued innovation and continuous experimentation developed. With greater freedom came a remarkable burst of creativity accompanied by an active search for new aesthetic and moral values. Yet this did not bring new ideals on which writers and artists could agree, let alone to a synthesis that could unite art with national life. Nor did it lead to a society in which artistic talent and creativity served to enrich the lives of the expanding middle classes. Most of the people liberated by the new affluence and leisure became consumers not of high culture but of the burgeoning mass variety. High art, even more than high science, became the province of an elitist subculture existing in a state of tension with American society at large.

## Culture and the Masses

If high culture in the 1920s can be seen as the creative outpouring of an estranged and increasingly autonomous subculture, the period's popular literature and art are best viewed as an array of commercialized responses to mass leisure and affluence. Coming together at the time were a growing mass demand for cultural products, a widening gap between high art and mass tastes, and an expanding structure of cultural industries attuned to mass markets. This convergence produced a rapidly growing sphere in which cultural experiences were manufactured for mass sale. And in this sphere — the sphere of popular writing, commercial showmanship, and pleasers of the popular ear and eye — the experiences provided depended less on their artistic merits than on their mass marketability or their capacity to meet tests imposed by elite or community censors.

One set of such cultural products became the means through which the newly prosperous sought a sense of upward movement into more refined social circles. For substantial numbers of Americans, upward movement had long been associated with the ability to afford cultural refinements. Now, as demand for these increased and older prescriptions for attaining them became suspect, cultural "developers" built ever larger markets for mass-produced and commercialized replicas of certified art and culture. If the 1920s had their "lost generation" and their breakthroughs in form and subject matter, the decade also witnessed the successful launching of the Book-of-the-Month Club, the rapid growth of pretentious theater and packaged cultural experiences, and an amazing proliferation of what arts critic Gilbert Seldes called "arty conglomerations of middle-class seriousness and bourgeois beauty." For some observers, this constituted evidence of rising tastes and the spread of cultural riches to a broader segment of the population. But whether those who made such enterprises prosperous were really enriched by the products consumed was debatable. In Seldes's view, the principal ecstasy provided was an unfulfilling snobbism.

Livelier and less pretentious were products purchased for amusement or escape rather than as symbols of social refinement. For these, too, the period brought larger mass markets, and as markets grew, the tendency was toward heavy reliance on set formulas, stereotyped characters, and habit-forming experiences. Much of the output was closer to the realm of narcotics than to that of art, and much of it was produced under stipulations that virtually forbade the expression of profound feelings or insights. Yet there was creativity of a sort, especially in building new media audiences, adapting to market changes, and frustrating the designs of cultural uplifters. If the movie, radio, and musical industries showed little concern for creative art, they did attract organizers, technicians, and artisans of the first rank and often turned out well-crafted and superbly organized productions of mass melodrama and fantasy. From these standpoints there was much to admire in the screen spectaculars of Cecil B. De Mille, the musical revues of Florenz Ziegfeld, and the production teams that adapted older entertainment forms to radio audiences. Genuine art, moreover, was easier to find in the mass output of the 1920s than it would be in that of later decades. In the comedy of Charlie Chaplin and Harold Lloyd, the films of D. W. Griffith, and the comic strips of George Herriman (creator of "Krazy Kat"), the period yielded works that had both mass appeal and the qualities appreciated by the nation's intellectual and artistic elites.

The 1920s were also notable for the emergence of new themes in popular culture. Its creators now found growing audiences for the glamour of youthful rebellion and urban sophistication, the rhythms and romances of city life, and the triumphs and trials of the machine age. Yet even as these audiences grew, works that reasserted earlier values and ideals enjoyed immense popularity. Large numbers of Americans immersed themselves in romanticized celebrations of heroic frontiersmen, noble primitives, and self-sufficient individualists. Partly because ethical certainty was under attack, millions found comfort and reassurance in works celebrating the triumph of traditional standards and virtues. Measured solely in terms of mass sales, the great popular works of the decade were the fictionalized sermons of Harold Bell Wright, the western morality tales of Zane Grey, the "Tarzan" adventures of Edgar Rice Burroughs, and the sugary myths of Gene Stratton Porter.

For still other Americans in the 1920s, however, the popular culture most in demand was that in which the new appeared as terrain still inhabited and rendered worthwhile by the old. Eager for the benefits of progress yet deeply troubled by the transforming effects of economic and social change, they hungered for heroic figures who performed great feats in the modern world yet remained embodiments of traditional virtue. Such, for example, were the media images of big sport's Babe Ruth, big entertainment's Will Rogers, big industry's Henry Ford, and big administration's Herbert Hoover. Such was also the image of the decade's greatest media hero, Charles A. Lindbergh, conqueror of the Atlantic through his solo, nonstop flight to Paris in May 1927. With slight variations and adaptations, figures of the same sort peopled the pages of inspirational works, juvenile literature, and personal success stories. Vicariously at least, one could function and rise in the modern world without losing one's soul, and in one stream of related literature, that seeking to sanctify the "new capitalism," this message was made particularly explicit. The most prominent examples were the best-selling works of advertising executive Bruce Barton, especially *The Man Nobody Knows* (1924) and *The Book Nobody Knows* (1926). In these he offered comforting parallels between the activities of early Christianity and those of modern American business.

Much of the popular culture in the 1920s clearly supported the

The front page of the *New York Times* for May 22, 1927, which announced Lindbergh's triumph. *(Culver Pictures, Inc.)*

existing order, either by embracing its ideals and prescriptions for progress or by providing safety valves through which cultural strains and tensions could be eased. Yet New Era leaders were not entirely happy with what the cultural "developers" of the period were doing. They saw connections between certain themes in the popular culture and the aggravation of such problems as urban corruption and lawlessness, anti-institutional attitudes, and popular resistance to modern technology and its organizational imperatives. They worried also about the impact that the marketers of popular pleasures and cultural experiences were having on the work ethic, the drive to get ahead, and the pool of talent from which institutional leadership had to be drawn. A portion of the associational code system through which they were seeking to regulate economic and social behavior was pushed into the sphere of popular culture, producing there a network of rules and ethical standards governing the output of motion picture producers, radio broadcasters, organized baseball, and mass-oriented publishers. In the New Era establishment there seemed to be much more concern with keeping popular culture in line than with the negativism and alternative values of high culture.

This concern, moreover, was persistent, reflecting to some extent the weaknesses of the control system but indicating as well that popular culture could develop a life of its own and follow paths incongruent with those in the economic sector. If it remained estranged from high culture and the core of scientific thought, portions of it also remained in conflict with the New Era economic and organizational visions. These portions seemed capable of sustaining themselves as still another manifestation of cultural fragmentation.

## Impulses toward Differentiation and Separatism

Another form of cultural fragmentation in the 1920s stemmed not from divergent and conflicting responses to economic and social modernization but rather from the determination of particular groups to have their own cultures and maintain them as separate entities with unique perspectives on the human condition. One manifestation of this phenomenon was the effort to throw off European domination and establish "American" styles in serious art and music. Another was the continuing effort of a few radicals to create "proletarian" art and literature expressive of working-class perspectives. A third was the reassertion and defense in the cultural sphere of particular regional experiences. Each of these, however, would become much more pronounced after 1930 than before. The more prominent manifestations in the 1920s were those associated with ethnic and racial minorities, a separate youth culture, and the much publicized rebellions against middle-class respectability and lifestyles.

Ethnic-oriented cultural activities were in part a reaction to the expanded Americanization programs of the period. They were the work in particular of culturally aware individuals, often the children or

grandchildren of immigrants, who were torn between pride in an ethnic heritage and pressures to renounce it. Such individuals were determined to awake fellow members of their ethnic groups to an appreciation of their cultural heritage. They were also convinced that creativity
could flow from the unique perspectives provided by their back-
grounds and experiences. Although they produced little that approached the status of great art, they were successful in establishing
new cultural programs and in sustaining alternatives to the cultural
experiences being manufactured for mass sale. Their critique of assimilation also helped to raise doubts about its application elsewhere. Another development during the decade was the appearance of a movement recognizing the value of Native American cultures and seeking
ways to recover, preserve, and expand on them.

Developing along similar lines but with wider ramifications and
generating greater creativity was the movement whereby black artists
and intellectuals could proclaim their racial heritage and exploit it for
cultural purposes. Joining in what became known as the "Negro Renaissance," they were responsible not only for new cultural recovery
and appreciation programs but also for an outpouring of ethnic-oriented novels, poems, plays, drawings, and music. Especially prominent
were such writers as Langston Hughes, Claude McKay, Jean Toomer,
and Countee Cullen, all of whom focused on the situation of blacks in
American society and in doing so produced some of the best prose and
poetry of the decade. Of lesser stature was the work in music, painting,
and drama, but it too had admirers far beyond the borders of the black
community.

Also developing as a separate entity during the period was a set of
youth-oriented cultural activities glorifying the special perspectives
and capabilities of the young and depicting the attitudes and teachings
of elders as being outmoded, harmful, or absurd. Helping to make this
possible was the prolongation of adolescence resulting from higher
living standards, fewer child laborers, and extended education. Involved as well was an institutional gap opened by the weakening of
traditional authority and left open when modern substitutes proved
unable to channel all youthful endeavor into preparation for adult roles
in the new organizational society. Youth, those who resisted such socialization were told, was a time for experimentation, daring adventure,
and rejection of the hypocrisies and false ideals that had poisoned
human relationships. Those who possessed it had the potential either to
redeem society or to collect experiences that made life worth living.
Rebellious youths and their allies and exploiters in the intellectual
community began to identify appropriate forms of cultural activity and
defend them against critics who regarded such forms as immature,

mindless, or pathological. As the decade progressed, the new subculture acquired its own distinctive literature and art, its own forms of expressive behavior and social intercourse, and above all its own forms of music and dance. Jazz, once the music of New Orleans brothels and the black ghettos, owed much of its rise and development to its association with the new youth culture and its activities.

Indeed, the "jazz culture," as it had developed by 1929, can be seen as the product of the ongoing interaction between an ethnic folk culture, the new youth culture, and commercial packaging of cultural experience. In its origins, jazz was mostly a black art form, born, as music historian Irving L. Sablosky has put it, when "spirituals, blues, and vestiges of voodoo had come together with rags, street band music, and the musical experiences of Creole Negroes." But it had left behind much of its folk origins as it moved from New Orleans to other cities and was taken up by young white musicians and youthful rebels. In some respects it became the music of a counterculture rather than a folk culture. At the same time, commercialized forms of it were taking their place in the larger popular culture. Increasingly, recordings were made for a mass market, performances featured extended solos, bands grew to satisfy the preference of dancers, and such bandleaders as Paul Whiteman demonstrated how far America's "syncopated music" had come from its "primitive" origins.

One final manifestation of cultural separatism in the 1920s was the much publicized growth of a bohemian counterculture centering in the cafés and gathering places of New York's Greenwich Village and elsewhere. An object of fascination to journalists then and since, this growth has been much exaggerated, but clearly the number of Americans embracing bohemian lifestyles did increase, the circles in which they were admired widened, and visits to the Left Bank in Paris were followed by efforts to re-create its spirit and values in the United States. A significant subculture emerged, loosely joined in various ways to the youth, ethnic, and intellectual rebellions yet also embracing a substantial number of people who were neither adolescents, members of minority groups, nor genuine connoisseurs of artistic genius and intellectual achievement. Their central bond was a shared aversion for ordinary pursuits and bureaucratic organizations, and it was around activities through which they could assert, justify, and act out this aversion that the new subculture was built.

As America entered the 1930s, cultural consensus seemed further away than ever. The advance of science and the weakening of traditional authority had not, as some observers had hoped, brought unity between intellectual and popular life. Major portions of the cultural sector had not followed the central thrusts of economic development.

Nor had discordant subcultures disappeared from the national scene. On the contrary, new impulses toward fragmentation and separatism had shown surprising strength, and by invoking the values of tolerance, diversity, and freedom of expression, these had been able to sustain themselves against mass standardization and against pressures for imposing and enforcing a cultural orthodoxy.

Yet it was by no means clear that the failure to achieve cultural coherence and stability acted as a bar to creativity or subtracted from the quality of American life. If cultural conflict and disorder allowed vulgarity, pretense, and irresponsibility to flourish, they also helped to stimulate the burst of intellectual and artistic creativity for which the 1920s are now remembered. And if they made the tasks of economic and political leadership more difficult, they also served as checks against those who would organize an end to individual liberties. The totalitarian-minded of the period also had their visions of a new order, with controlled scientific and cultural activities used to build and sustain it. Whether there could have been greater cultural "rationalization" without opening the way to such designs or to something resembling the wartime abuses in the cultural sphere is difficult to tell.

# CHAPTER 11

# The New Day and the Great Crash

## 1928–1930

 For some Americans the year 1927 revealed a flawed underside to the New Era's dreams and assumptions. In Chicago dozens died in gangland warfare, a manifestation, it was said, of the lawlessness that Prohibition had bred. In western Pennsylvania coal operators evicted striking miners from their company homes, organized private armies, and imported strikebreakers by the thousands. In the lower Mississippi valley a disastrous flood exposed both the emptiness of engineering claims and the appalling conditions of the people at the bottom of the South's rural social structure. In Michigan, Henry Ford closed down his plants for retooling, laying off thousands and aggravating a slump in business activity and employment totals. And in Massachusetts, Nicola Sacco and Bartolomeo Vanzetti, convicted of murder in the nation's most celebrated case of "red scare" justice, were denied pardons and died in the electric chair. The "American system" had its victims as well as its beneficiaries, and as some people saw it, any system that allowed such victimization was in need of drastic changes.

For the great majority, however, these were minor flaws in a system that was still moving toward ever higher levels of technical achievement, material benefits, and spiritual enrichment. During the same year Lindbergh had crossed the Atlantic, Babe Ruth had hit sixty home runs, Warner Brothers had brought the marvel of sound to the silver screen, and Owen D. Young, dedicating the new Baker Foundation at the Harvard Business School, had proclaimed the arrival of professionalized business orders intent on ending the "economic blot" of unemployment, creating modern substitutes for local community opinion, and establishing an economy in which all people were free to

157

develop culturally and all worked with "zest and spirit and pride of accomplishment." The slump, moreover, had seemed to respond well to the monetary and educational correctives applied by public and private authorities. Even the flood area had become one more arena in which Herbert Hoover could demonstrate his organizational and administrative prowess. As head of the President's Flood Relief Committee, he had mobilized and coordinated a remarkably effective set of cooperative endeavors, thus validating, it seemed to many, his organizational and social ideals.

As the year 1928 dawned, most Americans seemed more inclined than ever to credit New Era claims and formulas. If they saw defects in the existing order, their solution was to broaden the area in which managers like Hoover could exercise their organizational talent. And to a remarkable extent, the story of American history from 1928 to 1930 revolved around the figure of Herbert Hoover. It was the story, first of all, of increasing acclaim for the Great Engineer, his prophecies of a "New Day," and his efforts to create a presidency suited to the realization of his designs. It was the story, second, of the failure of the New Era's managerial apparatus, especially its failure to check the economic imbalances and irrational behavior that it was supposed to prevent. And it was the story, third, of a stabilization and countercyclical program based on Hooverian prescriptions yet unable to halt the forces that would soon make a mockery of his campaign promises. In sum, the period from 1928 to 1930 witnessed both the high point of a dream and the first stages of an economic nightmare.

## A New Kind of President

In the presidential nominating conventions of 1928, both major parties chose men who differed markedly from those chosen in the past. The Democratic nominee, Alfred E. Smith of New York, came neither from the rural hinterland nor from the older middle and upper classes. He was a representative instead of the urban metropolis and of that immigrant-invaded, polyethnic, boss-ordered America to which nativists and hypernationalists were so averse. And though the Republicans nominated a man of sterling respectability and village origins, they also broke with their pattern of rewarding electoral success, party work, and standing in the older professions. Herbert Hoover was the first presidential candidate to emerge from the managerial and technical elites spawned by the organizational revolution, and at the time his choice seemed to signify a closing of the gap between the new economic and technical order and the older American polity.

When the Republicans met in Kansas City on June 12, it was clear that Hoover would be their nominee. Coolidge had taken himself out of the contest by declaring, the previous summer, that he did not choose to run again. Such contenders as Vice-President Charles G. Dawes and former governor of Illinois Frank O. Lowden had failed to develop substantial followings, and neither the skeptical party regulars, the antibusiness progressives, the disgruntled McNary-Haugenites, nor the anti-Hoover elements of the financial community had been able to find a candidate strong enough to check the Hooverites and their energetic gathering of convention delegates. On the first ballot, Hoover received 837 of the 1,084 votes cast, and in subsequent action the convention chose Senator Charles Curtis as his running mate. In his acceptance speech, the Great Engineer praised the blend of individual and cooperative endeavor that had been developed over the preceding eight years and promised that its continued development would eventually banish poverty from the land.

The Democratic convention, meeting in Houston on June 26, was more colorful but equally devoid of surprises. The Smith forces had won control of most of the nonsouthern states and had no difficulty this time in mustering the two-thirds majority needed to nominate their candidate. Concessions followed in the hope of making Smith's candidacy more palatable to the South, one being the nomination of Senator Joseph T. Robinson of Arkansas as Smith's running mate and another being the absence of a platform plank favoring repeal of the Eighteenth Amendment implementing Prohibition. But Smith still reserved the right to work for repeal.

In the campaign that followed, Smith won strong support among urban ethnic groups, anti-Prohibitionists, Roman Catholics, and anti-Hoover elements in the farm, business, and welfare communities. Indeed, his carrying of the nation's twelve largest cities has been seen as a major milestone in the evolution of a new urban-oriented Democratic party. But his following was no match for Hoover's. Although the latter had no great appeal for ethnic minorities, he was able in 1928 to bridge the gap between modernists and traditionalists, hold the Republicans together, and win the votes of anti-Smith Democrats in the South and the West. Many of them, responding to anti-Smith campaigns carried on by such Protestant leaders as Bishop James Cannon of Virginia, decided that they simply could not vote for a man who was Catholic, against Prohibition, and associated with an urban culture alien to the American heartland. When the votes in the November election were counted, Hoover had won by a landslide; he had even cracked the solid South and carried seven southern states. He had polled 21,392,190 votes to Smith's 15,016,443 and in the electoral college had won by a vote of 444 to 87.

In the wake of the election, the new president-elect toured Latin

America, considered possible cabinet appointees, and laid plans for implementing his campaign pledges. His vision of the future, what he had called during the campaign a "New Day," had apparently been overwhelmingly endorsed by the American people, and presumably his prescriptions could now become operative over ever widening areas of national life. Yet he was now entering an arena in which technocratic skills would have to be supplemented with the political arts of compromise, bargaining, and popular appeal. This was particularly true since the congressional majority elected with him consisted chiefly of old-guard politicos and anti-Hoover progressives and agrarians. To complicate matters further, the campaign had involved him in ethnocultural issues in which lack of consummate political skills could leave him isolated between polarized extremes. In his quest for votes he had welcomed the support of the anti-Smith Democrats and had thereby committed himself to stronger enforcement of the Prohibition laws, new efforts to reduce urban disorder and lawlessness, and party reforms that could give the Hoover Democrats a permanent home in the Republican party. The nation was about to inaugurate a new kind of president. But how he would fare in a polity that had not yet "rationalized" its lawmaking bodies, its party structures, and its ethnocultural divisions remained to be seen.

## Before the Crash

In staffing the new administration Hoover gave some consideration to politics. Andrew Mellon remained secretary of the treasury; the State Department went to the eminent Republican architect of the Nicaraguan settlement, Henry L. Stimson; and the War, Agriculture, and Post Office departments went respectively to James W. Good, Arthur M. Hyde, and Walter F. Brown, all of whom had played major roles during the election campaign. Attorney General William D. Mitchell, however, was nominally a Democrat, and prominent among those who shared Hoover's vision of the future and his organizational prescriptions for attaining it were Ray Lyman Wilbur as secretary of the interior and Robert P. Lamont as secretary of commerce. Below the cabinet level, moreover, were numerous other "Hoover men," among them F. Trubee Davison in the War Department, Julius Klein in Commerce, Ernest Lee Jahncke in Navy, and Charles J. Rhoads as commissioner of Indian affairs.

The early days of the administration brought a variety of efforts to establish coordinating mechanisms. Plans were quickly made for a massive study of social trends and for an accompanying series of conferences on such problems as child welfare, housing, recreation, education, and public health. Plans were also made for a series of economic studies and conferences. More immediately, there were efforts to rationalize oil production and to set up a national economic council in which both public and private organizations would be represented. In June 1929 the administration convened a national oil conference and sought support for cooperative drilling programs and an interstate conservation compact, and in May and June it gave serious consideration to a proposal for formal linkages between federal administrators and representatives of organized business, labor, and agriculture. In neither of these cases, however, was the president willing to push matters, especially if it meant revising the laws governing private combinations and public-private relations. In neither case did the envisioned agencies and programs materialize.

The major area in which the administration did seek congressional action was that of agricultural organization and relief. Redeeming a campaign pledge, the president called a special session of Congress to deal with the farm problem. Although his proposals for agricultural tariff revision bogged down and were carried over to the regular session, Congress did pass a measure embodying the Hoover farm relief plan. Under the Agricultural Marketing Act of June 1929, the Federal Farm Board, organized to represent the various interests in agriculture, was to become the agency for building and financing a set of marketing associations. Given an initial sum of $500 million, it could provide technical and promotional assistance, make loans to facilitate orderly marketing, and form emergency stabilization corporations to deal with demoralized markets. To head the agency, Hoover turned to Alexander Legge, a former member of the War Industries Board, and by late 1929 Legge had most of the major commodities organized.

These actions in agriculture were accompanied by other reform initiatives, some unsuccessful but some laying the basis for more substantial changes later. The administration failed to secure repeal of the national origins provision in the immigration law and was eventually unsuccessful in efforts to transfer western grazing lands to state control. But it moved quickly to rationalize the system of veterans' benefits, reform and improve the educational and health services of the Indian Bureau, and establish new procedures for making judicial appointments. It also strengthened its relations with labor when a special railroad board endorsed a broad view of employer responsibilities. Following a prison riot at Leavenworth, it opened a campaign of prison reform that eventually produced eight pieces of remedial legislation. The central figure in this was Sanford Bates, a nationally recognized penologist who left his position as head of the Massachusetts state system to take charge of the Federal Prisons Bureau.

In addition, the administration became involved in the troubled areas of liquor control and party reform. Spurred on by pressures from the "drys" and by reactions to new outbursts of gangland warfare, it proceeded to reorganize and "depoliticize" the Prohibition enforcement agencies, thus setting the stage for a mounting clash with urban politicians and advocates of repeal. At the same time it organized still another major exercise in fact finding, a national study commission on law enforcement chaired by George W. Wickersham. As for party reform, the administration sought to bring the Hoover Democrats into the Republican party by lending its support to the "purging" of corruptionists from the southern party organizations — often, it turned out, corruptionists who happened to have black skin. Ironically, the major result was to alienate much of the northern black community. In the South the Democrats quickly reestablished themselves as the party of "respectable" whites, in part by pointing to Hoover's previous ties to black leaders, his continuing concern with improving economic opportunities for blacks, and his wife's decision to entertain Mrs. Oscar De Priest, the wife of Chicago's new black congressman, at a White House tea. From the standpoint of the National Association for the Advancement of Colored People, the president was a racist, but from the standpoint of southern whites he was not racist enough.

Both the southern policy and Prohibition policy seemed likely to involve more political costs than gains. Nor had the administration's handling of the tariff question, the oil problem, and public land reform done much to enhance its political reputation. Yet in mid-October, as the president journeyed to Michigan for the dedication of the new Edison Institute of Technology, he could still be hailed as the architect of a new political economy. His actions still seemed to be moving the nation toward a "New Day," and few observers suspected that his ideas and prescriptions were about to face their severest test.

## Panic and Contraction

The panic selling that gripped the American stock market in October 1929 marked the culmination of a series of speculative excesses that New Era institutions had been unable to prevent. In 1923 and again in 1926 the market had seemed to check itself: speculation had not become excessive and had been followed by mild setbacks that the economy had quickly absorbed. But the new bull market that began developing in 1928 was accompanied by a get-rich-quick psychology that proved readily exploitable by high-pressure securities merchants and promoters with exaggerated and irrational visions of the future. Seemingly intoxicated by the potentialities of the "new economy," Americans were eager to bid against each other for chances to participate in what was being touted as an astounding phase of development. They also had mounting savings with which to conduct the bidding contest, and partly because the international situation seemed to demand a low-interest policy that would discourage the flow of gold to the United States, they were able to borrow on easy terms. Once the bidding started, it fed on itself. The upward spiral in stock prices drew in more bidders and increased willingness to keep borrowing even after interest rates began moving rapidly upward. By the time the Federal Reserve Board took steps to curb credit and reduce its use for speculative purposes, it was too late.

By March 1929, speculative activity had developed a momentum that was difficult to check. It was not about to yield to the new president's efforts to coax warnings from key public and private figures or to his pleas for greater responsibility on the part of investment bankers and securities merchants. Throughout the spring and summer the upward spiral in stock prices accelerated. Over the previous year many leading stocks had doubled and tripled in price, despite the fact that corporate earnings statements told of mounting business difficulties. The demand seemed insatiable. Promoters were now busy organizing holding companies and investment trusts for the express purpose of manufacturing more stock. Unscrupulous stock sellers had little difficulty in finding gullible customers, and public deference to the new set of "financial wizards" had opened the way to a variety of market-rigging abuses.

Eventually, though, the bubble would have to burst. The market could not sustain itself once the supply of new bidders began to falter, and by September 1929 this point was being reached. Buy orders were no longer sufficient to fuel the price spiral. As this became apparent, a number of investors who had bought for speculative purposes began looking for the right moment to take their profits. Under the circumstances, any downward movement in stock prices could trigger a selling panic, and should the movement become substantial, it could force a wave of involuntary selling. Stocks that had been bought with borrowed money and pledged as collateral would have to be sold to cover the loans.

As it happened, the first break in stock prices came as a result of developments abroad. In late September there was a large withdrawal of funds in London, initially triggered by a scandal on the London Exchange and then deliberately encouraged through actions taken by the Bank of England. Prices on the New York Stock Exchange fell, and big speculators started liquidating their holdings. For a time others seemed reluctant to follow suit. But on October 15 a new wave of selling got under way, and by October 24, as brokers began unloading the stock that had been pledged as collateral, this wave was approaching flat-out panic. A bankers' pool then stepped in. Under the leadership of the House of Morgan, it began buying stock and succeeded in holding the line for a few days. Its efforts, however, could not reverse the panic psychology that was now developing, and on October 29, "Black Tuesday," the bottom fell out. Over 16 million shares (more than three times what had been considered normal) exchanged hands that day, and many leading industrials dropped as much as forty points (for U.S. Steel a 20 percent drop in market value) in this single day's trading. By the end of October stocks that had been worth $87 billion at the peak of the boom were now worth only $55 billion, and by 1933 they would be worth only $18 billion.

The impact of the stock market debacle was twofold. First, it created an atmosphere of gloom that dampened both investment and consumer spending. Whereas Americans had once cherished rosy visions of their future, they were now inclined to be cynics and pessimists. Second, it ended the speculative boom that had hidden and temporarily offset serious weaknesses in the New Era system. Had this been working as its theorists claimed, the new setback might have been relatively short-lived. But it was not working that way. Structurally the reality differed from the theory in ways that now became increasingly apparent.

For one thing, the system was not as balanced or as expansive as New Era theorists argued. It did recognize the importance of mass purchasing power. But it had not yet found ways of expanding this fast enough to absorb the goods being produced. This gap was reflected both in the massive growth of consumer debt and in the increasing resort to hard-sell techniques. Investment opportunities had also become a growing problem. Despite the faith in a new scientific and technical frontier, the late 1920s had not brought forth industries and technologies comparable to those responsible for earlier investment outlays. Nor were these weaknesses the only ones. To make matters worse, the balance wheels that were supposed to come into play when demand faltered were in 1929 largely nonexistent. Construction demand had been largely exhausted by 1927, not built up as a countercyclical reserve. Production for inventory, even if credit could be arranged, seemed highly irrational at a time when consumers and investors were retrenching. And foreign demand had already reached its practical limits, at least without major changes in tariff, debt collection, and foreign-loan policies.

Indeed, not only was the system lacking in balance wheels, but it was now mined with booby traps whose triggering could transform a modest downturn into a severe economic contraction. A relatively small number of layoffs or wage cuts could have strongly negative effects on the market for consumer durables and thus trigger more layoffs or wage cuts. A relatively small dose of retrenchment could force overcapitalized holding company pyramids into bankruptcy and liquidation, thus triggering stronger pressures for retrenchment. Any new shrinkage in agricultural markets could push the commodity-holding operations of the United States and other nations beyond their available resources, thus triggering "dumping" measures that would cause even greater distress in rural areas. Any new decline in the export of American capital could bring down an international trade and monetary system predicated on its continued outflow. And any one of these developments could trip what was perhaps the greatest booby trap, a banking system rigged to collapse when subjected to pressures for monetary liquidity, the desire to hold money. Each of these could reinforce the downward impetus, and organizational development had now greatly reduced the ability of the marketplace to force the readjustments needed for expansion. In a contracting economy the business institutions that were supposed to organize continuous and orderly growth could become institutions for blocking needed liquidation and protecting vested capital interests, thus keeping the market from producing its own recovery.

Thus in the wake of the stock market crash, the tendency of the New Era economic system was toward continuing contraction. Although there would be brief halts and temporary reversals in this process, contraction would nevertheless be the dominant feature of the economy's behavior for four years. During the first year after October 1929, new investment declined some 35 percent, the gross national product fell about 8 percent, and unemployment climbed from an estimated 3 percent of the work force to an estimated 9 percent. And this was only the beginning. By 1933 new investment would dwindle to virtually nothing, GNP (adjusted for deflation) would stand at only 67 percent of the 1929 level, and unemployment would reach 25 percent.

## Hooverism on Trial

For Hooverism the beginnings of economic contraction provided a major test. Since 1920 the Great Engineer had been associated with business cycle control, and in 1929 he was quick to accept the challenge and apply the formulas worked out over the past nine years. As he saw it, the potential for continued economic growth was still there and could still be realized, not through liquidation or statist measures but through cooperative programs that would counteract the psychological effects of the panic and induce compensatory spending. In November 1929 he called the leaders of the economic establishment into a series of conferences at the White House, and by early 1930 three new programs were in operation. The National Business Survey Conference, functioning as an adjunct of the Chamber of Commerce through a committee representing some 170 trade associations, was seeking to dispel gloom and obtain compliance with pledges of wage maintenance and new investment; the National Building Survey Conference, also operating through trade organizations, was seeking to implement pledges of new or expanded construction; and the Division of Public Construction in the Commerce Department was working to speed up federal building projects and obtain compliance with state and municipal pledges to increase expenditures on public works.

To these programs Hoover added supplementary measures. He obtained a temporary tax cut, a $400 million increase in public works appropriations, a "labor peace" pledge from union leaders, and monetary expansion measures from the Federal Reserve Board. In addition, the new Farm Board swung into action by forming government corporations to purchase surplus wheat and cotton. Yielding to arguments that domestic stabilization required temporary sheltering from foreign competition, the president also worked to secure an appropriate tariff law. He did not, however, show much sympathy for business leaders who wanted to tie macroeconomic stabilization to the legalization of protective cartels. On the contrary, he seemed strongly supportive when his new antitrust officials and a new majority on the Federal Trade Commission scrapped the policies of the late 1920s, refused further advisory opinions on projected business agreements, and attacked the more restrictive features of the industrial codes and trade association operations. These, Hoover explained, protected the wrong kind of concerted action.

That the Hoover program had much chance of working is doubtful. But in the spring of 1930 the indexes measuring production and employment did turn up, and even stock prices seemed to be recovering. Addressing the annual convention of the Chamber of Commerce on May 1, the president expressed the conviction that the worst was over and that rapid recovery was in the offing. A "great economic experiment," he declared, had "succeeded to a remarkable degree," and once recovery was complete, he hoped to organize another great national investigation in which economists would join with business, labor, and farm representatives to discover ways of achieving greater future stability. He was also enthusiastic about the prospects of growth in new industries, especially in aviation, where the recently implemented Air Mail Act had provided the tools for building a national passenger service.

The latter half of 1930, however, brought new downturns and a growing divergence of business expectations from those projected by the Hoover agencies. Strengthening this divergence, moreover, was the inability of the Hoover programs to counter the effects of downward pressures. As summer gave way to fall, the economy reeled under the impact of a severe drought in the South and the West, a collapse of commodity-holding operations abroad, and an intensifying international trade war aggravated by the new Smoot-Hawley Tariff Act that Hoover (ignoring a petition signed by 1,038 members of the American Economic Association) had signed into law on June 17. It also suffered from a rising rate of bank failures, especially late in the year as farm and drought distress intensified the strain on rural banks. Between November 1 and December 31 a total of 609 banks with combined deposits of $550 million went under.

Confronted with this worsening situation, the Hoover administration took action. In August it organized the National Drought Committee, hoping to mobilize drought relief in much the same way that flood relief had been mobilized in 1927. In October it added a similar agency for unemployment relief, setting up for this purpose the President's Emergency Committee for Employment. The president also deemphasized developments abroad, arguing that recovery could come along national lines. When Congress met in December, he recommended new expenditures for public works, further support of his cooperative programs, and limited antitrust relief for the natural resource industries. Still, as the year drew to a close, contraction was accelerating, and the number of Americans who believed that Hooverism had failed and should be abandoned was now increasing.

## Welfare, Prohibition, and the Southern Strategy

By late 1930 Hoover's difficulties were compounded by growing dissatisfaction with his welfare, law enforcement, and southern policies. In each of these areas he was losing political support, and in the press his "political ineptitude" was now being played up. More and more journalists felt that he was trying to manage the news through canned releases and press favorites, and the tendency among them was growing to give credence to Democratic publicity portraying the president as an insensitive political bungler.

In social welfare the administration's plans for new rationalizing

A breadline at New York City's Hippodrome. Meals at MacFadden's restaurant were a nickel each. *(Brown Brothers)*

and coordinating mechanisms continued to unfold. The prestigious Research Committee on Social Trends began its studies; the National Advisory Committee on Education produced a design for improved educational organization; a national conference on child welfare led to a new body of recommendations and a new network of committees; and by the end of 1930 the planning for a similar conference on housing was well advanced. Social workers and welfare organizations, however, were not impressed. As unemployment put new pressure on welfare budgets and traditional sources of funding, demand for federal aid was growing. And as shrinking profits put pressure on corporate welfare programs, the advocates of a tax-supported social security system were gaining new adherents. Throughout 1930, Hoover resisted such proposals, arguing vehemently that federal action of this sort would undermine the institutions essential to American freedom and progress. But his stand was interpreted as hardhearted rejection of humanitarian considerations, an unmasking, as it were, of his pretentious claims to the label of the "great humanitarian."

The Prohibition issue also continued to fester, with "wets" arguing now that repeal could stimulate recovery and reduce the burden of existing taxes. Alarmed "drys" reacted by talking about a "whiskey rebellion," and Hoover's policies now were being criticized from both sides. In practice, it seemed, better administration and more scientific study could not prevent further polarization. In any event, a law transferring the Prohibition Bureau from Treasury to Justice had not deflated the issue. Nor had the Wickersham Commission, which Hoover had set up to undertake a scientific study of law enforcement, been able to produce a scientific solution.

At the same time, efforts to reform the Republican party in the South were now having political repercussions that Hoover had never intended. They had brought not a more respectable southern Republicanism but an alienation of black pressure groups, intensified factionalism in the southern party organizations, and an acerbation of the president's relations with southern Democratic members of Congress. They were also at least partly responsible for the curious coalition of blacks, laborites, and southern Democrats that was fighting Hoover's nomination of Judge John J. Parker to fill a vacancy on the U.S. Supreme Court. An able jurist from North Carolina, Parker had in his earlier career upheld "yellow dog" contracts — in which employees promised, as a condition of employment, not to join a labor union — and had advocated that blacks be completely excluded from the political process. But the crucial factor that produced the 41 to 39 vote against confirmation was the identification of Parker's appointment with Hoover's "southern strategy." The contest marked the emergence of the National Association for the Advancement of Colored People as an important political pressure group, and it was a significant milestone along the route that would eventually drive most blacks out of the Republican party.

One indicator of the changed political climate was the strong Democratic showing in the midterm elections of 1930. In the South the gains that the Republicans had made in the 1920s were virtually wiped out. In northern state contests candidates associated with Hoover fared badly. And in Congress the massive Republican majorities disappeared. In the Senate the new division was 48 Republicans, 47 Democrats, and a lone Farmer-Laborite; in the House of Representatives, which the Democrats would eventually organize, it was initially 217 affiliated with each of the major parties and one Farmer-Laborite holding the balance of power. If Congress had been uncooperative in 1930, it was likely to be more so in the future.

## Setbacks in the Quest for World Order

The year 1930 also brought setbacks in the New Era quest for an Americanized world order. In this sphere, as in domestic policy, the Hoover administration had hoped to build on and improve the system developed in the 1920s. But here too some impressive early achievements failed to correct fatal flaws in the economic structure, and the result by late 1930 was the beginning of an economic breakdown that would usher in a decade of destructive economic nationalism and growing political disorder.

The most impressive of the initial achievements was the Hoover administration's success in extending and expanding the naval limitations system. Its key contribution was adopting the "yardstick principle," which took into account a navy's age, armaments, and other fighting capabilities as well as its tonnage, thereby allowing the British to accept parity with the United States while retaining a larger cruiser tonnage. At the London Naval Conference, meeting from January to April 1930, the new formula produced a treaty under which Britain, the United States, and Japan agreed to fixed limitations on the construction of cruisers, destroyers, and submarines. France and Italy did not sign, primarily because the United States still refused to give guarantees of French security and Italy would accept no limitations unless the French did so. But all five powers did agree to extend the Washington Treaty limitations on capital ships for another five years.

Three other developments were also hailed as proof that the New Era approach was still working. One was a formula under which the United States again committed itself to membership in the World Court. Worked out by an international committee under the chairmanship of Elihu Root, it became the basis for a treaty submitted to the Senate in 1930. The second development was the passing of a Far Eastern crisis that dominated the international scene in late 1929. American efforts to invoke the Kellogg-Briand Pact and arrange for mediation were rebuffed by the Soviet Union, but fears of a general war subsided when the Russians and the Chinese made peace on the basis of the previous status quo. Finally there was the renewed movement toward the pan-American ideal. Fresh from his goodwill tour, Hoover moved to upgrade the diplomatic service in Latin America, encourage new forms of economic cooperation and cultural exchange, and solidify the Nicaraguan and Mexican settlements. He also endorsed the repudiation of the Roosevelt Corollary to the Monroe Doctrine as set forth in the Clark Memorandum, and despite pressure from American investors he made it clear that there would be no collection of debts by force. The one sore spot during his first year was the situation in Haiti. There a new wave of rioting erupted in late 1929, some of it directed against the American military government. But even here Hoover responded rationally and sympathetically. More marines were rushed in, but this action was quickly followed by the creation of a special commission to devise a plan for American withdrawal.

However, the Hoover administration was not successful in protecting the Latin American economy from the effects of the American financial panic and the Smoot-Hawley Tariff Act. For this purpose the cooperative system of the 1920s seemed inadequate, especially since it was now under investigation by critics in Congress. Yet suggested alternatives — such things as government investment guarantees, government loans and grants, or special trading arrangements — were still regarded by the Hooverites as certain to cause more difficulties than they resolved. Consequently, by late 1930 the Latin American economies that had been linked to the United States were entering a vicious cycle of debt repudiation, capital withdrawal, and shrinking markets, which in operation would soon make a mockery of the hopeful visions of the past decade.

In Europe, too, the Hoover administration failed to find ways of enabling the rickety economic structure of the 1920s to withstand the loss of American capital and markets. There 1929 had brought another committee of experts, chaired this time by Owen D. Young; from its recommendations had come the Young Plan, which readjusted German reparations downward, linked a portion of them to Allied war debt obligations, and set up an international bank to facilitate collection. To Young's dismay, however, the Hoover administration strongly criticized the linkages between reparations and Allied war debts and rejected all suggestions of official participation in the new bank. Nor was it amenable to the economic relief proposals put forth by European statesmen in 1930. Throughout the year it rejected suggestions for trade concessions, monetary support, and debt readjustment; from mid-1930 on, the international debt structure became increasingly difficult to sustain. Finance ministers committed to the task were putting increasing strain on their nations' monetary systems and laboring populations and by doing so were setting the stage for the collapse and disorders of 1931.

For the heralders of a "New Day," then, 1930 was not a propitious year. In 1928 and 1929 the Hooverian vision of national and international progress had reached the apogee of its acceptance and influence, and for a time in early 1930 it had seemed to be proving itself in another major trial. But as 1930 gave way to 1931, its architects were on the defensive and would soon be fighting desperately for their political lives.

# CHAPTER 12

# The Hoover Vision
# at Bay
## 1931-1932

For the American people the twenty months from January 1931 to August 1932 constituted one of the bleakest and most unsettling periods since the 1890s. As during that decade, frontiers seemed to be closing, institutions seemed out of control, and a long search for liberal ordering mechanisms seemed to be ending in failure. The Hoover prescriptions, although they continued to bring forth new programs and agencies, seemed incapable of putting idle resources to work. Yet to many Americans the alternatives being proposed seemed to involve forms of coordination that would require the sacrifice of fundamental freedoms and cherished national dreams.

If bleak and unsettling, however, the period was also one of major significance for the future course of American development. Economically it was a period during which depression spread worldwide and reached depths beyond even what the most pessimistic had been predicting in 1930. In America manufacturing output declined some 35 percent, farm prices fell to record lows, another 3,000 banks went under, and another 5 million workers joined the ranks of the unemployed. The land of promise became one of increasing distress, and it was under pressure from these worsening economic conditions that two interrelated stories continued to unfold and to dominate national life. One was the story of an administration fighting desperately to restore faith in its wisdom and to block what it considered prescriptions for bureaucratic despotism and social degeneration. The other was the story of growing support for politicians once outside the mainstream, especially those who envisioned other kinds of institutions as the tools through which New Era goals could actually be realized. Much of what would eventually be incorporated in or attempted by the New Deal was now emerging, and once the Hooverian barriers crumbled, the American search for a "new liberalism" would veer onto these new paths.

## Prelude to the European Crash

During the four months that preceded the European financial panic of May 1931, the American economy seemed to be stabilizing and showing signs of recovery. As a result, much of the political debate in early 1931 revolved not around alternative recovery programs but around such issues as liquor control, drought relief, veterans' benefits, power development, employment service reform, and oil imports. Congress was in a rebellious mood. But this was reflected less in an alternative economic or social program than in particular congressional blocs seeking to pass specific pieces of legislation that the administration opposed.

Two of the most heated debates were over Prohibition and the drought relief program. The former reached a new intensity in January 1931, when the Wickersham Commission finally confessed its inability to agree on a solution and filed a badly divided report that each side tried to use for its own purposes. Journalists had a field day satirizing the report, and it meant further embarrassment for a president who had made expert commissions an integral part of his leadership strategy. Nor did the workings of drought relief, presumably an area in which the president was himself an expert, do much to reestablish his personal and political standing. There his commitments to working through the Red Cross, the business establishment, and local community institutions collided with mounting evidence of severe distress and inadequate resources. And although he won victories—placing limits on federal feed and seed loans, blocking federal appropriations for the Red Cross, and restricting the use of a special $20 million loan fund—they cost him dearly in political credits. Many people agreed with Will Rogers, who remarked that the more generous congressional proposals were unlikely to give drought-stricken farmers "the gout," and for years Hoover would be subject to the taunt that he was willing to feed the area's livestock but not its starving human beings.

Two other congressional initiatives that the administration strongly opposed were those calling for federal loans to veterans and federal development and operation of the Muscle Shoals facilities. To each of these the president reacted with a veto, but only on Muscle Shoals was he able to make this stick. There his blockage of the latest version of the Norris bill seemed to open the way to his own proposals for a development commission made up of regional and organizational representatives. But in the area of veterans' benefits an overridden veto left the initiative in the hands of the veteran's lobbies. In 1931 the holders of World War bonus certificates gained the right to borrow up to 50 percent of their certificates' maturity value, an operation that eventually involved about $1.4 billion in federal loans, and by 1932 this same group was pushing for immediate redemption at full maturity value.

Also vetoed in 1931 was a bill to establish federally financed state employment services. Introduced by Senator Robert F. Wagner, a liberal Democrat from New York, it had won the support of numerous labor and welfare groups. But in the eyes of the Hoover administration it would destroy a developing system of federal, local, and private cooperation, coordinated by the existing Employment Service. The president, however, did agree to a special $500,000 appropriation for expanding and overhauling the Employment Service's existing work. And he did sign into law a measure authorizing a new public works planning agency, an agency first known as the Federal Employment Stabilization Board that would eventually develop into the New Deal's National Resources Planning Board. This was also sponsored by Senator Wagner, but in signing it the president took pains to link the measure to the public works planning movement of the 1920s and give credit to such men as Edward Eyre Hunt and Otto Mallery.

A final set of political debates swirled around proposals for the legalization of cartels in especially demoralized industries. Oil, coal, lumber, sugar, and textiles were all pushing their cases. But the president's answer was still negative. In his mind there was a clear distinction between associationalism (which he considered to be legal under the Sherman Act) and cartelization, and it was the former that he continued to prescribe. While rejecting the cartelization proposals, the administration did take actions intended to strengthen the associationalism in distressed industries, claiming that this would make competition more intelligent rather than doing away with it.

When Congress adjourned in March 1931, both the business and the political communities were sounding cautious notes of optimism. The indexes of employment, payrolls, and production had steadied, and were rallying slightly; as some analysts saw it, a period of relief from congressional activities and the accompanying political quarrels might induce them to move up more rapidly. This was an analysis, moreover, in which the president seemed to join. In late April, speaking to the Gridiron Club in Washington, he expressed the view that "mobilized voluntary action" had "proved its strength" and noted that recovery from every major depression in the past had "begun in the summer." At the time he was largely unaware of just how threatening the situation in central Europe had become.

## Worldwide Depression

Seen in long-range perspective, the European crash of the spring and summer of 1931 was a product of wartime dislocations that the peacemakers and New Era diplomats had never dealt with adequately. It was, as the Hooverites would say again and again, the price paid for such follies as the reparations assessment, the breakup of the Austro-Hungarian Empire as an economic entity, and French intransigence toward German reconstruction. Yet one could hardly claim, as the Hooverites frequently did, that American actions and decisions had played no part in this story. American policies, after all, had been largely responsible for the emergence of an international exchange system financially dependent on a continued outflow of capital from the United States. It was the loss of American capital and markets that subjected this system to the severe strains of 1930 and early 1931. And it was American rejection of the relief proposals of 1930 that rendered the development of compensatory programs exceedingly difficult. Although the United States had now replaced Britain as the center of world finance, it refused, in the words of economist Charles Kindleberger, to accept the "role of underwriter" that Britain could no longer play.

The immediate triggering of the crash, however, was largely the result of German, Austrian, and French actions rather than decisions made in the United States. One factor was a March 1931 proposal for an Austro-German customs union, offered as a way of reviving trade but regarded by the French as a projected breach of the Versailles Treaty system. The French reaction made it increasingly difficult for Austria's overextended banking system to obtain needed funds. In early May, when it was learned that the Credit-Anstalt in Vienna had become the beneficiary of special governmental support operations, the result was a run on the institution that finally forced it to close its doors. Panic liquidation then followed. The next two months brought exchange crises and bank runs throughout central and western Europe. Gold flowed out of Germany and Austria in massive amounts, its owners apparently convinced that the financial system was doomed and that revolution from either the left or the right was imminent. As capital fled or went into hiding, a hard-pressed German government was forced into austerity measures and crisis taxes.

In the United States the European crisis brought new downturns in the economic indexes. But throughout June and July the Hoover administration had hopes of reversing these through a new set of international initiatives. As early as June 5 the president had decided to propose a one-year moratorium on intergovernmental debts; once he had overcome the resistance of his Treasury Department and obtained pledges of cooperation from congressional and financial leaders, he arranged for an appropriate request from Germany and proceeded to announce his plan. This came on June 20, but it was not until July 6 that the moratorium finally took effect. The French, irritated at not being consulted beforehand, were not inclined to be cooperative, and only after Hoover threatened to leave them outside any international agreement was their endorsement finally obtained. To deal with a continuing banking crisis, the Germans then requested fresh loans, but this proposal won little support in either Britain or the United States. The only further relief was a standstill agreement on withdrawals of foreign credits, hammered out at a conference in London in late July.

Through such measures Hoover had hoped to restore confidence in the European financial system, gain a year during which armament burdens could be further reduced, and allow the American economy to escape additional deflationary pressures. His hopes, however, were not realized. In Europe there was further liquidation, manifested now in a flight from sterling that finally led the British to abandon the gold standard. The result was an intensified trade war, fought with retaliatory currency devaluations, higher tariff walls, and a variety of exchange controls. And as European difficulties intensified, the American depression entered an even deeper phase. The late summer and fall brought sharp breaks in commodity and security prices, new declines in foreign trade, and further drops in industrial production. Late September and early October also brought major losses of gold, and when Federal Reserve authorities responded with deflationary credit policies, the result was a new wave of bank failures and bank runs. Between September 30 and November 1 private cash hoards increased by an estimated $500 million, and another 522 banks, with $471 million in deposits, closed their doors.

Subjected to this new pressure, a number of the earlier Hoover programs broke down and were abandoned, including the National Business Survey Conference's wage maintenance program and most of the Farm Board's operations. Having already invested most of its funds in surplus wheat and cotton and having failed in efforts to bring about voluntary acreage reductions, the Farm Board shut down its emergency support programs and began liquidating its holdings. Yet even as the earlier programs collapsed, the president's response to the latest economic setbacks was further attempts to mobilize cooperative action. In August, Walter S. Gifford of American Telephone and Telegraph agreed to head a new President's Organization on Unemployment Relief. In October a conference in New Orleans produced an agreement under which organized southern bankers would help to finance cotton-holding operations. And in early December the long-planned national housing conference became the vehicle for organizing new efforts to promote construction and make mortgage money available.

In addition, the president moved to establish a cooperative credit pool that could be used to aid banks in temporary distress. Meeting with key financial leaders on October 4, he persuaded them to organize a new National Credit Association and through it to set up a reserve fund of $500 million from which loans could be made on collateral not eligible at the Federal Reserve banks. The financiers, however, were decidedly skeptical about the new program. Their action was conditioned on the president's pledge that should the measure prove inadequate, he would ask Congress to establish a governmental lending agency similar to the old War Finance Corporation.

If the bankers were now skeptical of Hooverian diagnoses and formulas, this was even more the case with many other Americans. The new phase of the depression was now bringing forth not only new applications of the Hoover approach but also a burgeoning anti-Hooverism that was beginning to move beyond its purely negative stage and generate rival diagnoses and prescriptions.

## The Anti-Hooverian Alternatives

For relatively few Americans, the events of 1931 were proof not merely of Hooverism's loss of contact with reality but of the need to replace liberal capitalist institutions with a different social order. In intellectual circles there were new admirers of Stalin's Russia, Mussolini's Italy, and America's preindustrial aristocracies. And in farm and labor circles, anticapitalist radicals enjoyed more receptive hearings than at any time since 1922. They developed followings among coal miners, textile workers, sharecroppers, agrarian protesters, and ethnic minorities, and they were active in organizing hunger marches, strike activities, agrarian resistance to foreclosure proceedings, and defenses of civil rights. Yet even among those who were most receptive to such radicalism, its appeal tended to be limited and tenuous, and among other groups it was rejected as being both impractical and incompatible with American ideals and values. For the overwhelming majority of Hoover's critics, the alternative was not a rejection of the capitalist system but institutional reforms that would make it function properly.

For a relatively large group of such critics, moreover, the reforms needed were not in the core of the Hooverian apparatus but rather in support mechanisms that Hoover had failed to develop properly. In particular they saw such things as the new tariff structure, monetary mismanagement, and defective publicity as being responsible for the larger economic failure. Even though they believed that Hoover had committed grievous errors, they tended to see these as being confined to one particular policy area. Such was the case with "old Wilsonians" like Cordell Hull, who were now prescribing tariff reductions and reciprocal trade treaties; with a wide spectrum of monetary reformers prescribing new monetary bases or banking systems; and with critics envisioning different tools of informational and public opinion management.

For a second and expanding group, however, the fault did lie with the central core of ordering and coordinating mechanisms. The failure of Hoover's economic programs, these critics argued, stemmed from the fact that they lodged or left economic power in the wrong hands and thus allowed it to be used in ways that left imbalances uncorrected and resources idled. The organizations that were expected to implement the programs were either too weak or too lacking in system consciousness to do so. To remedy this, the critics proposed either to place more power in the hands of the truly enlightened or to restore an order in which natural forces would act to compel proper economic behavior.

One set of prescriptions was concerned primarily with new ways to obtain the spending decisions that were necessary for renewed growth. The main line of development came directly from the economics of William T. Foster and Waddill Catchings as publicized by such groups as the Planned Prosperity League. As the depression deepened, Foster and Catchings began to sound like major prophets, and by late 1931 their notion of a new sector of public spending used to offset destabilizing private decisions had become embodied in a wide variety of compensatory spending proposals. Public spending, geared to different needs from those recognized by the Hooverites and in theory financed so as to enhance price stability, was now emerging as a major alternative to Hooverian recovery policies. Not surprisingly, the theory that made it a means of recovery was being seized upon by groups who saw needs to be met but were unable to secure funding from traditional sources. Welfare and relief workers, the depressed construction industries, would-be subsidizers of industrial and railroad modernization, advocates of a larger and better equipped military, and spokesmen for commodity price supports were all developing arguments to show that the funding of their programs would foster general recovery.

As the "spending" challenge developed, a second major challenge was also taking shape, this one manifested in new planning proposals that rejected Hooverian formulations and called for stronger planning agencies backed up by stronger sanctions. Of these the largest number still envisioned planning as taking place only in particular industries or sectors. In essence they would use the new agencies to deal with "sick" or "chaotic" areas, the argument being that restoring economic health to these areas would allow the economy as a whole to recover. But there were also proposals for planning that would embrace the economy as a whole. Former war administrators, especially Bernard Baruch and William Gibbs McAdoo, were suggesting that recovery could be organized through a "peace industries board." Liberal intellectuals, notably Stuart Chase, Charles A. Beard, and George Soule, were setting forth schemes that would use a national planning board and cooperating functional syndicates to correct economic imbalances and put idle resources to work. And of greatest importance for the immediate future, the business movement for antitrust relaxation was now generating proposals for lending governmental power to a planning and welfare system administered through industrial cartels. By late 1931 the leaders of the Chamber of Commerce were pushing one plan of this sort, Gerard Swope and Owen D. Young of General Electric were pushing another, and associates of the National Civic Federation had developed still others.

Paradoxically, though, while the events of 1931 propelled these planning and spending challenges to the fore, they also sparked a return to classical economic fundamentalism. For a number of economic and political leaders, the New Era and New Day deviations from this established wisdom had become the explanation of why the depression persisted. From those analysts came a third major challenge to Hooverian policy, one that manifested itself in proposals for unleashing or revitalizing natural market forces and allowing them to compel the kinds of behavior that would restore the economy to working order. In most of these the central prescription was for recovery through government shrinking, the argument being that this would broaden the area subject to market imperatives. But there were also theorists who wished to use government to shrink the domains in which private institutional power served as a shield against the market. A group of antitrusters saw strengthened antitrust laws as the answer, and a group of antiunionists saw recovery coming through government-supported wage cuts and union busting.

In late 1931 the great majority of Americans remained committed to liberal and capitalist institutions. There was no political polarization of the kind occurring in Germany during this same period. Yet the number committed to the Hooverian version of a "new liberalism" was rapidly dwindling. In this sense what had once been the center was eroding. As it did so, more and more of Hoover's energies were going into defensive or containment struggles. Increasingly unable to make his system work, he still saw it as the fount of future progress, and he was determined if at all possible to save it from critics who would substitute another kind of liberalism.

## A New Set of Programs

Throughout the summer and fall of 1931, Hoover seemed to dread the coming of the new Congress. It was, he realized, likely to reflect the challenges to his programs and philosophy. As part of an effort to forestall or contain congressional initiatives, the Hoover administration opened campaigns to expose the "fallacies" in the new proposals and rechannel the demands for action into beneficial forms of planning, economizing, and reflating. The Commerce Department began a drive to expand orthodox associational activity and persuade business groups to steer clear of the "grandiose schemes" now being proposed, and the president held a series of "economy conferences," intended to draw distinctions between desirable cutbacks and undesirable ones.

It also became clear now that the National Credit Association could not restore confidence in the banking system, which led the administration to swing its support behind a new program of public-private cooperation in the credit field. As outlined in the president's message to the incoming Congress, this would involve a new federal lending institution similar to the War Finance Corporation, a new system of home loan discount banks, new lending powers for the Federal Reserve and Federal Land banks, and new measures to hold down the federal deficit and safeguard the gold standard.

As Hoover had expected, the challenges to his approach quickly made themselves felt in the new Congress. The Senate Committee on Manufactures, chaired by Robert M. La Follette, Jr., promptly opened hearings on the new planning proposals. The farm, labor, veterans', and "government economy" blocs quickly pushed forward measures incompatible with the administration's recovery design. Bills calling for large-scale federal employment and relief programs were introduced and promoted by such legislators as Robert Wagner, Edward Costigan, and David Lewis, and a presidential veto ultimately became necessary to block a measure altering the powers of the Tariff Commission. Yet despite these displays of independence, Congress also proved willing to enact the legislation needed for the president's new credit program. In early 1932 it authorized the creation of the Reconstruction Finance Corporation (RFC), empowered to lend up to $2 billion to credit institutions and needy railroads. Congress also passed measures expanding the lending powers of the Farm Loan and Federal Reserve systems. In July, after several frustrating delays, a new system of discount banks for home mortgages came into existence. Discarded along the way were several credit and banking reforms that the president had desired. But the final result was remarkably close to what he had recommended in late 1931.

The Hoover program of 1932 also came to include a wide range of other actions. Three supplements to the new credit measures were the Citizens' Reconstruction Organization, set up to conduct a campaign against hoarding; a reconstruction conference organizing a public-private division of railroad credits; and a new network of Banking and Industrial Committees, set up in each Federal Reserve district to promote credit expansion. Another was the Glass-Steagall Act of February 1932, authorizing the use of government securities as backing for Federal Reserve notes and thereby countering the credit contraction caused by gold withdrawals. Also enacted by June 1932 were a surplus disposal law, authorizing Farm Board surpluses to be turned over to the Red Cross for distribution to the needy; a revenue act intended to increase federal revenues and thus quiet fears about the soundness of government credit; and an economy act cutting federal salaries and services and authorizing administrative reorganization.

Still, as enacted and implemented, the new Hoover program seemed to have no greater success than similar programs in 1930 and 1931. New government loans and purchases were made, but these were used primarily to enhance the liquidity of the borrowers and to build up excess banking reserves, not to release new flows of private credit and put them to work. Private lenders were reluctant to lend and borrowers to borrow. Whereas Hoover ascribed the blame for most of this to congressional perversity, his critics contended that the fault lay with his continued reliance on private groups, his acceptance of a diagnosis that ignored the system's crucial structural defects, and his perverse belief that raising taxes would somehow stimulate more private spending.

Any real answer, the critics insisted, must involve a rejection of the Hooverian formulas themselves; for some of them, the only new measures of any real value were those that Congress had forced on the reluctant president. They thought it fortunate, for example, that a congressional rebellion led by Congressman Fiorella La Guardia had been able to block passage of a federal sales tax and thus prevent the Revenue Act from doing even more damage. They were pleased when Congress insisted on retaining a veto over administrative reorganization. And they looked on the Norris–La Guardia Labor Relations Act of March 1932, a measure that Hoover signed with some reluctance, as one of the few truly progressive measures. Under it labor unions gained further immunity from the antitrust laws, and court injunctions could no longer be used to enforce antiunion employment contracts or to prevent strikes, boycotts, and peaceful picketing.

Despite the new programs, then, Hoover's support continued to erode. In business, labor, and farm circles the idea of compulsory planning through corporative institutions kept gaining new adherents. Also prominent by June 1932 was a movement among former war administrators, supported by industrial groups and the American Legion, urging the establishment of an "economic government" under a revitalized Council of National Defense. While these movements attacked Hooverism from one quarter, those for market restoration and compensatory spending were also becoming stronger. The former was unsatisfied with the Economy Act, and the latter had now brought forth two major challenges to the president's definitions of sound and desirable federal expenditures.

One of these, on the verge of passage by late June, was the Garner-Wagner relief bill, a measure calling not only for emergency RFC credits to state and local governments (as Hoover was now advocating) but also for a new $2 billion federal works and loans program. The other was Wright Patman's bonus bill, calling for maturity-value redemption of the World War bonus certificates with the money to be raised through the issuance of $2.4 billion in greenbacks. After gaining House approval on June 15, this had stalled in the Senate. But gathered in Washington now was a "bonus army" of nearly 20,000 veterans, disappointed by the Senate's action but determined, its leaders said, to force reconsideration. Unless something intervened, the steamy Washington summer promised to be hot in more ways than one.

### Responses to International Disorder

By mid-1932 it had also become increasingly clear that Hoover's hopes for the international arena were unlikely to be realized. In February a world disarmament conference had finally convened in Geneva, and in proposals on April 11 and June 22 the United States had urged the outlawing of certain offensive weapons and a flat one-third reduction in all military forces. But the Hoover administration was not receptive to French proposals for substituting an international police force and collective security guarantees, and the Allied powers were loath to concede the arms equality now demanded by the Germans. Given these differences, no agreement seemed possible, and the subsequent German decision to withdraw from participation, announced on August 31, would make the outlook even bleaker.

Disarmament seemed particularly inappropriate at a time when Japanese imperialism was reasserting itself in the Far East. There, in September 1931, the Japanese army in Manchuria had manufactured an incident along the Japanese-owned South Manchurian Railway, blamed this on the Chinese, and proceeded to seize Mukden and several other Manchurian cities. For a time the moderate elements in Japan had resisted further military commitments. But in December a reorganized government under Premier Inukai had decided to occupy all of Manchuria, and by early 1932 this had been completed and a new puppet government installed. The Japanese militarists, moreover, were in no mood to brook retaliation against their actions. Their response to Chinese economic warfare was to occupy the city of Shanghai and hold it until the boycott had been lifted. When a League of Nations investigation branded the Japanese as "aggressors," they reacted by withdrawing from the League. Their conquest of Manchuria stood as a major and, as it turned out, irreparable breach in the Versailles system.

The conquest also constituted a major breach in the Washington Conference system and the moral commitments created by the Kellogg-Briand Pact. This the Hoover administration realized, and in early 1932, through an enunciation of what became known as the Stimson Doctrine, it tried to invoke the moral sanctions that were supposed to repair such a breach. On January 7, U.S. Secretary of State Henry L. Stimson informed Japan and China that the United States would never recognize any changes in the area that were brought about in violation of the principles set forth in the Nine Power Treaty and the Kellogg-Briand Pact. Subsequently the United States also cooperated with the League's investigators and threatened to reconsider its pledges not to fortify its outlying island possessions in the western Pacific. But none of this seemed to have much effect on Japanese behavior, and the president was opposed to and quickly repudiated the idea of threatening economic sanctions. Such an action, he feared, would only strengthen the Japanese militarists and bring the kind of confrontation from which the United States stood to lose much more than it could gain.

Even if the president had favored stronger actions, it seems doubtful that he could have mobilized the support needed to take them. Public opinion at the time attached little value to the maintenance of the "open door" or the preservation of China's territorial integrity, and many Americans were now in favor of liquidating American holdings and commitments in the Far East rather than expanding them. As economic conditions had worsened, the movement for giving the Philippine Islands their independence had picked up strong support from Americans who wanted to exclude Filipino products and immigrants. A Filipino independence bill, complete with severe trade and immigration restrictions, had passed the House of Representatives, and as of mid-1932 it was becoming increasingly doubtful that administration opposition, even if it came to a presidential veto, could keep such a measure from becoming law.

In Latin America the Hoover administration faced no crisis comparable to that in the Far East. There were further debt repudiations and political upheavals in the region. But despite these the administration stuck by its pledges of nonintervention, its refusal to serve as debt collector for private creditors, and its program for gradually liquidating the Haitian occupation. The only displays of military force were limited to upholding the settlement in Nicaragua and providing coastal protection for Americans in Honduras, and the refusal to recognize changes of government was used only in Central America and Chile. Yet this kind of "good neighborism" did nothing to halt the further collapse of the economic structure erected during the 1920s. The Hoover administration gave no support to a debt moratorium or standstill agreement for Latin America, and it remained firmly opposed to the kinds of trade concessions, investment guarantees, and special aid programs that would-be revivers of a pan-American economic community now believed necessary.

Similar efforts to refloat the European economic structure were also opposed. As German distress and disorder grew, the Allied powers met with German representatives at Lausanne, Switzerland, where in June 1932 they finally agreed to cancel most of the reparations if a satisfactory agreement could be reached on the war debts owed to the United States. But the Hoover administration would have none of this. Though Stimson was sympathetic, the president was unwilling to go beyond a possible reapplication of the "capacity to pay" formula to each individual country.

The chief ray of hope in the international economic picture of mid-1932 was the plans being made for a world monetary and economic conference. The British had agreed to be the hosts, and the president and his advisers hoped that the conference would find some way to reestablish a prosperous, peaceful, and progressive world order. But this was in the future. The more immediate concerns in the summer of 1932 were with the impact of continuing distress on the domestic situation.

## The Summer of 1932

Economically the summer of 1932 brought slight upturns. But politically it was a time of continuing failure for the Hoover administration. In its battles against federal relief, its handling of the "bonus army," and its efforts to deflate the pressures for compulsory planning and cartelization, it took actions and positions that further eroded its political base and strengthened its opponents.

The relief issue came to a head on July 9, when Congress ignored administration warnings and proceeded to pass a modified version of the Garner-Wagner relief bill. Two days later the president responded with a stinging veto message. Such a measure, he declared, would put the government into business in such a way as to violate the very principles on which the nation had been founded. When it became clear that the veto could not be overridden, the sponsors of the measure agreed to settle for what the president would allow. As finally approved on July 21, the Emergency Relief and Construction Act authorized the RFC to lend up to $300 million to needy states, the money to be repaid by reducing appropriations for federal-aid highways. In addition, the agency could lend up to $1.5 billion for self-liquidating public works, and it was now required to report all its loans to Congress. The latter was a provision strongly opposed by the administration, but the president finally accepted it when congressional leaders promised to keep the information confidential.

In one sense Hoover had been victorious. The new legislation was essentially of the kind that he had proposed in May, and RFC control meant that *need* and *self-liquidating* would not be loosely defined. But in terms of his political future the struggle had been costly. His opponents had depicted him as hardhearted and callous, talking about "moral fiber" and "social principles" at a time when millions were without basic necessities and therefore thoroughly fraudulent in his pose as a "great humanitarian." Even more damaging politically, they established him in the public mind as a social reactionary defending a "trickle-down approach" that allowed government aid only for bankers, railroad owners, and other millionaires. For many Americans he had now become a tool of entrenched wealth and privilege rather than a builder and manager of socially progressive institutions.

What was true of the relief debate, moreover, was even more true of administration policy during the "bonus riot" of July 28, 1932. Anxious to get the "bonuseers" out of Washington, the administration had secured legislation under which they could borrow money to pay for their transportation back home. But when approximately 8,000 of them still refused to leave, it also decided to press matters by evicting them from federal properties along Pennsylvania Avenue. The result, on the afternoon of July 28, was violence in which two of the veterans were killed. Acceding to a request from the District of Columbia Commissioners, the president decided to use the troops being held in readiness. Under the command of General Douglas MacArthur, a specially trained riot force of about 550 men entered the area, used tear gas, bayonets, and cavalry charges to clear it, and as of 9 P.M. appeared to be carrying out its orders to force all rioters into the camp at Anacostia Flats and take such actions as were necessary to identify and arrest

Bonus marchers battle the Washington, D.C. police at the Capitol building. *(UPI/Bettmann)*

those responsible for the rioting. At this stage, however, General Mac-Arthur decided to take matters into his own hands. Convinced that the "bonus army" had now become a radicalized insurrectionary force, he authorized operations that routed the veterans out of Anacostia and finished burning those hovels that they had left standing. By morning the "bonus army" had been reduced to a jumble of ragged and confused groups wandering through the streets and seeking any means of leaving.

The president was not pleased with MacArthur's actions. But after meeting with the general and with Secretary of War Patrick Hurley, Hoover too was convinced that the "bonus army" had been a dangerous group controlled by communists and criminals. His decision was to defend MacArthur's actions rather than repudiate them, and not surprisingly a subsequent investigation did its best to document the allegedly subversive character of the "bonuseers." The public, however, was not much impressed with the flimsy and contrived evidence that was offered, and the outcome of the investigation was a strengthening of the belief that Hoover was insensitive, vindictive, and paranoid. To the image of harshness and reaction was now added that of a man who had turned the nation's arms against the very people who had saved it twelve years earlier.

Meanwhile, during the same period that the relief and bonus issues were coming to a head, the president was also planning an operation that might simultaneously promote recovery and deflate the pressures for compulsory planning and cartelization. It was to take the form of another great voluntary effort, built primarily around the new Banking and Industrial Committees in the Federal Reserve districts but calling as well for new agencies to spread work, stimulate capital expenditures, and cope with disorderly markets. In addition, the relief and welfare agencies were to be mobilized again, and farm distress, which was now generating threats of "farm strikes" and mob action against foreclosing judges, was to be relieved through new agricultural credit associations and mortgage relief conferences. In August and September much of this new plan was put into effect, at least on paper. At conferences in Washington and Chicago the agencies were created and a framework provided for what Hoover called "coordinated effort on the economic front." The nation, so he told the conferees, had now won its economic "battle of Château-Thierry." It had brought its financial structure "safely through the worldwide collapse." But it must now re-form for its economic "battle of Soissons."

War metaphors notwithstanding, recovery still did not come. On the contrary, late September brought another economic downturn that Hoover attributed to fears about the coming elections but that his critics quickly seized on as proof that he was still clinging to a discredited and unworkable approach. Nor was he able to deflate the movements for compulsory planning and cartelization, whose advocates could now point to the new failures as further evidence that obstructive and shortsighted business groups must be forced into line. Ironically, some segments of this latest administrative framework would become vehicles for promoting the kind of governmentally enforced cartelization that the administration had hoped to block.

As the summer of 1932 ended, the Hooverites still had hopes of carrying their designs for a "new liberalism" safely through the economic storm and making them the basis of a new era of economic growth and social progress. But that they could do so had now become increasingly doubtful. The worldwide collapse of 1931, the failure of the new programs of late 1931 and early 1932, and the seeming impotence of the latest set of recovery agencies had continued to undermine the credibility of Hooverian formulas. In the political arena anti-Hooverism had now become a potent force, and along the economic policy front the lines that Hoover was still holding against the new schemes for recovery had become perilously thin. The era of "Hooverism at bay" seemed about to give way to an era in which alternative formulations of a "new liberalism" could no longer be contained.

CHAPTER 13

# From Hooverism to
# the New Deal
## 1932–1933

 Viewing each other across the transfer of power in 1933, the Hooverites and the New Dealers tended to see much greater differences than recent historical scholarship has been able to discern. The Hooverites, it now seems clear, were not the laissez-faire fundamentalists excoriated in New Deal rhetoric. Nor were the New Dealers the collectivizing anti-capitalists depicted in Hooverian oratory. Both are best seen as seekers of a managed capitalist order committed to the realization of traditional liberal ideals. Both had also drawn much of their inspiration from the organizational experience of the war period. And the early New Dealers, at least, were remarkably similar to the Hooverites in their willingness to work through established organizational elites and concerts of organized interests. Far from being an application of socialist theory or a radical kind of redistributionism, much of the early New Deal might more aptly be labeled "Hooverism in high gear."

Nevertheless, within the broader story of America's continuing search for liberal ordering mechanisms, the transfer of power in 1933 stands as a major watershed. It marked the end of efforts to implement a "new liberalism" that in theory could allow Americans to meet modern needs without developing a welfare and regulatory state. It removed the barriers against the kind of government-backed cartelization, public works spending, and administrative state that the outgoing administration had strongly resisted. It also brought to power a group of leaders who were less committed to a particular set of ordering mechanisms and more open to pressures from insurgent groups and antiestablishment critics. In the realm of public psychology, moreover, as distinct from public policy, the watershed was even greater—a fact that may explain the persisting myths that quickly grew up around it. On one side of the dividing line, as much of the American public perceived it, stood a demoralized society rejecting a discredited leader, a man who had been exposed now as cold, uncaring, doctrinaire, and incapable of acting against the causes of popular distress. On the other side, again as widely perceived, stood a reinvigorated society infused with optimistic activism and responding to a new and dynamic leader, a man of warmth, vitality, immense political skill, and an almost magical capacity to ferret out and foil the enemies of the people.

In part, then, the history of the American nation from September 1932 to March 1933 is a story of heritages bequeathed across a political and rhetorical divide. In part it is a story of public policy breaking into new paths and embracing new instruments. And in part it is a story of a society under stress looking for scapegoats and saviors and inclined to accept perceptions of the period that provided them. Each of these deserves careful scrutiny, and it is to this story of a troubled, myth-shrouded, and multidimensional transition that we now turn.

## Election and Interregnum

For Herbert Hoover and his supporters the month of September 1932 was one of shattered hopes and mounting frustrations. At the Republican convention, meeting in Chicago on June 14, the president and vice-president had been easily renominated, and through August there were still hopes that the new recovery organizations, coupled with concessions to the anti-Prohibitionists, could somehow turn their political fortunes around. But September brought new economic downturns and the full backlash of the relief debate and the "bonus army" episode. It also brought Democratic victories in traditionally Republican Maine, an indication of how low Republican fortunes had now fallen. Hoover might and did claim that his programs had been effective, particularly in saving the country "from a quarter of a century of chaos and degeneration." But people who believed this were now a dwindling and dispirited band. Many more saw him as the apostle of what his political opponents were calling the four $D$'s: destruction, delay, deceit, and despair.

It was clear, moreover, that the Democrats had now found a leader who could unite their party and allow it to take full advantage of pervasive anti-Hooverism. Triumphant in the gubernatorial contests of 1928 and 1930, Franklin D. Roosevelt of New York had emerged as the man capable of fusing Smith's new urban Democracy with the old Wilsonian coalition. He had gathered about him a group of astute political managers and articulate intellectuals, and at Chicago, where the Democrats met on June 27, a "stop Roosevelt" movement had been of no avail. On the contrary, House Speaker John N. Garner had quickly swung his delegates over to Roosevelt's support, thus giving the latter the nomination on the fourth ballot. And following Garner's nomination for vice-president, Roosevelt had decided to break with tradition and deliver his acceptance speech at the convention. Speaking there on July 2, in an atmosphere of buoyancy and excitement that contrasted sharply with the mood at the earlier Republican proceedings, he had pledged himself and his party to "a new deal for the American people."

To the political columnist Walter Lippmann, the Democratic candidate was essentially a "nice young man who would like very much to be president." But as the campaign unfolded in 1932, it offered an early illustration of the appeals and strategies that would enable Roosevelt to remain in the White House until his death in 1945. One element was rapport with the masses, created through a mixture of antiestablishment appeals to the "forgotten man" with a charismatic radiation of warmth, confidence, compassion, and even vigor despite his crippled legs, the legacy of a 1921 bout with polio. A second was the invocation of a political demonology, in this case the Hooverites and the other architects of disaster and injustice that they were allegedly protecting. A third was the accommodation or balancing of conflicting prescriptions and pressures. In speeches addressed to each of the anti-Hoover groups, Roosevelt mixed denunciations of the Republican tariff with calls for greater economic nationalism, condemnation of Hoover for centering "everything in Washington" with talk of a new economic planning, and biting criticism of Hooverian extravagances and deficits with proposals for greater relief and works expenditures.

Long before election day it was clear that Roosevelt would win. On occasion, Hoover spoke with force and feeling and was well received. But often the crowds were cold or hostile. When the votes were finally counted, the man who had once promised a New Day for the American people was delivered an even more decisive defeat than he had handed Smith in 1928. Roosevelt received 27,821,857 popular votes to 15,761,841 for Hoover and 884,781 for Norman Thomas, the Socialist candidate. In the electoral college Hoover carried only four New England states, Pennsylvania, and Delaware, for a total of 59 electoral votes to Roosevelt's 472. Nor did Republican congressional candidates fare much better. In the Senate the Republican contingent was reduced to 36 and in the House of Representatives to only 117. The election was a major milestone in the history of the American party system: the

Democrats had become — and would long remain — the nation's normal majority party.

In his message to the lame-duck Congress in December 1932, the defeated president outlined another legislative program that would allegedly assist in getting recovery started again. He urged, in particular, new economic and budget-balancing measures, another commission to renegotiate inter-Allied war debts, liberalization of the branch banking and bankruptcy laws, and speedy ratification of a Canadian-American treaty calling for joint development of the Saint Lawrence Seaway. Subsequently the administration also gave serious consideration to a land withdrawal program for agriculture and to concerted reemployment plans underwritten by federal credit. But in Congress attention was focused on the president-elect and his plans for action. Of the administration measures, only the bankruptcy reform bill was enacted into law. And of the measures that emerged from congressional initiatives, the only one to get past a presidential veto was a Philippine independence act with features so harsh that the Filipinos themselves subsequently rejected the offer. In addition, this last session of the 72nd Congress completed action on a proposal to repeal the Prohibition Amendment. Submitted to the states on February 20, 1933, it would be quickly ratified and would take effect before the year ended.

The legislative stalemate at the time was accompanied by a stalemate in international negotiations. There the president's hopes were now tied to the projected world economic conference and to his plans for negotiating new debt settlements in accordance with the "capacity to pay" principle. But efforts to secure Roosevelt's cooperation in implementing this approach were to no avail. Legislation for a debt commission remained bogged down in Congress. And by March 1933, two developments abroad had virtually ensured that neither the world economic conference nor the reconvened world disarmament conference would find ways to reestablish the kind of liberal international order that Hoover envisioned. One was the decision of the French and then other nations to default on their war debts and risk whatever retaliatory action the United States might take. The other was the emergence of Adolf Hitler, head of the National Socialist or Nazi party, as Germany's national leader. On January 30 he had assumed the chancellorship, and by late March a Nazi dictatorship was firmly established.

As the international situation deteriorated, economic contraction began bringing down portions of the banking system that the Reconstruction Finance Corporation had saved in late 1931 and early 1932. A foretaste of what was in store had come during the week before the election, when the governor of Nevada declared a banking holiday to avert the failure of an important chain of banks in his state. But the acute phase of the crisis began in mid-February 1933, when presidential and RFC efforts to arrange new loans for a banking group in Detroit ended in failure. On February 14 the governor of Michigan declared a banking holiday, and in the two weeks that followed, spreading panic was manifested in bank runs, increased hoarding of gold, and more banking holidays. Also contributing to a loss of confidence were revelations made at hearings conducted by the Senate Banking and Currency Committee. Some of the leading banking figures of the 1920s were confessing to malpractices that, in the lame-duck president's words to his attorney general, had been far more injurious to the American system than "all the followers of Karl Marx" and "all the incidental operations of Al Capone." By the end of February popular confidence was on the verge of complete collapse, and during the first two days of March so many states joined the bank holiday parade that a nationwide closing seemed all but inevitable.

Hoover blamed part of the situation on the publicity being given to RFC loans. But the real culprit, he believed, was fear of the unsound monetary policies that the new Democratic administration might adopt. Hence his principal attempt to curb the panic took the form of a plea to the president-elect urging that he commit himself to balancing the budget and maintaining the gold standard. Roosevelt, however, was in no mood to cooperate, particularly when the plea came in the form of a thinly veiled accusation that his election was responsible for the crisis. After a perplexing delay, attributed in the response to a "secretary's oversight," he replied that no mere statement could counteract the real trouble.

As the March 4 date for Roosevelt's inaugural neared, the deepening crisis seemed destined to leave the country without a functioning monetary system. Under consideration now, both at the White House and by Federal Reserve authorities, were plans for limited deposit guarantees, embargoes on gold withdrawals, issuance of a special scrip, and national closing actions. But disagreements over what should be done, doubts about the power to act, and the president's refusal to act without Roosevelt's formal endorsement prevented any of the plans from being implemented. On Hoover's last night in office the governors of New York and Illinois declared banking holidays, which meant that banks were now closed or operating under severe restrictions in nearly every state. It was against this somber backdrop of impending crisis and economic paralysis that the transfer of power took place. Had the New Dealers planned it that way (and Hoover suspected that they had), they could hardly have arranged a more damning exit for the administration they had defeated at the polls four months earlier.

## American Society in the Third Depression Winter

As the banking system collapsed, the accompanying economic contraction also subjected other kinds of institutions to increasingly severe strains. By February 1933 the ranks of the unemployed had swelled to nearly 13 million, savings and credit for workers laid off or on short hours were virtually exhausted, and federal relief loans seemed hopelessly inadequate to compensate for the accelerating collapse of corporate welfare programs, municipal relief systems, and private charity organizations. Social workers in this third depression winter reported increasing misery, malnutrition, and demoralization. Journalists wrote stories on the new migrants and vagabonds and on the shantytowns that the American public had labeled "Hoovervilles." A variety of social surveys documented increasingly strained family relations, drastic declines in educational enrollments and expenditures, and severely straitened circumstances for churches, health delivery systems, and cultural programs.

Fear that revolution or anarchy might be in the offing was frequently expressed, especially in pleas for federal aid or proposals for new welfare services. Yet when pressed on the matter, most of the doomsayers would concede that the potential anarchists and revolutionaries were still remarkably loyal and docile. More often than not, it seemed, unemployment led to feelings of apathy or personal inadequacy rather than anger and alienation. At work too was a kind of siege mentality that helped to maintain loyalty to established institutions and to make privations more endurable. Reducing the potential for radicalization still further was what proved to be an amazing capacity of the American social order to cope with the situation by reverting to more primitive forms of economic and social organization.

This backtracking was apparent in a variety of areas. Women and young people were moving back home and back to various kinds of household production. Recent migrants to the cities were moving back to the land and the villages. Agriculture seemed to be reverting toward its subsistence phase. Unable to find slots in the modern organizational economy, men and women were entering entrepreneurship at the lowest and least rewarding levels. Especially noticeable was the proliferation of hole-in-the-wall stops, street peddlers, and what sophisticated observers called "Mama, Papa, and Rosie" stores. All of this was facilitated by a resurgence of antimodernism that regarded such develop-ments as making for a healthier and more desirable society. Building on the antimodernism that had persisted during the 1920s, moral philoso-phers were telling Americans that the answer to their present difficul-ties lay in casting out the false gods of the New Era and returning to simpler and more wholesome forms of social organization.

Even under the conditions of 1933, then, American society re-mained remarkably resistant to radicalization. There were occasional outbreaks of violence, the most celebrated incidents being near-lynch-ings of foreclosing judges and mob seizures of public buildings and food stores. Militant organizations such as the Khaki Shirts, the Farm Holi-day Association, and Communist-influenced labor unions also gained a few adherents. But violence and militance were remarkably limited and tended, for the most part, to resemble frontier or community vigilant-ism rather than revolutionary action.

What radicalism there was tended to be more of an intellectual than a mass phenomenon. Its principal manifestations were not in mass-based political movements or a mass-supported set of alternative social institutions but rather in works by Marxist, syndicalist, and fascist theoreticians, the beginnings of a proletarian literature allegedly aris-ing out of social realities, and a brief reflowering of the technocratic designs that had first blossomed in the immediate postwar period. Designs were now emanating from a group called Technocracy, under the direction of Howard Scott, the eccentric engineer who had helped to form the Technical Alliance back in 1920. For a few months, in late 1932 and early 1933, the nation's newspapers carried lengthy discus-sions of the group's energy surveys, its plans for a new money based on units of energy, and its visions of an economic utopia run by technicians and engineers.

In theory, proletarian literature was supposed to mobilize the masses for action. In practice, it seemed to have little mass appeal and little effect in altering a popular culture that tended to enhance rather than reduce resistance to radicalization. Its capacity to provide escape valves for anxieties and frustrations remained. Consolation was still available in the form of packaged dreams and fantasies. The gangster and horror films that dominated popular cinema at the time provided both safety valves for antisocial impulses and moral warnings against tampering with established traditions and institutions.

A society resistant to radicalization, however, did not mean a soci-ety totally immobilized. If there was little response to radical social visions, there was much disillusionment with Hooverian prescriptions and congressional stalemates and hence a disposition to support the segments of the economic and political establishment that proposed to try something different and to expedite this with emergency executive powers. Limited change, in other words, could proceed along the paths outlined by the heirs of McNary-Haugenism, the movement for anti-trust revision and business planning, the agitation for compensatory spending and federal welfare supplements, and the advocates of utilities, tariff, and monetary reform. In each case energy was mobilized and ready for release by the president-elect. Many Americans were disposed to applaud this release and to believe that the man they had elected would somehow prove capable of coordinating the conflicting streams of energy, harnessing them to the attainment of national purposes, and correcting any abuses that might develop.

What was true of the masses was also true of many of the nation's intellectuals. Disillusionment with the New Era, they seemed to think, could become the basis for a society in which intellectuals would reassume their rightful place as the creators and defenders of integrating values. And while some embraced radical political movements as the tools for achieving this, a much larger group looked to the elevation of a powerful national leader who would help to restore intellectuals to their rightful place. For some the hopes once invested in Theodore Roosevelt and Woodrow Wilson were now being attached to the incoming president and his much publicized Brains Trust of intellectual advisers and academic experts. For a smaller group he was becoming the embodiment of a new politics capable of achieving ends that were once unrealizable politically. For a few he had become the instrument that Hoover should have been had not the latter been incapacitated by ideological blinders.

## The Watershed of 1933

Meanwhile, as much of the nation invested its hopes in the coming transfer of presidential power, Roosevelt was putting together a cabinet and choosing other advisers and administrators. Places were found not only for old-line party leaders but also for business backers, Republican progressives like Henry A. Wallace and Harold L. Ickes, and a woman, Frances Perkins, whose appointment as secretary of labor symbolized a commitment to social welfare and the advancing position of women. Brains Trusters Raymond Moley and Rexford G. Tugwell were to stay on as assistant secretaries in positions to help launch the New Deal. And in a series of conferences and agreements with groups pushing for new programs — most notably the agricultural organizations, the proponents of federal relief and federal works projects, and the champions of antitrust revision and business planning — the outlines of what was to come were becoming clear.

During the immediate preinaugural period, the banking situation received the most attention. The key development was neither linkages to demands for change in the banking community nor ties to the bank reform initiatives in Congress; it was rather a working association between Roosevelt's appointees and such outgoing treasury officials as Ogden Mills, Arthur Ballantine, and F. Gloyd Awalt, with the Hoover men supplying most of the recommendations that were incorporated in Roosevelt's plan of action and in the Emergency Banking Act that passed Congress on March 9. Hoover could never have dramatized the situation and restored public confidence in the way that Roosevelt would do. But the New Deal's first major piece of banking legislation, especially the scheme under which sound banks would be reopened, was shaped by the same general perspective that had produced the financial legislation of 1932.

There were other strands of continuity. The distribution of relief and credit, for example, remained mostly in the hands of the same local agencies that had formed the base of the Hooverian administrative network. The new schemes for agricultural and industrial controls, as embodied in the Agricultural Adjustment and National Industry Recovery acts, were to work through the same private or quasi-private bureaucracies that had been entrusted with implementing Hoover's farm and industrial programs. The purposes of the Economy Act of March 20, 1933, were difficult to distinguish from those of the Economy Act of June 1932. Beyond these particular strands of continuity, there was a broad identity of view as to ultimate goals, technological imperatives, and institutional gaps in need of filling. Some members of the new administration saw its programs as the route to a collectivist democracy. But they were far outweighed by those who saw them as the route to realizing the kind of America that Hoover had visualized in his New Day speeches of 1928.

The basic difference between the Hooverian system and the New Deal measures of 1933 lay in the latter's acceptance of a larger public sector and of a public obligation to enforce privately developed regulations found to be in the public interest. Involved were forms of public enterprise, federal welfare activities, and delegations of federal power that Hoover had regarded as incompatible with the maintenance of a liberal order. Involved as well was a rejection of the view that America could find ways of meeting modern needs without developing a welfare and regulatory state. Yet such innovations, important as they were, can easily be magnified. Much of the New Deal state was initially conceived of as an emergency government, resembling the emergency structures with which the Hooverites were willing to fight wars, cope with natural disasters, and ward off blows from abroad, and the rest was conceived of as supplementary to private and local programs. To a considerable degree the differences lay in divergent definitions of what constituted an emergency or a necessary supplement rather than in divergent theories of what constituted liberal governance.

Still, the departures from Hooverism in 1933 were significant. They foreshadowed the New Deal measures of 1935 to 1938 which did constitute a far greater break from Hooverian conceptions. In the public consciousness, moreover, 1933 would remain one of the great watersheds of twentieth-century American history. The lines of continuity were largely obscured by the contrasting personalities and public images of the two presidents, the frenetic activism that succeeded the stalemates of early 1933, and political oratory stressing Hoover's "do-nothingism" and Roosevelt's "radicalism."

Thoroughly imbedded in the public consciousness, too, were the images of an inaugural ceremony that seemed to symbolize the passing of an old order and the dawning of a new. As countless journalists and historians would write, March 4, 1933, was a drear and gloomy day, suited, it seemed, to a nation whose financial and economic machinery had come to a virtual standstill and whose outgoing president sat cheer-

The first inauguration of Franklin D. Roosevelt, who is being sworn in by Justice Charles Evans Hughes while Herbert Hoover *(far right)* looks on. *(The Bettmann Archive)*

less and immobile like the doomed figure in a Greek tragedy. Then the overcast seemed to break. A new national figure, standing in heavy braces yet exuding energy, confidence, and hope, was ready to turn crisis into challenge. He would banish paralyzing fear, restore the temple of civilization to "social values more noble than mere monetary profit," and seek "broad executive power to wage a war against the emergency." Nor was he ready to accept the constitutional arguments that some opponents of expanded government were now falling back on. "Our Constitution is so simple and practical," he declared, "that it is possible always to meet extraordinary needs by changes in emphasis and arrangement without loss of essential form." In reality the nation had a new crisis manager rather than a leader committed to building a new order, and essentially the crisis was not one of classical capitalism but of the economic system spawned by the organizational revolution and institution building of the 1920s. But public psychology was inclined to make the watershed far more pronounced than these realities warranted.

## The Heritage of a Search That Failed

In many respects the central story of the American experience from 1917 to 1933 is the story of a search that failed. It is the story of a people deeply influenced by the organizational experience of a democracy at war and seeking, against various obstacles, to draw from that experience a set of liberal ordering mechanisms suitable for peacetime economic, social, and international management. It was a search first manifested in the designs of Wilson and his reconstruction managers. But it did not end when the Wilsonians were ousted from power. It quickly reappeared in modified form and was soon holding forth the vision of an associational order capable of meeting the needs for coordination and control without creating a welfare, regulatory, or military state. For a time, it seemed that the goals of this vision were being realized. But in reality the new order, to the extent that it did come into existence, was unable to keep the economy in balance or to overcome the forces that produced the "great contraction" of 1929 to 1933. Its failure in this regard also subjected its international and social solutions to pressures they could not sustain. Finally, in 1933, the men who still held to the vision were removed from power and their places taken by men less resistant to statist coordination and support.

In one sense this search that failed ended up in a blind alley — or perhaps, as the Hooverites might have put it, it was on a road beset with perils from which Americans unwilling to endure temporary privations for the sake of future benefits impatiently turned aside. In any event, the ordering mechanisms it was able to establish proved incapable of doing what had been promised in the time that the American people were willing to allow. Yet in another sense the testing of these mechanisms was an important link in the chain of events leading to the New Deal innovations. The test reflected and reinforced the increasing abandonment of classical economic ideas and a growing belief that certain bureaucracies were necessary to make a modern economy function effectively. It provided a framework in which the ideology of scientific management moved out from the workplace to embrace whole industries, whole systems of social activity, and national economic life as a whole. Even as the failures of 1931 and 1932 brought a considerable revival of laissez-faire fundamentalism, they also led to the view that other bureaucracies with different outlooks and more power could be successful and to struggles for organizational survival that embraced this new view. Under the pressure of economic contraction the instruments that were supposed to manage an associational order tended to evolve into instruments for battering down the Hooverian barriers instead of supporting them.

The search that failed, then, had much to do with the creation of an intellectual and political setting in which the New Deal state could become the American response to economic adversity and idled resources. Beyond this it stimulated or allowed an organizational growth that was important in determining the eventual form that the New Deal took. Not only did the structures associated with this growth provide the New Dealers with ready-made units of administration, much as they had the Hooverites, but they also acted as a barrier against New Dealers who wanted to build an administrative or planning state comparable to those in Europe. Significantly, the great organizational changes of the New Deal years were not in the areas organized during the New Era but in the filling of certain organizational vacuums, particularly among mass production workers and urban ethnics and in the social welfare system.

Finally, it should also be noted that if the Hooverian designs for a "new liberalism" proved defective and politically unsustainable, the same was also true of substantial portions of the New Deal designs. Only a few portions of Roosevelt's National Recovery Administration experiment in government-backed cartelization were able to survive its failure to bring recovery and its generation of a backlash in favor of market restoration. Only isolated portions of the efforts to reunite high culture and national life survived into the 1940s. And as of 1939 the efforts to restore economic balance through attacks on business power, social security measures, and limited bursts of stimulative spending had not brought an economy capable of putting its idle resources to work and rewarding participants in it with rising material or social benefits. Full employment and new economic growth would come only with the installation of another war system resembling that installed during the Great War of 1917 and 1918. And the economic miracles of the period from 1945 to 1965 would come less from the heritage of the New Deal programs and initiatives than from new and more successful efforts to adapt the elements of this war system to peacetime needs.

If the would-be builders of an associational order in the 1920s opened the way to the political and statist measures of the 1930s, they also created institutions that shaped and limited the results of such measures and became the basis for the new organizational developments of the 1940s. In many respects their efforts and designs foreshadowed the institutional arrangements that would be hailed as the true basis of a "new liberalism" in the post–World War II years. Without their handiwork, the America that took shape on the other side of the watershed of 1933 might have developed along quite different lines.

# Bibliography

## General Accounts

Traditionally, study of America in the 1920s has begun with Frederick Lewis Allen's *Only Yesterday* (New York: Harper, 1931), a work that not only shaped popular stereotypes of the period but also reinforced the tendency of scholars to regard it as a frothy and frivolous interlude between progressivism and the New Deal. Writing on the decade long followed the Allen tradition, resulting in such works as Laurence Greene's *Era of Wonderful Nonsense* (Indianapolis: Bobbs-Merrill, 1939) and Henry M. Robinson's *Fantastic Interim* (New York: Harcourt, Brace, 1943). Not until the 1950s did historians begin to take a new look, focusing less on the period's bohemians, bootleggers, and Babbitts and more on its reformist aspects, its technical and organizational innovations, its cultural fragmentation and creativity, and its impulses toward and battles over social modernization. The beginnings of such research were reflected in William E. Leuchtenburg, *The Perils of Prosperity, 1914–1932* (Chicago: University of Chicago Press, 1958). But they had minimal impact on such surveys as Harold U. Faulkner, *From Versailles to the New Deal* (New Haven, Conn.: Yale University Press, 1955), Arthur M. Schlesinger, Jr., *The Crisis of the Old Order, 1919–1933* (Boston: Houghton Mifflin, 1957), and John D. Hicks, *Republican Ascendancy, 1921–1933* (New York: Harper & Row, 1960). Only recently has scholarship led to reinterpretations stressing the significance of the period in its own right and not merely for the light it can shed on the fate of progressivism or the origins of the New Deal. For perceptive discussions of these scholarly trends, see Burl Noggle, "The Twenties: A New Historiographical Frontier," *Journal of American History* 53 (September 1966), and Joan Hoff Wilson, *The Twenties: The Critical Issues* (Boston: Little, Brown, 1972). A recent popular history of the period is Geoffrey Perrett, *America in the Twenties* (New York: Simon & Schuster, 1982).

Historical reinterpretation of the 1920s has also been accompanied by changing perceptions of the periods immediately preceding and following the decade. The years 1917–1919 have become significant not only for their impact on liberal reformism and their responses to developments abroad but also for their institutional innovations and especially for their contributions to New Era designs for economic, social, and international order. For a review of recent work on the period, see the bibliographical essay in Burl Noggle's *Into the Twenties* (Urbana: University of Illinois Press, 1974). And at the other end, historians have been restudying the years 1930–1933, seeing them more as a crisis period for the managerial capitalism and associative designs of the 1920s than as a time of retribution for returns to "normalcy" and laissez-faire. For a discussion of this work, see especially Robert H. Zieger, "Herbert Hoover: A Reinterpretation," *American Historical Review* 81 (October 1976), and the bibliographical essay in Joan Hoff Wilson, *Herbert Hoover: Forgotten Progressive* (Boston: Little, Brown, 1975). For discussions of interpretive frameworks that have helped to change perceptions of the period, see Louis Galambos, "The Emerging Organizational Synthesis in Modern American History," *Business History Review* 44 (Autumn 1970), Irwin Unger, "The 'New Left' and American History: Some Recent Trends in United States Historiography," *American Historical Review* 72 (July 1967), and John M. Carroll, "Reassessing America's Past," in Charles Bussey, John M. Carroll, William MacDonald, and John W. Storey, eds., *America's Heritage in the Twentieth Century* (St. Louis, Mo.: Forum Press, 1978).

## The War and After, 1917–1920

Despite recent trends, the coming of war and the diplomacy of war and peacemaking still stand as the most intensively researched aspects of the 1917–1933 period. On each there are mountains of literature. Of the older works the most significant are Charles Seymour, *American Diplomacy during the World War* (Baltimore: Johns Hopkins Press, 1934), Charles C. Tansill, *America Goes to War* (Boston: Little, Brown, 1938), Ray Stannard Baker, *Woodrow Wilson and World Settlement*, 3 vols. (Garden City, N.Y.: Doubleday, Page, 1923), and Thomas A. Bailey, *Woodrow Wilson and the Lost Peace* (New York: Macmillan, 1944). The best of the recent studies are Ernest R. May, *The World War and American Isolation, 1914–1917* (Cambridge, Mass.: Harvard University Press, 1959), Arthur S. Link, *Wilson the Diplomatist* (Baltimore: Johns Hopkins Press, 1957), Daniel M. Smith, *The Great Departure: The United States and World War I, 1914–1920* (New York: Wiley, 1965), and Arthur Walworth, *Wilson and His Peacemakers:*

*American Diplomacy at the Paris Peace Conference* (New York: Norton, 1986). Also perceptive, especially in illuminating the Wilsonian vision of stability through liberalization, are Arno J. Mayer, *Politics and Diplomacy of Peace-making* (New York: Knopf, 1968), N. Gordon Levin, Jr., *Woodrow Wilson and World Politics* (New York: Oxford University Press, 1968), and Carl P. Parrini, *Heir to Empire: United States Economic Diplomacy, 1916–1923* (Pittsburgh: University of Pittsburgh Press, 1969). In addition, the subjects have been illuminated by a number of outstanding monographs, among which are Lawrence E. Gelfand, *The Inquiry: American Preparations for Peace, 1917–1919* (New Haven, Conn.: Yale University Press, 1963), Ralph Stone, *The Irreconcilables* (Lexington: University Press of Kentucky, 1970), Daniel M. Smith, *Robert Lansing and American Neutrality, 1914–1917* (Berkeley: University of California Press, 1958), and Lloyd Ambrosius, *Woodrow Wilson and the American Diplomatic Tradition: The Treaty Fight in Perspective* (New York: Cambridge University Press, 1988). Diplomacy is also stressed in Robert H. Ferrell's survey of the period for the American Nation series, *Woodrow Wilson and World War I, 1917–1921* (New York: Harper & Row, 1985).

The most detailed account of American military operations during World War I is U.S. Department of the Army, *United States Army in the World War, 1917–1919*, 17 vols. (Washington: Government Printing Office, 1948). Two more recent military histories, both substantial and scholarly, are Edward M. Coffman, *The War to End All Wars: The American Military Experience in World War I* (New York: Oxford University Press, 1968), and Harvey A. DeWeerd, *President Wilson Fights His War* (New York: Macmillan, 1968). Other studies that help clarify the operations of the military agencies, both at home and abroad, are Daniel R. Beaver, *Newton D. Baker and the American War Effort, 1917–1919* (Lincoln: University of Nebraska Press, 1966), Elting E. Morison, *Admiral Sims and the Modern American Navy* (Boston: Houghton Mifflin, 1942), David F. Trask, *The United States in the Supreme War Council* (Middletown, Conn.: Wesleyan University Press, 1961), and John Whiteclay Chambers II, *To Raise an Army: The Draft Comes to Modern America* (New York: Free Press, 1987). The role of black soldiers is examined in Arthur E. Barbeau, *The Unknown Soldiers: Black American Troops in World War I* (Philadelphia: Temple University Press, 1974), and Gerald W. Patton, *War and Race: The Black Officer in the American Military* (Westport, Conn.: Greenwood Press, 1981).

Historical study of the wartime mobilization and control agencies has come in three waves. The first produced such immediate postwar publications as Benedict Crowell and Robert F. Wilson, *How America*

*Went to War*, 6 vols. (New Haven, Conn.: Yale University Press, 1921), and Grosvenor B. Clarkson, *Industrial America in the World War* (Boston: Houghton Mifflin, 1923). The second wave, developing in conjunction with concerns about a new mobilization, led to such publications as William C. Mullendore, *History of the United States Food Administration, 1917–1919* (Stanford, Calif.: Stanford University Press, 1941), and Richard H. Hippelheuser, ed., *American Industry in the War* (New York: Prentice-Hall, 1941). The third wave, arising as one facet of neoinstitutional or managerial history, has produced such detailed analyses of bureaucratic formation and functioning as Robert D. Cuff, *The War Industries Board: Business-Government Relations during World War I* (Baltimore: Johns Hopkins Press, 1973), Burton I. Kaufman, *Efficiency and Expansion: Foreign Trade Organization in the Wilson Administration, 1913–1921* (Westport, Conn.: Greenwood Press, 1974), and Valerie Jean Conner, *The National War Labor Board: Stability, Social Justice, and the Voluntary State in World War I* (Chapel Hill: University of North Carolina Press, 1983). Also helpful in putting the wartime organizational experience into perspective are Frederick L. Paxson, *American Democracy and the World War*, 3 vols. (Boston: Houghton Mifflin, 1936–1948), William J. Breen, *Uncle Sam at Home: Civilian Mobilization, Wartime Federalism, and the Council of National Defense, 1917–1919* (Westport, Conn.: Greenwood Press, 1984), K. Austin Kerr, *American Railroad Politics, 1914–1920* (Pittsburgh: University of Pittsburgh Press, 1968), Robert H. Wiebe, *The Search for Order, 1877–1920* (New York: Hill & Wang, 1967), James Weinstein, *The Corporate Ideal in the Liberal State* (Boston: Beacon, 1968), and Murray N. Rothbard, "War Collectivism in World War I," in Ronald Radosh and Murray N. Rothbard, eds., *A New History of Leviathan* (New York: Dutton, 1972). On other aspects of the home front, see Stephen L. Vaughn, *Holding Fast to Inner Lines: Democracy, Nationalism, and the Committee for Public Information* (Chapel Hill: University of North Carolina Press, 1980), Maurine W. Greenwald, *Women, War, and Work: The Impact of World War I on Women Workers in the United States* (Westport, Conn.: Greenwood Press, 1980), David M. Kennedy, *Over Here: The First World War and American Society* (New York: Oxford University Press, 1980), Frederick C. Luebke, *Bonds of Loyalty: German Americans and World War I* (De Kalb: Northern Illinois University Press, 1974), and Horace C. Peterson and Gilbert C. Fite, *Opponents of War, 1917–1919* (Madison: University of Wisconsin Press, 1957).

Historical study of the postwar reconversion period had tended to focus on antiradical hysteria, setbacks for organized labor, race riots, and the breakup of the Wilsonian coalition. The best accounts of these matters are in Robert K. Murray, *Red Scare: A Study in National Hysteria, 1919–1920* (Minneapolis: University of Minnesota Press, 1955), David Brody, *Labor in Crisis: The Steel Strike of 1919* (Philadelphia: Lippincott, 1965), William M. Tuttle, Jr., *Race Riot: Chicago in the Red Summer of 1919* (New York: Atheneum, 1970), and David Burner, "1919: Prelude to Normalcy," in John Braeman et al., eds., *Change and Continuity in Twentieth-Century America: The 1920s* (Columbus: Ohio State University Press, 1968). The efforts to adapt wartime organization to peacetime needs have been less studied. But see Gary Dean Best, *The Politics of American Individualism: Herbert Hoover in Transition, 1918–1921* (Westport, Conn.: Greenwood Press, 1975), Robert Himmelberg, "Business, Antitrust Policy, and the Industrial Board of the Department of Commerce, 1919," *Business History Review* 44 (Spring 1968), Melvin I. Urofsky, *Big Steel and the Wilson Administration* (Columbus: Ohio State University Press, 1969), James R. Mock and Evangeline Thurber, *Report on Demobilization* (Norman: University of Oklahoma Press, 1944), and Stanley Shapiro, "The Great War and Reform," *Labor History* 7 (Summer 1971).

## New Era Politics

The most detailed account of the politics and policies of the Harding period is Robert K. Murray, *The Harding Era: Warren G. Harding and His Administration* (Minneapolis: University of Minnesota Press, 1969). Less favorable to Harding are Andrew Sinclair, *The Available Man* (New York: Macmillan, 1965), Francis Russell, *The Shadow of Blooming Grove* (New York: McGraw-Hill, 1968), and Eugene P. Trani and David L. Wilson, *The Presidency of Warren G. Harding* (Lawrence: Regents Press of Kansas, 1977). On the Coolidge presidency William Allen White's book *A Puritan in Babylon* (New York: Macmillan, 1938) still has value. But the best book is Donald B. McCoy's revisionist study, *Calvin Coolidge: The Quiet President* (New York: Macmillan, 1967). A conservative defense can be found in Thomas B. Silver, *Coolidge and the Historians* (Durham, N.C.: Carolina Academic Press, 1982). Other works that have helped to clarify New Era political behavior and dispel a variety of myths about it include Wesley M. Bagby, *The Road to Normalcy* (Baltimore: Johns Hopkins Press, 1962), Burl Noggle, *Teapot Dome: Oil and Politics in the 1920s* (Baton Rouge: Louisiana State University Press, 1962), J. Joseph Huthmacher, *Massachusetts People and Politics, 1919–1933* (Cambridge, Mass.: Harvard University Press, 1959), David Burner, *The Politics of Provincialism: The Democratic Party in Transition, 1918–1932* (New York: Knopf,

1968), Gilbert C. Fite, *George N. Peek and the Fight for Farm Parity* (Norman: University of Oklahoma Press, 1954), James H. Shideler, *Farm Crisis, 1919–1923* (Berkeley: University of California Press, 1957), Preston Hubbard, Jr., *Origins of the T.V.A.* (Nashville, Tenn.: Vanderbilt University Press, 1961), and Robert Zieger, *Republicans and Labor, 1919–1929* (Lexington: University Press of Kentucky, 1969).

The most prominent themes in recent work on New Era political history have been the persistence of progressive political modes, the building of administrative networks and domains, and the political manifestations of rural-urban and ethnocultural conflict. On the first of these themes, see Arthur S. Link, "What Happened to the Progressive Movement in the 1920s?" *American Historical Review* 64 (July 1959), Clarke A. Chambers, *Seedtime of Reform: American Social Service and Social Action, 1918–1933* (Minneapolis: University of Minnesota Press, 1963), George B. Tindall, "Business Progressivism: Southern Politics in the Twenties," *South Atlantic Quarterly* 62 (Winter 1963), and Paul Glad, "Progressivism and the Business Culture of the 1920s," *Journal of American History* 53 (June 1966). On administrative developments the most important works include Donald L. Winters, *Henry Cantwell Wallace as Secretary of Agriculture, 1921–1924* (Urbana: University of Illinois Press, 1970), Donald C. Swain, *Federal Conservation Policy, 1921–1933* (Berkeley: University of California Press, 1963), Craig Lloyd, *Aggressive Introvert: Herbert Hoover and Public Relations Management* (Columbus: Ohio State University Press, 1972), Philip T. Rosen, *The Modern Stentors: Radio Broadcasters and the Federal Government, 1920–1934* (Westport, Conn.: Greenwood Press, 1980), Evan B. Metcalf, "Secretary Hoover and the Emergence of Macroeconomic Management," *Business History Review* 49 (Spring 1975), Ellis W. Hawley, "Herbert Hoover, the Commerce Secretariat, and the Vision of an Associative State, 1921–1928," *Journal of American History* 61 (June 1974), Gary Alchon, *The Invisible Hand of Planning: Capitalism, Social Science, and the State in the 1920s* (Princeton, N.J.: Princeton University Press, 1985), and Ellis W. Hawley, ed., *Herbert Hoover as Secretary of Commerce: Studies in New Era Thought and Practice* (Iowa City: University of Iowa Press, 1981). On rural-urban conflict the most penetrating analyses are in George Mowry, *The Urban Nation, 1920–1960* (New York: Hill & Wang, 1965), and Don S. Kirschner, *City and Country: Rural Responses to Urbanization in the 1920s* (Westport, Conn.: Greenwood Press, 1970). And for the most divisive of the ethnocultural issues, see Andrew Sinclair, *Prohibition: Era of Excess* (Boston: Little, Brown, 1962), Norman H. Clark, *Deliver Us from Evil* (New York: Norton, 1976), David E. Kyvig, *Repealing National Prohibi-*

*tion* (Chicago: University of Chicago Press, 1979), John Higham, *Strangers in the Land* (New Brunswick, N.J.: Rutgers University Press, 1955), Norman F. Furniss, *The Fundamentalist Controversy, 1918– 1931* (New Haven, Conn.: Yale University Press, 1954), and Ruth C. Silva, *Rum, Religion, and Votes* (University Park: Pennsylvania State University Press, 1962).

The story of the anticapitalist left in the 1920s is well told in Theodore Draper, *The Roots of American Communism* (New York: Viking, 1963), David A. Shannon, *The Socialist Party of America* (New York: Macmillan, 1955), Robert L. Morlan, *Political Prairie Fire: The Nonpartisan League, 1915–1922* (Minneapolis: University of Minnesota Press, 1956), Melvyn Dubofsky, *We Shall Be All: A History of the Industrial Workers of the World* (Chicago: Quadrangle, 1969), and William E. Akin, *Technocracy and the American Dream* (Berkeley: University of California Press, 1977). The La Follette movement is carefully traced in Kenneth C. McKay, *The Progressive Movement of 1924* (New York: Columbia University Press, 1947), and the development of black nationalism is discussed in E. David Cronon, *Black Moses: The Story of Marcus Garvey and the Universal Negro Improvement Association* (Madison: University of Wisconsin Press, 1962). For the "radical right" of the period, see David M. Chalmers, *Hooded Americanism* (Garden City, N.Y.: Doubleday, 1965), Charles Alexander, *The Ku Klux Klan in the Southwest* (Lexington: University Press of Kentucky, 1965), and Kenneth T. Jackson, *The Ku Klux Klan in the City, 1915– 1930* (New York: Oxford University Press, 1967). See also Robert A. Goldberg, *Hooded Empire: The Ku Klux Klan in Colorado* (Urbana: University of Illinois Press, 1981), and Leonard Moore, *Citizen Klansmen: Ku Klux Klan Populism in Indiana during the 1920s* (Chapel Hill: University of North Carolina Press, 1991), both of which stress the antielitist and populist components of the Klan movement. For rightist groups other than the Klan, the best account, still unpublished, is George S. May, "Ultra-Conservative Thought in the United States in the 1920s and 1930s" (Ph.D. dissertation, University of Michigan, 1954).

## New Era Diplomacy

On American diplomacy between 1920–1932 there is a voluminous literature, much of it synthesized in such surveys as L. Ethan Ellis, *Republican Foreign Policy, 1921–1933* (New Brunswick, N.J.: Rutgers University Press, 1968), Selig Adler, *The Uncertain Giant, 1921–1941* (New York: Macmillan, 1965), and Warren Cohen, *Empire without*

*Tears: American Foreign Relations, 1921–1933* (Philadelphia: Temple University Press, 1987). Among the most important of the specialized studies are Thomas H. Buckley, *The United States and the Washington Conference, 1921–1922* (Knoxville: University of Tennessee Press, 1970), Robert H. Ferrell, *Peace in Their Time: The Origins of the Kellogg-Briand Pact* (New Haven, Conn.: Yale University Press, 1952), Akira Iriye, *After Imperialism: The Search for a New Order in the Far East, 1921–1931* (Cambridge, Mass.: Harvard University Press, 1965), Joseph Tulchin, *The Aftermath of War: World War I and U.S. Policy toward Latin America* (New York: New York University Press, 1971), Joseph Brandes, *Herbert Hoover and Economic Diplomacy* (Pittsburgh: University of Pittsburgh Press, 1962), Robert H. Ferrell, *American Diplomacy in the Great Depression: Hoover-Stimson Foreign Policy, 1929–1933* (New Haven, Conn.: Yale University Press, 1957), Alexander De Conde, *Herbert Hoover's Latin American Policy* (Stanford, Calif.: Stanford University Press, 1951), Edward M. Bennett, *Recognition of Russia* (Waltham, Mass.: Ginn, Blaisdell, 1970), Armin Rappaport, *Henry L. Stimson and Japan* (Chicago: University of Chicago Press, 1963), and Melvyn P. Leffler, *The Elusive Quest: America's Pursuit of European Stability and French Security, 1919–1933* (Chapel Hill: University of North Carolina Press, 1979).

In recent years a number of works have also illuminated the relationships between the New Era political economy and the diplomacy of the period. Among these are William Appleman Williams, "The Legend of Isolationism in the 1920s," *Science and Society* 18 (Winter 1954), Joan Hoff Wilson, *American Business and Foreign Policy, 1920–1933* (Lexington: University Press of Kentucky, 1971), Carl P. Parrini, *Heir to Empire: United States Economic Diplomacy, 1916–1923* (Pittsburgh: University of Pittsburgh Press, 1969), Michael J. Hogan, *Informal Entente: The Private Structure of Cooperation in Anglo-American Economic Diplomacy, 1918–1928* (Columbia: University of Missouri Press, 1977), Melvyn P. Leffler, "Political Isolationism, Economic Expansion, or Diplomatic Realism: American Policy toward Western Europe, 1921–1933," *Perspectives in American History* 8 (1974), Robert N. Seidel, *Progressive Pan-Americanism* (Ithaca, N.Y.: Cornell University Latin American Studies Program, 1973), and Robert F. Smith, *The United States and Revolutionary Nationalism in Mexico, 1916–32* (Chicago: University of Chicago Press, 1972). The theme of informal empire, cultural as well as economic, is also developed in Frank Costigliola, *Awkward Dominion: American Political, Economic, and Cultural Relations with Europe, 1919–1933* (Ithaca, N.Y.: Cornell University Press, 1984), and Emily S. Rosenberg, *Spreading the American Dream: American Economic and Cultural Expansion, 1890–1945* (New York: Hill & Wang, 1982).

## Economic Developments

The standard work on economic developments during the period is George Soule, *Prosperity Decade: From War to Depression, 1917–1929* (New York: Holt, Rinehart, 1947). Also good on particular aspects and sectors of economic behavior are Irving Bernstein, *The Lean Years: A History of the American Worker, 1920–1933* (Boston: Houghton Mifflin, 1960), Elmus R. Wicker, *Federal Reserve Monetary Policy, 1917–1933* (New York: Random House, 1966), and Wassily W. Leontief, *The Structure of the American Economy, 1919–1929* (Cambridge, Mass.: Harvard University Press, 1941). On business organization and practice during the period, see Thomas C. Cochran, *The American Business System: A Historical Perspective, 1900–1955* (Cambridge, Mass.: Harvard University Press, 1957), Louis Galambos, *Competition and Cooperation: The Emergence of a National Trade Association* (Baltimore: Johns Hopkins Press, 1966), Alfred D. Chandler, *Strategy and Structure: Chapters in the History of the Industrial Enterprise* (Cambridge, Mass.: M.I.T. Press, 1962), Robert F. Himmelberg, *The Origins of the National Recovery Administration: Business, Government, and the Trade Association Issue, 1921–1933* (New York: Fordham University Press, 1976), Loren Baritz, *The Servants of Power* (Middletown, Conn.: Wesleyan University Press, 1960), Stuart D. Brandes, *American Welfare Capitalism, 1880–1940* (Chicago: University of Chicago Press, 1976), Sanford Jacoby, *Employing Bureaucracy: Managers, Unions, and the Transformation of Work in American Industry, 1900–1945* (New York: Columbia University Press, 1985), and Morrell Heald, *The Social Responsibilities of Business* (Cleveland: Case Western Reserve University Press, 1970). For differing views on the origins and coming of the Great Depression, see John K. Galbraith, *The Great Crash* (Boston: Houghton Mifflin, 1955), Milton Friedman and Anna Schwartz, *The Great Contraction, 1929–1933* (Princeton, N.J.,: Princeton University Press, 1965), Peter Temin, *Did Monetary Forces Cause the Great Depression?* (New York: Norton, 1976), and Charles P. Kindleberger, *The World in Depression, 1929–1939* (Berkeley: University of California Press, 1973). Still useful as well is the President's Conference on Unemployment, *Recent Economic Changes in the United States*, 2 vols. (New York: McGraw-Hill, 1929).

## Social and Cultural Developments

For the social history of the 1920s, historians have continued to rely heavily on Robert S. Lynd and Helen M. Lynd, *Middletown: A Study in Contemporary American Culture* (New York: Harcourt, Brace, 1929), the President's Research Committee on Social Trends, *Recent Social Trends in the United States*, 2 vols. (New York: McGraw-Hill, 1933), and the relevant volume in the "History of American Life" series, Preston W. Slosson, *The Great Crusade and After, 1914–1928* (New York: Macmillan, 1931). Recent years, however, have witnessed the appearance of a growing number of specialized studies. Among these are Paul A. Carter, *The Decline and Revival of the Social Gospel* (Ithaca, N.Y.: Cornell University Press, 1954), Gilbert Osofsky, *Harlem: The Making of a Ghetto* (New York: Harper & Row, 1966), Paula S. Fass, *The Damned and the Beautiful: American Youth in the 1920s* (New York: Oxford University Press, 1971), Paul A. Carter, *Another Part of the Twenties* (New York: Columbia University Press, 1971), David Levering Lewis, *When Harlem Was in Vogue* (New York: Knopf, 1981), Kathy J. Ogren, *The Jazz Revolution: Twenties America and the Meaning of Jazz* (New York: Oxford University Press, 1989), Erick Barnouw, *A Tower in Babel: A History of Broadcasting in the United States to 1933* (New York: Oxford University Press, 1966), James J. Flink, *The Car Culture* (Cambridge, Mass.: M.I.T. Press, 1975), Raymond Callahan, *Education and the Cult of Efficiency* (Chicago: University of Chicago Press, 1962), Lawrence A. Cremin, *The Transformation of the School* (New York: Knopf, 1961), Roy Lubove, *Community Planning in the 1920s* (Pittsburgh: University of Pittsburgh Press, 1963), Daniel Nelson, *Unemployment Insurance: The American Experience, 1915–1935* (Madison: University of Wisconsin Press, 1969), and Ernest Sandeen, *The Roots of Fundamentalism* (Chicago: University of Chicago Press, 1970). In addition, see Gilman Ostrander, *American Civilization in the First Machine Age, 1890–1940* (New York: Harper & Row, 1970), Elizabeth Stevenson, *Babbits and Bohemians* (New York: Macmillan, 1967), Mark Sullivan, *Our Times*, vol. 6 (New York: Scribner, 1946), Gilbert Seldes, *The Seven Lively Arts* (New York: Sagamore, 1957), and Roland Marchand, *Advertising the American Dream: Making Way for Modernity, 1920–1940* (Berkeley: University of California Press, 1985).

Recent work on the experience of women in the 1920s includes Dorothy M. Brown, *Setting a Course: American Women in the 1920s* (Boston: Twayne, 1987), Susan D. Becker, *The Origins of the Equal Rights Amendment: American Feminism between the Wars* (Westport, Conn.: Greenwood Press, 1981), Nancy Cott, *The Grounding of Modern Feminism* (New Haven, Conn.: Yale University Press, 1987), Winifred Wandersee, *Women's Work and Family Values, 1920–1940* (Cambridge, Mass.: Harvard University Press, 1981), and J. Stanley Lemons, *The Woman Citizen: Social Feminism in the 1920s* (Urbana: University of Illinois Press, 1973).

The best survey of intellectual and artistic developments in the 1920s, and one upon which I have drawn heavily, is Roderick Nash, *The Nervous Generation: American Thought, 1917–1930* (Chicago: Rand McNally, 1970). Other works illuminating various aspects of these developments are Frederick J. Hoffman, *The Twenties: American Writing in the Postwar Decade* (New York: Viking, 1955), Robert M. Crunden, *From Self to Society, 1919–1941* (Englewood Cliffs, N.J.: Prentice-Hall, 1972), Nathan I. Huggins, *The Harlem Renaissance* (New York: Oxford University Press, 1971), Robert Faris, *Chicago Sociology, 1920–1932* (San Francisco: Chandler, 1967), Edward A. Purcell, Jr., *The Crisis of Democratic Theory: Scientific Naturalism and the Problem of Value* (Lexington: University Press of Kentucky, 1973), Ronald C. Tobey, *The American Ideology of National Science, 1919–1930* (Pittsburgh: University of Pittsburgh Press, 1971), David Felix, *Protest: Sacco-Vanzetti and the Intellectuals* (Bloomington: Indiana University Press, 1965), and Milton W. Brown, *American Painting from the Armory Show to the Depression* (Princeton, N.J.: Princeton University Press, 1955). See also John Malcolm Brinnin, *The Third Rose: Gertrude Stein and Her World* (Boston: Little, Brown, 1959), and Robert Crunden, ed., *The Superfluous Men: Conservative Critics of American Culture* (Austin: University of Texas Press, 1977).

## The Hoover Years

Two standard surveys of the Hoover programs and policies are Albert U. Romasco, *The Poverty of Abundance: Hoover, the Nation, the Depression* (New York; Oxford University Press, 1965), and Harris G. Warren, *Herbert Hoover and the Great Depression* (New York: Oxford University Press, 1959). Also useful within limits are such defenses as William Myers and Walter Newton, *The Hoover Administration* (New York: Scribner, 1936), Ray Lyman Wilbur and Arthur M. Hyde, *The Hoover Policies* (New York: Scribner, 1937), Edgar Robinson and Vaughn Bornet, *Herbert Hoover: President of the United States* (Stanford, Calif.: Hoover Institution Press, 1975), and Herbert C. Hoover, *The Memoirs of Herbert Hoover: The Great Depression* (New York: Macmillan, 1952). All these surveys, however, either predate or largely ignore the scholarship that has appeared since the opening of the Hoover papers at the Hoover Presidential Library in 1966. Among the most important of these recent works are Joan Hoff Wilson, *Herbert Hoover: Forgotten Progressive* (Boston: Little, Brown, 1975), David Burner, *Herbert Hoover: A Public Life* (New York: Knopf, 1978), Martin L. Fausold and George T. Mazuzan, eds., *The Hoover Presidency: A Reappraisal* (Albany: State University of New York Press, 1974), Martin L. Fausold, *The Presidency of Herbert Hoover* (Lawrence: University Press of Kansas, 1985), Donald J. Lisio, *The President and Protest: Hoover, Conspiracy, and the Bonus Riot* (Columbia: University of Missouri Press, 1974), Roger Daniels, *The Bonus March, An Episode of the Great Depression* (Westport, Conn.: Greenwood Press, 1971), Donald J. Lisio, *Hoover, Blacks, and Lily-Whites: A Study in Southern Strategies* (Chapel Hill: University of North Carolina Press, 1985), Jordan A. Schwarz, *Interregnum of Despair: Hoover, Congress, and the Depression* (Urbana: University of Illinois Press, 1970), James S. Olson, *Herbert Hoover and the Reconstruction Finance Corporation, 1931–1933* (Ames: Iowa State University Press, 1977), David E. Hamilton, *From New Day to New Deal: American Farm Policy from Hoover to Roosevelt, 1928–1933* (Chapel Hill, N.C.: University of North Carolina Press, 1991), and William J. Barber, *From New Era to New Deal: Herbert Hoover, the Economists and American Economic Policy, 1921–1933* (New York: Cambridge University Press, 1985). Among the seminal essays contributing to a revised view of Hoover and his presidency are William Appleman Williams, "The Central Role of Herbert Hoover in the Maturation of an Industrial Gentry," in *The Contours of American History* (Cleveland: World, 1961), Carl N. Degler, "The Ordeal of Herbert Hoover," *Yale Review* 52 (Summer 1963), Barry D. Karl, "Presidential Planning and Social Science Research: Mr. Hoover's Experts," *Perspectives in American History* 3 (1969), and Peri Arnold "Herbert Hoover and the Continuity of American Public Policy," *Public Policy* 20 (Fall 1972). The changing interpretations are also discussed in the essays published in Mark M. Dodge, ed., *Herbert Hoover and the Historians* (West Branch, Iowa: Hoover Presidential Library Association, 1989).

Finally, on the interregnum period and the coming of the New Deal, see especially Frank Freidel, *Franklin D. Roosevelt: Launching the New Deal* (Boston: Little, Brown, 1973), Susan Estabrook Kennedy, *The Banking Crisis of 1933* (Lexington: University Press of Kentucky, 1973), Rexford G. Tugwell, *The Brains Trust* (New York: Viking, 1968), and Raymond Moley, *The First New Deal* (New York: Harcourt, Brace, 1966). A dissent, both from the standard scholarship on the period and from the recent revisionism on the Hoover administration, is Elliot A. Rosen, *Hoover, Roosevelt, and the Brains Trust: From Depression to New Deal* (New York: Columbia University Press, 1977).

# Index